Teaching & Learning
English Literature

Teaching & Learning English Literature

Ellie Chambers & Marshall Gregory

⑤ SAGE Publications
London ● Thousand Oaks ● New Delhi

First published 2006

 SAGE Publications Ltd
1 Oliver's Yard
55 City Road
London EC1Y 1SP

SAGE Publications Inc
2455 Teller Road
Thousand Oaks, California 91320

SAGE Publications India Pvt Ltd
B-42, Panchsheel Enclave
Post Box 4109
New Delhi 110 017

British Library Cataloguing in Publication data

A catalogue record for this book is available from the British
Library

ISBN-10 0-7619-4171-1   ISBN-13 978-0-7619-4171-2
ISBN-10 0-7619-4172-X   ISBN-13 978-0-7619-4172-9 (pbk)

Library of Congress Control Number: 2005934569

Typeset by TW Typesetting, Plymouth, Devon
Printed in Great Britain by Athenaeum Press, Gateshead
Printed on paper from sustainable resources

Contents

Appendices
(on the book's website: www.sagepub.co.uk/chambers.pdf)
1 Text of 'Araby'
2 Teaching theoretical orientations: a tutorial
3 Sample curricula
4 Sample exam papers
5 Generic and graduate skills
6 Sample course assessment designs
7 Electronic sources

Acknowledgements

Many colleagues and students have contributed to this book – on both sides of the Atlantic, in formal discussion and conversation – sometimes unwittingly. To all of them, thank you. In particular, thanks should go to Wayne Booth, whose conversations and collaborations with Marshall Gregory over four decades have been foundational to Gregory's views about teaching, and to the many faculty members who over the years have participated in Gregory's pedagogy seminars. Conversations with them have given him a level of intellectual stimulation and motive for thinking through pedagogical issues that all too few faculty members are fortunate enough to receive.

In addition, we would like to acknowledge valuable contributions to the book from the following colleagues: Ann Dashwood, University of Southern Queensland; Dr Sara Haslam (Arts Faculty) and Dr Mary Lea and Simon Rae (IET), the UK Open University; Professor Graham Gibbs, University of Oxford, and Claire Simpson. We would also like to thank Professor Ben Knights (Director) and the staff of the Higher Education Academy *English Subject Centre*, Royal Holloway London, for use of their exemplary website.

Special thanks go to Nigel Blake, Philosopher of Education, who read and made insightful comments on all the draft chapters. And to our series editor, Jan Parker, who has carried out her task sympathetically and imaginatively. Our thanks, too, to Sage Publications and their editors: patient, forbearing and highly professional colleagues. Finally, we would like to thank our partners and families for their much appreciated encouragement and support throughout the composition and revision of the manuscript that eventually turned into this book.

Teaching and Learning the Humanities in Higher Education

SERIES EDITORS: Ellie Chambers and Jan Parker, The Open University

This series for beginning and experienced lecturers deals with all aspects of teaching individual arts and humanities subjects in higher education. Experienced teachers offer authoritative suggestions to enable beginning and experienced lecturers to become critically reflective about discipline-specific practices.

Each book includes an overview of the main currents of thought in a subject; major theoretical trends; appropriate teaching and learning modes and current best practice; new methods of course delivery and assessment; electronic teaching methods and sources.

Features include:

- discussion of key areas of pedagogy: curriculum development, assessment, teaching styles, professional development, appropriate use of C&IT;
- case study illustration of teaching certain problematic topics;
- the findings of educational research and sample material of all kinds drawn from a range of countries and traditions;
- suggestions throughout for critical decisions, and alternative strategies and follow-up activities, so that all teachers are encouraged to reflect critically on their assumptions and practices.

The series sets out effective approaches to a wide range of teaching and teaching-related tasks.

The books are intended as core texts for lecturers working towards membership of the Higher Education Academy, for adoption by training course providers, and as professional reference resources. The books are also suitable for PGCE, and Further and Higher Education courses. In countries with less formal plans for lecturer training but a longer tradition of serious attention to pedagogy within the higher education culture, the series will contribute to the scholarship of teaching and learning and professional and organisational development.

Series titles:
Modern Languages: Learning and Teaching in an Intercultural Field
Alison Phipps and Mike Gonzalez
Teaching and Learning History
Geoff Timmins, Keith Vernon and Christine Kinealy
Teaching and Learning English Literature
Ellie Chambers and Marshall Gregory

Ellie Chambers is Professor of Humanities Higher Education in the Institute of Educational Technology, The Open University, UK. Since 1974 she has worked as a pedagogic adviser, evaluator and researcher with colleagues in the university's Faculty of Arts. In 1992 she founded the interdisciplinary Humanities Higher Education Research Group and in 1994, with colleagues, the national Humanities and Arts Higher Education Network. She regularly addresses conferences internationally and has published widely in the fields of distance education and Arts and Humanities higher education – including the best-selling book for students, *The Arts Good Study Guide* (1997, with Andrew Northedge). Currently, she is founding Editor-in-Chief of *Arts and Humanities in Higher Education: An International Journal of Theory, Research and Practice* (Sage) and a Member of Council, the Society for Research into Higher Education.

Dr. Jan Parker is a Senior Research Fellow of The Open University's Centre for Research in Education and Educational Technology and chairs the Humanities Higher Education Research Group. Founding editor of the Sage journal *Arts and Humanities in Higher Education: An International Journal of Theory, Research and Practice* and Executive Editor of *Teaching in Higher Education* (Taylor and Francis), she still teaches and writes on her disciplinary specialisation, Greek Tragedy, and is a Senior Member of the Faculty of Classics, Cambridge. She is currently co-writing the *Teaching and Learning Classics and Classical Studies* volume of this series.

Foreword

Those of us working in the national English Subject Centre are acutely conscious of a paradox. That is that the family of English subjects in British universities study communication in a very sophisticated way, and harbour a wide variety of pedagogic methods. Since its inception, the subject has been committed to what we now know by the portmanteau phrase 'learning and teaching'. Yet, by and large, university teachers of English – in Britain at all events – find it hard to make their tacit pedagogic knowledge conscious, or to raise it to a level where it might be critiqued, shared or developed. In our experience, colleagues find it relatively easy to talk about curriculum and resources, but far harder to talk about the success or failure of seminars, how to vary forms of assessment, or to make imaginative use of Virtual Learning Environments. Too often this reticence means falling back on default assumptions about student learning, about teaching or about forms of assessment. There is a real question as to where new pedagogic understandings may be formed. Thus we are aware that many starting lecturers and their colleagues pass severe judgements on the university diploma courses they are required to take. Meanwhile, for those who seek to support English lecturers, there is a shortage of subject-specific material to recommend.

Ellie Chambers' and Marshall Gregory's timely book cannot provide all the answers, but it will be found an invaluable resource by new (and not so new) lecturers in English Literature. It is a thoroughly researched and stimulatingly detailed addition to the kind of dialogue that the English Subject Centre seeks to foster. While rich in practical ideas, it is not simply a compendium of tips. It sets out to ground its suggestions in a theorised account of the subject – an account which attends to the grammars that govern the interaction between teachers and students, the protocols of dialogue and assessment, and above all to the collaborative nature of the productive processes in which both teachers and students engage. The underlying argument is that 'content and pedagogy are inseparable' [p. 25]. The practical consequence is that the methods teachers choose should be sensitively attuned to the specific demands of what they are trying to achieve.

This book is articulated along two complementary lines of thought. The authors rightly refuse to be drawn into what they describe as the 'knee-jerk reaction that teaching is inherently suspect' [p. 42]. While we all have much to learn from the learner-centred orthodoxies of the last quarter century, teachers nevertheless have responsibilities towards their subject and towards their students. At the same time even a passionate commitment to the subject needs to be complemented by hard, careful thought about curriculum and module design, and about the structuring of seminars. For the other half of the argument is that 'we cannot assume that our students just know how to read a literary text' [p. 47]. Nor do they intuitively know how to take part in a seminar discussion. While the responsibility of the teacher is to create and hold the spaces in which learning can take place, that does not in itself entail a vow of silence. The teacher also has the role of modelling the discourse, and while it may sometimes be appropriate to withhold his or her superior knowledge, there are also occasions when it is just as appropriate to share it. In this light, Chambers and Gregory provide a wealth of detail about module design, seminar process, assessment, and feedback, modelling the process of dialogue as they do so.

The great strength of this book is that it is grounded simultaneously in pedagogic theory and in 'an approach to teaching in which literary experience is taken to be an important form of human learning ...' [p. 149]. Enriched by this dual focus, it promises to become a welcome contribution to the teaching of university English.

Ben Knights
Director, English Subject Centre
Higher Education Academy

Introduction

Whether or not the discipline of English Literature is 'in crisis' is something we consider right at the start of this book. But if not in crisis, it is certainly a discipline in the process of marked change. Curriculum, syllabus, teaching and student assessment methods all are pressured by significant social and political forces. In recent times, for example, these forces and government policies have produced:

- a 'massification' of higher education, with no commensurate increase in resource for teaching;
- a dominant discourse of the marketplace;
- a related instrumental pedagogic discourse of measurable 'learning outcomes' and skills 'transferable' to the workplace, underpinned by a so-called learner-centred ideology;
- increased resource for and dependence on information and communication technologies (ICTs);
- a convergence of distance and conventional education and the emergence of a 'blended' form of learning for all.

The study and teaching of English is also shaped by our students' purposes and the conditions in which they live and work, and by academics' shifting ideas about the nature of the discipline and its relationship to other, adjacent, fields. In the modern world, can we still talk about English Literature or should we substitute Literatures in English? What is Literature's wider relationship to Media and Film Studies, and Cultural Studies?

At the start of the book we take it as axiomatic that there is an identifiable discipline of English literature, that it has certain central characteristics and outer limits. But, as the book progresses and we examine the curriculum and our teaching and assessment methods in more detail, boundaries become less distinct. Perhaps limits come to seem more like limitations. Or maybe they just matter less.

Believing, with Max Weber, that man is an animal suspended in a web of significance he himself has spun, I take culture to be those webs, and the analysis of it to be therefore not an experimental science in search of law but an interpretive one in search of meaning.

(Geertz, 1975: 5)

Perhaps, after all, the search for meaning is something that unites the Humanities.

If this hypothesis is worthy of at least provisional acceptance, it follows that the study and teaching of literature will play a central role – and has always played a central role – in human beings' search for meaning. Literature, as a subset of story, acts, as do all other forms of story, to perform such all-important functions as telling human beings what is important in life, telling us what's worthy of our admiration or our contempt, telling us what it's like to be those who live in different circumstances and in other historical times and in other gendered bodies, telling us what we should pay attention to and what we can afford to ignore, and, in short, telling us how life might be lived *this* way rather than *that* way. Among the many different ways that the Humanities search for meaning, deploying our resources for reading literature well and teaching it effectively must be among the most important resources we can deploy in general, not just for disciplinary purposes but for the more broadly educational purposes of preparing our students for their overall lives, for their careers, for parenthood, for civic responsibility and for moral and ethical thoughtfulness.

The book differs somewhat in its aims from others of its kind (for example, Showalter, 2002; Agathocleus and Dean, 2002; Widdowson, 1999). Written by a US English professor and an educationist with an academic background in Literature, it aims to introduce its audience to an analysis of how educational ideas – both 'classic' texts and recent research – illuminate our subject. Literature is always at the heart of things, but from there we try to move 'out' to make fruitful connections to current educational thinking. Readers may, or may not, like to follow those leads. In the UK, where new university lecturers will soon be required to gain a teaching qualification, the need may be most pressing. We hope that the book will at least get them started – and from a basis in the discipline.

The first three chapters are designed to act as an introduction, especially for those who are beginning or relatively new teachers of Literature. There we 'show' as well as tell, demonstrating a close-reading seminar class and (on the book's website) a tutorial on an approach to teaching literary theory and criticism. We also discuss approaches to teaching essay writing, specifically via the writing workshop. And so we explore some of the main 'problems' involved in teaching Literature (teaching close reading, theory and writing) while also demonstrating some of Literature's main teaching methods (the seminar, tutorial and workshop).

Thereafter, we hope that the book's appeal is broader. Chapter 4 onwards takes the reader from planning the curriculum and courses in Literature, through a range of modern teaching-learning methods, to the issues surrounding student assessment – and finally, in Chapter 7, to evaluation of our work and performance as teachers. This whole planning process, perhaps presented somewhat seamlessly, is in reality messier. But, nonetheless, we trust that discussion of it raises some important issues for teachers, illuminated by the sample course outlines (including essay and exam questions) and assessment regimes presented on the book's website.

These example courses and regimes are drawn mainly from practice in the UK (although readers may use the web addresses offered in the Bibliography and Appendix 7 on the website to access literature course models from Australia and North America). This emphasis reflects the fact that, in the UK, the government and its agencies now make certain demands of teachers of all disciplines. For example, the UK Quality Assurance Agency requires that teachers in higher education should stipulate certain demonstrable 'outcomes' of their programmes, as regards the students' content knowledge and skills, to specified standards. And we demonstrate in the book that similar accountability and quality assurance measures are being introduced elsewhere. Looking at the situation in the UK – the 'worst case', as it were – is therefore instructive all round.

But, in addition to this, some educators are becoming involved in what is now termed a 'scholarship of teaching' (discussed in Chapter 7) – incorporating new media in their teaching, taking a more systematic interest in what goes on in the classroom or online and in their students' learning, asking questions about what they do and why. For them teaching is becoming less a job and more an intellectual activity worthy of serious consideration and investigation. This might just put an end to what George Levine (2001: 7) describes as 'the split between our work as teachers and our work as scholars'. Although he acknowledges that at present 'within the scholarly universe of the profession, knowledge about teaching does not for the most part count as 'knowledge' ', he goes on to say:

> *Teaching literature is a subject, and a difficult one. Doing it well requires scholarly and critical sophistication, but it also requires a clear idea of what literature is, of what is entailed in reading and criticizing it. It requires, in fact, some very self-conscious theorizing. But beyond the questions that ought to feed any serious critic's sense of what doing literature might mean, there are questions about the relation between such sophistication and the necessities of the classroom: what, how, and when are students most likely to learn?*

(Levine, 2001: 14)

If this book helps to stimulate such questioning among literature teachers, its authors will be well pleased.

1

The discipline today

IN CRISIS?

Culture wars

No Literature academic, long established or just beginning, can be unaffected by the 'culture wars' that in the last two decades or so have ravaged our scholarly community, and indeed the Humanities generally. Western governments' neglect of the Humanities, even to the point of repudiation, and their concurrent outpourings of resource for research and teaching in the so-called productive areas of the higher education curriculum – business, technology, the applied sciences – undoubtedly galvanised many humanists, but in ways that commentators (especially in North America)[1] have identified as an aspect of 'the crisis' itself. That is, in such a situation of dwindling resource for the discipline and perceived loss of its status within the academy, colleagues tended to turn on each other

> in culture wars and canon wars that feature campus radicals versus conservative publicists, proponents of multiculturalism versus defenders of tradition, scholars who insist on the political construction of all knowledge versus those who would preserve the purity and beauty of a necessarily nonpolitical, because objective, truth.
>
> (Scott, 1995: 293)

And these activists, in both traditionalist and radical camps, joined in (always justified?) scorn of their more utilitarian, entrepreneurial colleagues who, then and now, would 'sell' their services within the favoured, well-resourced domains – offering courses in medical ethics, for example, or communications for business managers, or in logical thinking, problem-solving and other so-called generic and transferable skills – for either their compliance or their debasement of a once-precious coinage.

'Marketing' higher education

Meanwhile, many of us look on in perplexity, fearing the worst as humanities departments continue to be merged or axed, faculty numbers and class-contact hours cut and our once coherent curricula reduced to short modules which students pick and mix like outfits from the shopping mall. At the same time, we are exhorted to introduce 'flexible' learning methods to cope with periodic bouts of expansion in student numbers (video-taped lectures, virtual seminars via computer conferencing), and to focus increasingly on our students' employability and acquisition of related skills. Insult adds to injury when such 'developments' are held up as progressive: as the elements of an architecture of client-centred Lifelong Learning, or some similarly opaque assertion our education has taught us to question and fully equipped us to demolish. For many academics in the Humanities, and perhaps especially in literary studies, vehemently reject such a retail model of higher education – a model in which every institution's first concern is to keep the paying customers coming through the door, and teachers are the floor clerks who keep those customers happy.

However, it's not all gloom and doom. It is clear that the apprenticeship model of higher education – in which disciplines are 'tribes', with their different, clearly marked out, well defended 'territories' (Becher and Trowler, 2001) and their academics busy training the next generation of scholars – is giving way under the pressures of national and international competition and of students' buying power to looser curriculum formations and an economy that is demand- as well as supply-led. These are shifts of emphasis that many in the academy welcome. And they may simply be inevitable in the situation of widening access to higher education in the age of the Internet (see Edwards and Usher, 2001). The main danger is of course a dumbing down of higher education generally, as newspaper headlines about Mickey Mouse courses attest (especially in some of the newer fields, such as Media Studies) and as many academics themselves fear. In this connection, we would just point to the widely acknowledged high academic standards of the UK Open University, which since 1969 has successfully offered a modular programme predicated on the widest possible choice to adult students who need have no previous educational qualifications at all. Dumbing down is a danger, then, but it is not inevitable.

Understanding global forces

And, at least, humanities disciplines are not alone in all this. Indeed, it is now widely accepted that there is 'a global crisis of rising demand for higher education which races ahead of the public funding to meet it' (Channon, 2000: 255, citing Goddard). We may conclude that, after all, the 'crisis' of the Humanities reflects an infrastructural crisis in all higher education, even if humanities disciplines perhaps come off worst. Furthermore, if (with Bourdieu, 1988) we first distinguish between the cognitive and the social structures of the disciplines – their academic (knowledge/actively intellectual) and their social (power/socially reproductive) dimensions – and, second, identify some disciplines as clearly located at the cognitive end of the spectrum (e.g. natural science) with others (such as business studies) at the social/temporal end, we may then locate the Humanities towards the cognitive end, in a state of some tension between the poles. This analytical framework (which, note, does not entail judgements of disciplinary value) can help make sense of the bewildering array of forces currently acting upon higher education and its effects. For the world-wide trend towards mass higher education systems is a phenomenon that emphasises the social/temporal dimension of *all* disciplines (Kelly, 2001) – an emphasis that is likely to have especially distorting effects on those disciplines located towards the cognitive end of the spectrum.

That is, as ever-larger numbers of students enter higher education systems, these systems – yoked as they are to the economic demands of an ever more global marketplace – are increasingly geared to the students' future employment and capacity to contribute to national wealth. A major aim of a higher education, then, is that students should acquire marketable skills. In the UK, for example, these skills are to be demonstrated by the students' competent performance of the 'learning outcomes' that their teachers must stipulate for them in advance – with teachers' own performance measured accordingly and controlled for 'quality'. Thus we all become constrained to think about our teaching goals and methods in similar terms, whether our field is Biology or Business or Literature. It is as if, when it comes to teaching, the structure, purposes and pedagogy of all disciplines were one and the same. And it is as if students themselves may have no educational goals or preferences of their own.

Truce and federation

While the particular tensions such constraints give rise to will of course differ within and among humanities as well as other disciplines, we should try to understand our own situation in a way that inspires something more productive than either panic or paralysis. With respect to Modern Languages, Kelly's solution to avoiding disciplinary fracture and marginalisation – to achieving both the social unity needed to address issues of power and the cognitive diversity required to create new knowledge – is 'federation': large departments or units that may 'speak with one voice', acting on behalf of all their members and, at the same time, fostering and sustaining a wide range of intellectual interests (Kelly, 2001: 55). If the situation of Modern Languages is in its essentials representative of other humanities then might not such a notion of federation profitably be extended to the Humanities as a whole, including Literature? Clearly, this would entail a truce in the culture wars and a genuine coming together to forge new understandings.

Indeed, it seems that the worst of the conflict is behind us now (Gregory, 2002). A recent contribution to the debate from another American academic, who was a student at the height of the culture wars (Insko, 2003), suggests teaching for democratic citizenship as a way forward, while Gregory himself (2001: 87) recommends the 'humanization of the social order'; Bérubé (2003) promotes ways of valuing the 'utility' of cultural work; Gerald Graff (2003), by 'teaching the conflicts', suggests yet another possibility. And evidence that there is a will to forge new understandings emerging widely in the Humanities came our way in response to a proposal in 2001 to establish an academic journal of Arts and Humanities higher education (*Arts and Humanities in Higher Education: An International Journal of Theory, Research and Practice*, Sage Journals (www.sagepub.co.uk)). Variously, the (anonymous) international respondents pointed to the need:

● ... *for a potential rallying-point for the politics of those dedicated to a remarkably resilient yet systematically slighted area of education. We don't get the big grants ... but we do get the students, and the interest ... we're big education providers/cultivators for post-industrial societies. After all, by and large, we insist on education (not training alone), and flexibility and adaptability (not narrow vocationalism).*

- ... *for ways to cut the humanities coat according to the shrinking cloth on the one hand, developing arguments that may at least have some potential to reverse this trend on the other.*
- ... *genuinely to bring together top-level thought on research-led pedagogy across humanities disciplines, which strengthens links between those disciplines without denying their separate identities.*

However, as we have seen, certain indicators are plain discouraging. Internally, some humanities disciplines are deeply fractured, perhaps especially Literature. It appears that within the Humanities generally there exists little agreement about desirable purposes, curricula and teaching practices – partly as a consequence of differences in response to the external pressures just noted, and also owing to different underlying conceptions of the disciplines themselves (see Chambers (2001) for discussion of traditional, radical and utilitarian views of Literature as a discipline). In starting this book with such sobering reflections we recognise no more than is true and no more than beginning academics will indeed encounter. It is because of this backdrop that what we say in it has urgency. And of course through the book we aim to point up the distinctiveness of our discipline, and to help achieve the kind of unity of purpose and understanding that will sustain its vitality.

Disciplinary vigour

In any case, we must not lose our nerve. Literature courses have traditionally attracted large numbers of students and they continue to do so. In spite of the difficulties involved when resources for teaching are far from commensurate, what this means is that many people actually *want* to study Literature. If they didn't, the discipline's 'crisis' would more likely be the discipline's demise. And these people we now see in our classrooms (or, in a mode such as distance education, perhaps don't see at all) could hardly be more heterogeneous: of all ages, and social and ethnic backgrounds; with a range of previous experience of education and of qualifications from virtually nil to standard higher education entry requirements and beyond. In the UK, a series of assessment visits made in 1994–5 to 72 per cent of university English departments revealed that in over a third of the departments 'the quality of education was judged to be excellent' (and of the remainder, to be satisfactory in all but three cases). The assessors continue:

Excellence was identified across a variety of programmes, institutions, approaches to subject delivery and assessments of the curriculum. Positive features included: vigour in the curriculum; success in attracting capable, enthusiastic students; widening of access – particularly to mature, returning students – without any diminution in quality; high retention rates; student achievement that in general reflects considerable intellectual challenge . . .; positive views held by past and present students about the quality of their learning experience; and excellent staff–student relations.

(QAA, *Subject Overview Report – English*, 1995;
Summary: at www.qaa.ac.uk – accessed March 2004)

So there is much that is encouraging.

It remains to be seen *why* students might want to study Literature and just what kind of education it is that they want or expect. But first we step back a bit, to consider where we're 'coming from'. Given the focus of the book, our starting point is of course pedagogy.

From ancient pedagogy . . .

Traditional pedagogy in literature classes has its roots in the ancient pedagogy of classical language instruction. This was a pedagogy aimed mostly at students 'getting it right'. The beginning stages of Latin and Greek do not provide occasions for student 'interpretation'; students can't *have* independent opinions about semantics, syntax, tenses, inflections and the like. Thus, the very pedagogy that is so much maligned today – students mimicking and parroting their teachers' knowledge and injunctions – was the pedagogy that for centuries was successful in beginning Latin and Greek classes. Once beyond the beginning stages, the content of classics classrooms was of course not language as such, but Greek and Latin philosophy and literature (Horace, Cicero, Seneca, Homer, Sophocles, Plato, Thucydides, Aristotle), and in translating these complex and nuanced texts questions of interpretation and judgement would increasingly come to the fore. Nonetheless, these roots in the pedagogy of Greek and Latin instruction partly explain why, historically, literature pedagogy of a 'top-down' kind has had so much momentum and why it has taken so long to alter or modify it.

Literature pedagogy

When Classics and Literature finally went their separate disciplinary ways, and literature teaching was mounted on the platform of students' own language rather than difficult and dead 'foreign' languages, the pedagogy of Literature could be loosened considerably. The issue in reading literature was no longer tied to students 'getting it right' as a matter of necessity. They could be encouraged to develop their own interpretive opinions. However, the magisterial rightness as represented by the teacher was a strongly entrenched tradition in the academy and did not immediately melt away. Throughout the latter part of the nineteenth and much of the twentieth century, students in literature classes were still taught as if their job was to 'get it right', if not tenses and inflection then interpretations and meanings. The right interpretations and meanings came not from student thought, inquiry or questioning, and certainly not from student 'opinion', which most teachers until recently (and some still, if truth be told) viewed in quotation marks, but from the instructor. 'Right opinion' was what the teacher thought. Today, given the challenges the discipline faces, there is even more reason willingly and imaginatively to jump outside the authoritarian frame that teachers and students may sometimes still inhabit.

Perhaps, therefore, the most helpful thing we might say about pedagogy at this early stage of the book is to recommend not this or that 'local' strategy, such as 'do seminars, not lectures' or 'do workshops, not seminars', but to discuss a 'global' approach designed to help teachers help students think more deeply than they might about the possible uses and value of literary study. Later, in Chapter 5, we discuss such local teaching strategies as lectures, seminars and so on, but, for now, we'll explore some ideas that may help teachers acquaint students with a deeper sense not of how to do literary study, but *why* do it at all.

In what follows we want to explore three sets of ideas. First, we want to investigate what kinds of connection students can make with literary works that contribute to their overall education, to the development of their minds and knowledge. Second, we want to suggest that the framing action of pedagogy is a more important variable in students' learning than teachers often think. Third, we want to describe in outline a particular pedagogical approach that helps students make a personal and educational connection with literary works: a pedagogic framework that is 'ancient' in the sense of enduring, and enduringly human.

Student connections: connected students

The kinds of connection that many students want to make to the literature they study can be called, for lack of a better term, existential, that is connections between literature on the one hand, and the basic, enduring terms and conditions of human existence on the other. A line of iambic pentameter in a Shakespeare play or a Keats sonnet may be a thing of beauty forever, but it may not seem so, initially at least, to an 18-year-old freshman or to a 35-year-old adult returning to education in the midst of pressures from employment or parenthood. For both of these students, as different as their circumstances may be, the invitation from a literature teacher who – perhaps kindly, but sometimes cluelessly – thinks her or his own enthusiasm for the technicalities of literature should generate similar enthusiasm in the student, winds up convincing both the 18 year old and the 35 year old of literature's irrelevance to the reality of their everyday lives. Such teacherly enthusiasm is often a bit myopic: what the teacher finds interesting may be a very small blip on any student's radar screen. Teachers need more than their own interests and enthusiasms in order to make a case to students for the value of literary study.

One way to make such a case is to provide a pedagogical frame for literary instruction drawn from conditions that affect all students because they affect all human beings. These conditions include but are not exhausted by: the need for growth, doubts and fears about success, the need for affiliation with others, the unavoidability of dealing with families, the need for friends and companions, the uncertainty of luck, the commonality of the physical senses, the frailty of the flesh, the certainty of loss and grief, the inevitability of death.

The human condition
It is of course very difficult to get contemporary students raised on TV and the literary equivalent of Pop-Tarts to feel any sort of personal connection with the strange behaviour, values and language of such literary artists and moralistic thinkers as the Beowulf poet, Chaucer, Milton, Swift, Pope and Samuel Johnson. And much talk about the benefits of education seems premised on the shallow assumption that students' only interests in it are material and financial. But we all

know that life's most fundamental conditions have little to do with money and are not generally solved by money. How does money solve the problems of grief, sickness, loss, rejection, disappointment?

Novels and poems don't solve those problems either, of course, not in any direct way – literary study is not a form of therapy; rather, as Sidney says, it is a form of learning – but it is the case that novels and poems *address* the griefs and losses of life and, in the means and manner of that address, offer literature students a wide array of stances, attitudes, concepts, insights, subtleties, ethical deliberations and both practical and intellectual remedies that they may adopt or store up for future consideration and possible use. Life for no one comes with a 'how-to' manual – nor is a destiny programmed into one's DNA – and, in the absence of both explicit external instructions and internal determiners, human beings have developed many strategies to help them sort out life's conundrums, to impose patterned meaning on the chaotic data of experience and to help them interpret or create the meanings of things. Science, religion, history, art, social sciences, games and legal systems all qualify as such strategies, but the most comprehensive and ubiquitous of all human strategies for both finding and creating meaning is the telling and consuming of stories. Hence the existential importance of literary study.

Relevance

Of course it is good for students to have stable, high-paying jobs – literature teachers these days may wish their own jobs were more stable and high paying – but having a good job does not absolve anyone from facing certain conditions of life common to human beings as such, regardless of income. It is humanity's *universal* set of conditions that literary study can help students face, and it is to this set of conditions that students refer when they ask their teachers about the relevance of literary study. If teachers cannot answer the question 'Why do we have to read this stuff?' with something more substantive than 'Because it's required' then we do little to counter the bean counters of the world who view literary study as a mere trifle, an anomalous deviation from the bottom line. Thus the concern to help students *connect* with literature.

However, teachers cannot forcibly create those connections. Nor is it helpful for teachers to rely on exhortation. Telling students they must like the literature of Milton and Johnson because it is, by God, *good* for them and implying that they'd better buy the teacher's literary goods or else, is merely a way of teachers losing their own focus and forfeiting their students' trust. Such bullying claims – seldom meant as bullying by well-intentioned teachers, to be sure, but sometimes seen in this light by students nevertheless – are not only ineffective but are usually false. They are false in the sense that the world does not operate this way. Many people who are *not* dolts know nothing at all about Milton or Johnson. More importantly, perhaps, such claims do not invite learning but sound like threats. Teachers need to remember that there is a big difference between a thing being interesting and a thing being important, especially to students; a difference that some teachers conflate as they innocently assume, prima facie, that what is interesting to them is also – or even therefore – important to their students.

Literary pedagogy and liberal education

The difference that students are likely to see between important and interesting throws light on the significance of pedagogical *frames*. What most students make out of the texts they read, literary or non-literary, is not what they make out of them on their own but what they are invited and, indeed, led to make out of them by the pedagogical guidance of their teachers. In literary studies, of course, this pedagogy encourages contributions from fellow students in seminars and through collaborative assignments, among other things. We do not intend to suggest that students learn only from their teachers, who transmit their knowledge and understanding seamlessly, but we do mean to be clear that nonetheless it is teachers who provide the framing pedagogy: that this is their job. Pedagogy frames course content and different frames invite different kinds of understanding of content.

Intellectual and personal development

Teachers of Literature have many specific disciplinary and cognitive goals, but their most general, foundational, goals are developmental. Through education, we want our students to grow intellectually, to mature personally, to develop socially and to become more sophisticated emotionally. We are not talking here about an educational perspective suitable only (or even mainly) for young students. All of us – whether adults out in the world, young people just beginning higher education or people returning to school after years away from the classroom – all of us have room in our lives to grow in these ways. Some adults returning to education may be much more mature in these respects than 18-year-olds, but all teachers who commonly teach adults know that those who return to education after years on the job very often hold goals of personal and intellectual development, along with their goals of financial advancement, even more steadfastly than their younger counterparts. What these adults have learned while out in the world is precisely the importance of personal development, not just as an employee on a job but as a human being dealing with the exigencies of living.

Affective engagement

But these are general teaching objectives. What do literature teachers want in particular? It seems to us that the overarching effect most literature teachers want is for their students to experience the same kind of exciting involvement with literature that *they* felt as students: namely vicarious identification and emotional transport. Those students who have not thought much beyond the employment benefits of higher education may have few conscious thoughts about this educational aim. But, when vicarious identification and transport do indeed occur, it is transparently clear to both students and teachers that such moments constitute the best moments of students' education. They may seldom ask for this experience because they may have no idea that it is available to them, but once they experience it they never ask for a refund on the grounds that it doesn't promise to increase their income. They ask instead for second helpings. Just like athletes playing their games, musicians playing their instruments or philosophers playing with their arguments, students do not feel that the learning that intensifies and enlarges their sense of life and sense of self needs further justification. These experiences can suddenly open a window on life through which a reader learns to see the world in new ways or, in many cases, learns to see new worlds altogether. This is the kind of education most literature teachers received when they first read Chaucer, Shakespeare, Dickens, Austen – and this is probably why, in the end, they became teachers of literature. One can enjoy this sort of thing in private for a lifetime. To decide that you want to *teach* literature must mean that the special adventures of mind and spirit offered by literary study are adventures that you want to share with others, not merely possess on your own.

A literary example that not only creates this experience but that talks about it is the poem the 21-year-old John Keats wrote to his teacher, Charles Cowden Clark, after the two of them stayed up all night reading George Chapman's translation of Homer. In this well-known sonnet, Keats uses two metaphors of the reader: the reader as an explorer of distant lands and the reader as an astronomer who has just discovered a new planet in the heavens. He expresses amazement that such transport is available to human beings, amazement at its beauty, amazement at its significance and amazement that it could take one's imagination so far. The importance of Keats's lines for us as teachers – not as literary critics or scholars of Romanticism but as teachers – is that Keats's feelings of transport exemplify what every student of literature most desires, even if he or she cannot say it. Students want this because we all want this. That is, we want to be taken places in our imagination and feelings that make life seem fresh, bracing and important. Sometimes it is one thing that can do this for us, sometimes another.

Narrative power

But vicarious identification and emotional transport are neither limited to nor solely defined by literary experience. Who can doubt that the success of narratives in the mass media is rooted in the power of stories to take us out of ourselves, to help us define what is important, to help us identify our longings and desires, and to help us achieve a sense of the intensity and vividness of life? For the purposes of this present argument, it does not much matter that many critics blast the mass media for offering only an ersatz vividness and a fake intensity; the point here is that whether or not the identification and transport offered by mass media are good for us or bad for us, they happen, and, as the term 'mass media' asserts, they happen on a massive social scale and go on constantly. Anyone in our contemporary world can go through a whole life avoiding the poems of Pope and the tales of Chaucer, but no one can go five minutes without running into the products of mass media: songs, political ads and DJ patter on the radio, dramas and sitcoms and commercials on TV, billboards in our faces, movies in our malls, newspaper headlines on our doorsteps and running like electronic banners around public buildings. Pop songs are constantly making claims about the most intense forms of love, TV games are constantly hooking us with images of human desire and achievement, movies are constantly enticing us to assent to everything from worlds we can hardly imagine to encounters with people who look like engaging versions of our neighbours.

The contents of vicarious identification and emotional transport offered by literature differ – often but not always – from that offered to us by mass media, but the psychology of the phenomenon is the same in all these cases. It is an eagerness to go outside of ourselves, to find out who we are by triangulating our experience with that of others, and to feel that we are a part of something larger than our own solitary existence. Literary travelling consistently and persistently achieves such identification and transport across generations, races, ethnicities, genders, classes and cultures. There have never been any non-storytelling cultures. *Only* human beings tell stories but *all* human beings tell stories (Gregory, 1995).

Literary experience and learning

To teachers, the desire to help students discover this sense of literary enlargement is not based on its entertainment value for them or its ego gratification for us. Few teachers are such purists that they think any entertaining class is sordid or cheap, nor are they so selfless that ego never plays a role in the desire to be a good teacher. However, most teachers do not want merely to entertain or merely receive on their course evaluation forms such dubious compliments as 'You made tragedy seem very enjoyable'. Most teachers can easily tolerate failure to make the death of Hamlet enjoyable, but what they cannot tolerate is for their students to miss out on the contribution that literary study makes to their liberal education, to the growth of mind, enlargement of self and the complication of feelings and judgement that constitute intellectual growth and personal maturation. As much as teachers tend to value literary experience for its own sake, they do not value it – for themselves or for their students – if 'its own sake' means supposing that it exists, or could exist, apart from the everyday lives in which human beings laugh, suffer, fear, love and die.

It has been difficult since at least the heyday of New Criticism to speak about literary experience as an important form of human learning. If literature is said to be all aesthetic strategies of unity, as the New Critics insisted, or if it is all textual indeterminacy, as the Derridians insist, or if it is just the automatic recycling of hegemonic master scripts, as the Foucauldians insist, or if it's just the inevitable excrescence of cultural and economic forces, as the New Historicists insist, or if it's merely a set of cues that prompt readers to rewrite each text in the reader's own image, as some of the reader-response critics insist, then there is not much learning to be acquired from literary study. But it has never been the case that the kind of human learning that lies at the heart of literary experience exists in an either/or relationship with postmodern views that in effect depreciate it. Literature is both aesthetic strategies *and* human learning, both textually slippery *and* textually determinate, both master-scripted *and* a critique of master scripts. But most of all it is learning.

Through the looking glass

For example, when teachers and their students read the 'Pardoner's Prologue' and the 'Pardoner's Tale' together, they learn something about the practices of the Catholic Church in the Middle Ages; they learn something about enduring human vices such as avarice, hypocrisy, deceit, passion and pride; they learn something about acts of language such as irony, hyperbole, metaphor and rhetoric; and they learn something about the moral criteria by which people like the Pardoner can be judged. As teachers and students surf their way through literary periods and genres, they find many human types different from the Pardoner – the misers, the lechers, the ambitious, the nitwits and so on – and likewise find many situations (comic, tragic, satiric, political, racial . . .) which differ greatly from the types of people and situations they encounter in their everyday life. Thus everyone's involvement with literary representations of what is strange and unfamiliar educates us about how the worlds on the other side of the looking glass might feel and look, what importance such worlds may have and how the people who live in those worlds may evaluate their own ends and methods of living. There is no way anyone can claim that this is not really learning, or that such learning does not enter into the life blood of anyone's everyday existence.

Literature undoubtedly encompasses not only the most comprehensive survey of the massive range of human types and situations to be found on the other side of the looking glass, but embodies this survey in concrete representations that actually invite its readers to assume, through the vicarious imagination, modes of living, feeling and judging that they may otherwise never learn about at all. This is exactly the process that defines a liberal arts education: a process that invites students to perform two significant acts of self-development.

First, it invites students to work explicitly on the development of basic human capacities such as language, reason, imagination, introspection, moral and ethical deliberation, sociability, aesthetic responsiveness, physical embodiment and so on: capacities that are fundamental to self-understanding in relation to others. Second, a liberal education invites students to avail themselves of the resources of their culture, as embodied in such traditions of research and knowledge as the arts and sciences, in order to gain that perspective on their own lives without which one finds it nearly impossible ever to leave the home base of ego. Never leaving the home base of ego presents a great obstacle to ever gaining any rich sense that one's own biography, one's own circumstances, one's own communities and one's own views are not the centre of the universe.

A framing pedagogy: existential 'sidebar' issues

One effective strategy for helping students engage with literary study in existential terms is to develop in class at the beginning of the course a set of *sidebar topics* which, for lack of a better term, one could call 'existential issues'. These sidebar issues can be developed during the whole semester or course. Their value consists of the assistance they give students in finding their own grounds for deciding that Chaucer and Shakespeare and Milton might possess a surprising relevance even in the age of I-Max theatres, rap music, gourmet pizzas, the World Wide Web, Nike sports shoes and the Hubble telescope.

Human physicality

The sidebar topics that we call existential issues refer to those universal conditions of the human experience encountered by all human beings in all times and in all cultures, regardless of their gender, class, race or ethnicity. To begin with, there are the universal facts of human physicality that provide the grounds of common transcultural experience. These include such obvious and common physical facts, for example, as bipedalism, binocular vision, colour perception, prehensile thumbs, male fertilisation, female gestation, sexual intercourse, physical pain, physical pleasure, eating, eliminating, getting sick, ageing, dying and the common human senses of smelling, touching, tasting, hearing, and seeing.

At one level it seems simple-minded to remind everyone of these facts of human physicality, yet much of human experience just *is* grounded in the universal physical facts of tasting and touching, eating and eliminating, grasping and walking, feeling healthy and getting sick, procreating and dying. George Lakoff and Mark Johnson, in fact, in their book *Philosophy in the Flesh*, go so far as to argue that the universal properties of the body are the basis of human conceptuality. This is not the place to recapitulate their whole argument, but their central thesis is both provocative and relevant to teachers who are interested in thinking about a pedagogy that links literary study with existential issues.

> *Think of the properties of the human body that contribute to the peculiarities of our conceptual system. We have eyes and ears, arms and legs that work in certain very definite ways and not in others. We have a visual system, with topographic maps and orientation-sensitive cells, that provides structure for our ability to conceptualize spatial relations. Our abilities to move in the ways we do and to track the motion of other things give motion a major role in our conceptual system. The fact that we have muscles and use them to apply force in certain ways leads to the structure of our system of causal concepts. What is important is not just that we have bodies and that thought is somehow embodied. What is important is that the peculiar nature of our bodies shapes our very possibilities for conceptualization and categorization.*
>
> (Lakoff and Johnson, 1999: 18–19)

Multiculturalism

It is precisely the universality of these experiences that creates much of literature's transcultural power. If difference really were the whole story about human groups and individuals, how could anyone love, respect, be educated or moved by stories of people in other lands, in other cultures or of other races and gender? But nothing is more common than that such ties are felt by readers every day (not to mention music lovers and movie watchers). If the differentness of the Other were indeed absolute – if difference were always already 'uncapturable' difference – then multiculturalism would be nothing but the delusory reach for an impossibility. Multiculturalism, in order to have a programme, demands the transcultural accessibility of common human experiences, many of them grounded in the fact that all human beings share the same bodies.

Reflecting on human physicality shows us how deeply our connectedness with all other human beings lies, for not only do all human beings everywhere and anytime live under the domination of these physical facts, but *all human beings prefer some versions of these facts to others*. All of us – regardless of gender or race, culture or era – prefer to be well rather than sick, prefer to be mobile rather than paralysed, prefer taste to the deprivation of taste, prefer to feel pleasure rather than pain, prefer to eliminate rather than be incapacitated for it, prefer sight to blindness, and so on. Even those who deliberately choose some negative version of one of these pairs – as monks choose not to procreate, for example, or as some swamis may choose immobility – do so for special reasons that they by no means construe as norms for all humanity. After all, if everyone did what swamis do then there would be no point in swamis doing it.

Human sociability

Even more important to us as teachers than the sidebar issues of human physicality, however, are the existential issues deriving from human sociability: the fact that living with other human beings is a universal reality for everyone in all times, places and conditions. None of us – with no ethnic, gender, race or class exceptions – can become human at all, much less flourish, except in the company and conversation and caring of other human beings. The existential issues created by universal facts of human sociability include but are not limited to:

- companionship (the need for it, the pleasures and annoyances and betrayals of it, the grief over loss of companions, sexual companionship, and so on);
- familial relations (the need for families, the complex dynamics of them, the primal pull of family loyalty, the grief over loss of family connections, and so on);
- moral criteria (there are no societies devoid of moral criteria for defining such features of life and conduct as goodness/badness, success/failure, cowardice/bravery, wisdom/foolishness, loyalty/betrayal, just/unjust, fair/unfair, and so on);
- views about the origins and meaning of life (views about what human beings are for, where they came from, what their basic nature and destiny are, and so on);
- views about death (whether death is a punishment, a stage of life, an absolute termination, a passage to some sort of continued, non-physical existence, and so on);

- views about religion (there are no societies devoid of religious beliefs and believers; even non-religious persons have to define their secularity *against* prevailing religious beliefs);
- experience of art (there are no societies devoid of art and artists and no individuals who can evade their society's forms of artistic representation and manipulations of graphic, architectural, representational or ornamental design); and finally
- stories (there are no societies devoid of stories and storytellers and no individuals who do not negotiate at least in part, often large part, a sense of self, reality, the nature of others, and the operation of the world with the representations of just these very things in stories).[2]

Calling these realities 'truths' and emphasising their universality is descriptive, not normative. They are simply empirically true descriptions of certain facts about human existence in all times and places. Among other things, what teachers value about these truths for their students is their power to help students separate the trivial from the serious in human experience. That is also what *they* value about these truths. Regardless of their age or social background, all students today live in a world composed so thoroughly of superficial images, and they are so much aware that these images are designed to manipulate them by making them buy certain products or by making them believe someone's self-interested 'spin' on ideas, and they are so influenced by the image of 'cool' from television shows such as the late-departed *Seinfeld* and *Friends*, that some of them have a hard time identifying a truly serious human issue grounded in a universal, existential fact.

Literary invitations

All of us mere human beings have instincts for grasping serious issues, but none of us receives much help from our culture in developing those instincts. Yet even amidst the linguistic thickets of unfamiliar reading, when students encounter Shakespeare's Sonnet No. 73 about 'That time of year thou mayst in me behold/When yellow leaves, or none, or few, do hang/Upon those boughs which shake against the cold,/Bare ruined choirs where late the sweet birds sang', or when they read Milton's sonnet about going blind at age 43, or when they read the final sentence of Johnson's Preface to his great dictionary in which he says that his work has been protracted until all the people he wished to please with it are dead and that other people's judgements of his success or failure are meaningless to him, then even young and immature students *know* they are in the presence of serious and permanent issues that describe the human condition. Older students often feel the importance of these issues even more keenly because they have more personal experience that resonates with them. But young and old alike – all of us in whatever conditions – are equally vulnerable to grief, to the loss of companions, to the need for courage, and to the certainty of death.

Far from being depressed by considering these grimmer facts of life as probed by literature, students seem braced by them; a little sobered, perhaps, when in the presence of writers who confront these facts without employing the euphemisms we are all used to in popular culture, but glad nevertheless to have their chance to face at least vicariously the circumstances they know all human beings face.

Literary travel

So what does all of this have to do with our students and Keats's travelling in the realms of gold and feeling like 'stout Cortez', 'visiting a peak in Darien'? Everything. The shock of discovery when students find that they are not alone in their feelings, anxieties and thoughts; when they discover that even long-deceased divines such as John Donne know about sexual passion, romance and love; when they discover that even quiet college dons such as Thomas Gray know about the anxieties of young people who wonder if they will ever meet their own expectations of themselves; when they discover that a deeply religious person such as Sir Thomas More can envision a society better than ours even without religion; and when they discover that even the erudite and lofty Samuel Johnson can feel absolutely bereft upon the death of his poor dependant and good friend, Robert Levet: all this discovery is like travelling in foreign lands. It helps students gain a better understanding of their own circumstances through the study of others' circumstances. As C. S. Lewis's most troublesome student in the movie, *Shadowlands*, says, 'we read to learn that we are not alone', and for those of us who wonder sometimes if our own interior lives are so idiosyncratic that no one else could ever understand them, an education in literature provides the supplementary knowledge – supplementary to life itself – that there is, indeed, nothing new under the sun, no human circumstance that has not been faced by someone, somewhere, and that despite the real possibility of failure and defeat in life, good luck and victory are also possible. To study literature from the perspective of existential issues makes it live for students of all ages and circumstances.

If as teachers we can help students discover not just that a sonnet has 14 lines with a particular rhyme scheme and metre, but that these formal features of the sonnet are vehicles for a set of invitations – to feel in new ways, to see in new ways, to think in new ways and to judge in new ways – then we are helping students learn to combine their technical knowledge and the circumstances of their lives. To encounter the elemental realities of the human condition in literature can indeed, as Keats says of reading Homer, strike one dumb with awe and gratification, feelings which Keats captures in the image of stunned amazement on the faces of the first Europeans, looking out on the vastness of the Pacific Ocean.

Literary techniques

The reference to 'technical knowledge' raises one last issue that will close this discussion. All the talk about teaching and learning literature in relation to existential issues is not meant to suggest that technical content in literature classes is less valuable than it ever was or that it should be given short shrift. In learning to understand the power of literature's probing of existential issues, it is imperative that students also learn that this power is generated not by general and vague authorial effusiveness, but is always generated by the *specific aesthetic and rhetorical strategies* that constitute a work's material structure: the imagery, the diction, the tone(s), the descriptions, the characterisations, the narrative techniques, the sound values and rhythms of language, and so on. Thus in order to know how it is that literature *can* resonate with our circumstances requires that students learn the techniques of detailed analysis.

To suggest that students acquire a deeper sense of literature's relevance to human life by framing the study of it with existential perspectives is not to suggest that classes should invite general effusiveness from students either. Both authors and students have to learn to deal with the detailed and concrete realities of language and expression. A trout fisherman's beautifully hand-wrought fly is not much use if it never catches any trout. The general purpose of both the fly and of studying literature provides a reason to go fishing or reading in the first place, but it is also true that within the context of that general purpose, both fishermen and readers have to learn how the object before them is made of many complicated details and sub-structures which account not only for its beauty but also for its utility. In the absence of some account of utility and beauty no one would ever have any reason either to fish or to read.

To reiterate, the pedagogical frame for students' connectedness with literature that has been our subject here is just that: a frame, the 'sidebar' to study. While it provides an existential context for studying literature – constantly keeping before students *why* they study – it does not and should not substitute for detailed analysis of literary techniques. Indeed, it is perhaps this combination of Literature's analytical, intellectual rigour and its expressiveness and 'connectedness' that attracts so many students to study it.

And with that, on to the *what* of study.

. . . TO THE MODERN ACADEMY

Despite all that has been said about the primary importance for students of a framing, guiding pedagogy, for most academics-as-teachers the curriculum (or 'content' to be taught) is a major focus of interest, and perhaps the main focus. So that is where we pick up again the discussion of the discipline today, nonetheless in the hope of persuading you later (should you need it) that pedagogic considerations are at least as important for teaching and that indeed, to students, content and pedagogy are inseparable.

The academic agenda

Course provision

Here at the start of the book it will be helpful to sketch the main contours of course provision in Literature in order to establish some common ground and terminology.

- *Periods and styles.* The period course, such as 'Medieval Literature', 'Seventeenth Century Literature' or 'Victorian Literature' – and style-labelled courses such as 'Romantic Poetry', 'Modernist Literature' – with a focus on close reading of a range of canonical texts and inculcation of scholarly values, practices and skills.
- *Authors.* The 'single author' and 'major author' course: 'Shakespeare' or 'Milton', or courses focusing on clusters of authors such as 'Tennyson, Browning and Arnold', 'The Brontës' Fiction'.

- *Genre(s)*. Courses that focus on genre – the novel, poetry, drama – and on sub-genres such as the short story, lyric poetry, slave narrative, and so on. Sometimes genres and periods are combined, as in 'The Nineteenth Century British Novel', 'Anti-Apartheid Themes in South African Literature 1945–1975', or 'American Short Stories of the 1950s'. Courses on comedy and tragedy also come into this category.
- *Women's writing/feminism*. Courses that focus on women writers and related issues. This is not just a matter of teaching women authors, such as Jane Austen, Edith Wharton, Katherine Mansfield, Nadine Gordimer or Pat Barker, but of teaching them in ways that position their themes, characterisations and visions in relation to women's history, politics, social roles, etc. And women are not the only authors studied; male writers whose attitudes and values help clarify such issues are also read.
- *Themes*. For example, 'Myth, Legend and Literature', or 'Values in Literature' or 'American Visions'. Some courses combine themes with periods and/or genres, styles, e.g. 'Comedy and Politics in Restoration Drama' or 'Visionary Mysticism in Romantic Poetry'.
- *Regional literatures*. Courses such as 'South American Writers', 'Modern Irish Literature', 'Introduction to Australian Literature' or 'African-American Literature'. While departments rarely appoint regional specialists, they will look to use the specialisations that faculty staff bring with them or may develop over the years.
- *Postmodern issues and themes*. Except for feminism, no single issue or theme is likely to orient a course by itself but will usually be included among a cluster of postmodern orientations, such as:
  - '*queer theory*', which holds roughly the same relation to 'gay power' as 'black power' used to hold to the goal of integration. Queer theory is uninterested in accommodation or 'integration' of gay people or gay issues in mainstream societies, but insists on a more radical advocacy designed to change fundamentally social structures and the content of discourse with regard to sexual orientation. But rather than being overtly programmatic, the rhetoric of queer theory is abstrusely theorised and often deeply infused with postmodern notions of the slipperiness of language or with Lacanian ideas about the subconscious;
  - '*new historicism*', which immerses literary texts within the context of the other forms of discourse and sometimes political

practice that characterised the historical period in which the texts were written, such that a Shakespeare text can be claimed, from this point of view, to be as much 'about', say, economics as it is about the humanist themes that have formed the traditional stuff of Shakespeare criticism;

- *'Bakhtinian dialogics'*, which employs the notion of the carnivalisation of language and the tension between monologic and dialogic forms of discourse in order to analyse a literary text's tendency to be open to response, or its tendency to close off response – to have the last word, so to speak – such that the more 'open' texts are usually valorised against those that are said to be 'closed', 'authoritative' or monological;

- *'deconstruction'* or *'Derridean' perspectives*, which, according to the theories of language and text proffered by Jacques Derrida, hold that textual meaning is infinitely deferred – non-graspable in any ordinary sense of determining stable meaning – and, rather than offering the experience of determining what the text is 'about' or what it 'means' offers instead the experience of riding among and through its sliding meanings, such that the reader confronts an ever shifting perspective *not of the world, but of language itself* – a language that seems to head for stable references but is unaware of the moments and places where it slips into contradiction and 'deconstruction';

- *'Foucauldian'* and *'Marxist' approaches* (often taken in tandem with the literary theories of Roland Barthes and Frederick Jameson), which challenge traditional humanistic approaches to literature by emphasising literature's potential to oppress the reader (the way it allegedly colonises the reader's mind and values, for example), and its complicity with the politics of what might be considered a Euro-American hegemony. Foucauldian approaches stress literature's tendency to re-inscribe, on or within the reader, society's 'master scripts' that allegedly are designed to seduce citizens into internalising status-quo values such that they maintain deferential postures toward established authority, without realising the extent to which they are policing themselves, thus allowing the state to avoid exercising the conventional apparatus of authoritarian controls that inspire resistance. Marxist approaches stress literature's participation in economic practices that, properly understood, undermine notions of 'intrinsic' literary excellence and value;

– *'postcolonial' approaches*, which draw heavily on Marx, Foucault, Barthes and Said, specifically focus on both the literature composed by writers *of* the colonising and postcolonial classes (or races or ethnic groups) and the literature composed *by* writers of the colonised classes, etc., primarily with the aim of analysing how these literatures reflect and, depending on the time at which they were written, also helped shape, reinforce or challenge the colonial process;

– *'cultural studies' approaches*, which tend not to rest on a particular theory so much as constitute a general set of strategies of literary interpretation and pedagogy that favour 'contextualising' literary study within historical practices, political configurations and social situations rather than engage with questions of literary quality or value. Such strategies often involve an interest in studying non-canonical, 'popular' literature or fictions, including romance novels, science fiction, soap operas, films, comics ... and may also include performance studies and other approaches designed to underscore the arbitrary, historical nature of the 'old' canon and to suggest that study of a much wider range of kinds of literary representation is both educationally progressive and politically liberating. Like postcolonial studies, cultural studies engage with non-Euro-American ethnic and multicultural literatures.

Compared to the situation even twenty years ago, this represents an explosion of possibilities.[3] The question is, what sort of impact has it had? What does the contemporary curriculum look like? These are questions we return to in Chapter 4. But undoubtedly social, economic and political conditions beyond literature departments have a shaping and constraining influence on the curriculum and courses, as on almost every aspect of contemporary university life.

External conditions

We have touched on some of these conditions already, which, although the details vary, are prevalent in many countries: a dwindling of resources for teaching (for academic staff, library stocks, accommodation, etc.); increasing numbers of students enrolled as a result of 'widening participation' initiatives, many of them relatively unprepared for university-level study, and greater numbers of mature

Hostility to national policy developments among UK academics in English departments is clearly demonstrated in this survey conducted on behalf of the national English Subject Centre (www.english.heacademy.ac.uk) to which 53 (or 40 per cent of) departments responded. In reply to the question *Please describe what changes in the HE environment nationally . . . are having the most impact on your department*, those most often cited in a range of categories were (in descending order):

- excessive bureaucracy/managerialism/central control/audit culture/new initiatives;
- lack of funding/under-funding of increasing student numbers;
- poor funding for research/RAE causing staff to work excessive hours/poor staffing levels;
- need to incorporate skills-based activities/vocational emphasis;
- student debt/all students effectively part-time.

In commenting on these responses, the report's authors also note 'concerns . . . about the ways in which the humanities were suffering by the predominance of a science model in much policy at national level' and 'about the deleterious effects of management-speak, an increasingly detached management tier, and "buzz words" producing reflex actions'. They conclude: '*Responses . . . indicated an overwhelming lack of faith in national policy initiatives*'.

(Halcrow Group et al., 2003: 81–2, emphasis added)

FIGURE 1.1   *UK Higher Education Academy English Subject Centre survey, 2002.*

and part-time students; an emphasis on students' employability and related skills; demands for accountability and quality assurance increasingly exercised over academic departments by university authorities and over the academy by government and its agencies. We sketched a situation of sustained, rapid change on all fronts, much of it inspired by governments' educational policies in turn driven by 'economic necessity'. (For UK academics' responses see Figure 1.1.)

Funding and accountability

In the UK in recent years, for example, the higher education system and its staff have experienced mounting stress. Over a short period an elite system has become a 'mass' system, with a current objective of 50 per cent participation among those under 30 years by 2010 (Department for Education and Skills, 2003). A periodic national 'Research Assessment Exercise' (RAE) mounted by the Higher Education Funding Councils determines each department's research funding for five to six years ahead, based mainly on its academics' publications, their records of attracting external grants and their 'national and international standing'. Academics are therefore required to undertake ever more research; in the case of the Arts and Humanities, in the absence of adequate funding for it. From time to time each department's teaching has also been externally assessed, and graded, in a Subject Review (now an institutional audit system) run by the national Quality Assurance Agency for Higher Education (QAA). Both exercises are costly and time-consuming, and have resulted in 'league tables' of universities and their departments published in the national press. (See Strathern (2000) on the 'audit culture', and the now classic account by Readings (1996), *The University in Ruins*.)

North America

In the USA, if we substitute state for central government agencies, the upshot is not very different: '... we have been witnessing transformations in the economy that have led to the imposition of corporate models on the university ... At the same time, we cannot avoid noticing that classes are getting bigger and the professoriate is shrinking ... States ... are feeling over-drawn by university budgets, and a broad public is increasingly eager to tell us how to do our jobs' (Levine, 2001: 16). In Canada the community

> *during the past decade has suffered slashed budgets and hiring freezes, increased class sizes and crushing teaching loads ... There are now 11 per cent fewer faculty in Canadian universities than in 1992. On average universities have replaced only half of all faculty departing as a result of retirement, disenchantment or both. Reduced government support for the universities is the single greatest reason for shrinking faculty numbers: since 1993, funding has dropped by 20 per cent ...*
>
> (Demers, 2002: 13–14)

Australia and South Africa

In Australia and South Africa, as in the UK, increasingly central control is exercised over the higher education system. In Australia, public institutions' self-monitoring – confirmed by rounds of institutional audits and sealed with differential funding for teaching – has been superseded by the requirements of the Australian Universities Quality Agency, under the aegis of the Department of Education, Science and Training (DEST). These requirements are that universities submit an Institutional Quality Assurance and Improvement Plan annually, along with implementation strategies and the performance indicators used to judge their success. The Plan must include the results of two national surveys: the Course Experience Questionnaire, which assesses graduates' perceptions of the teaching they received, and the Graduate Destination Survey that assesses the employment success of recent graduates. The Plans are described as 'the means of public accountability in the area of quality assurance for Australia's publicly funded universities' (www.dest.gov.au/highered/quality.htm, accessed September 2004).

As regards the Arts and Humanities in particular, discipline-based departments have tended to give way to cross-disciplinary schools. Although student numbers have grown since 1990, staffing has been cut; there is a widening staff/student ratio and expected hours of work by academics has risen; semesters have been reduced in length to reduce the cost of teaching alongside widespread introduction of electronic teaching-learning methods (Pascoe, 2003: 13–14). Recently, the Australian Academy of the Humanities (www.humanities.au) – and especially its new offshoot, the advocacy body CHASS (Council for the Humanities, Arts and Social Sciences: www.chass.org.au) – has mounted an active campaign to have the funding formula for the Arts and Humanities revised in favour of these disciplines and to ensure their involvement in major government initiatives aimed at wealth creation.

In post-apartheid South Africa

the focus of the democratic government . . . has shifted from the need to achieve equity in relation to access to higher education [by the black majority] to the need to achieve greater efficiency in terms of the way the tertiary system functions as a whole. One result of this shift is that debates about what it means to provide 'epistemological access' in terms of curricula and teaching methodologies have been sidelined in favour of the need to develop curricula which will allow students to become members of the global workforce.

(Boughey, 2003: 65)

One of the first pieces of legislation was the National Qualifications Framework (administered by the South African Qualifications Authority), introduced in 1995 to 'standardize and assure the quality of qualifications across [the] system', linked to the introduction of Outcomes Based Education and a focus on skills (including entrepreneurship) at all levels (SAQA, 2000: 68). A preponderance of vocationally-oriented courses was also designed to shift student enrolment away from the Humanities and Social Sciences, which have been most popular with students, towards the Sciences and Technology.

Benchmarking

In many countries, then, control is increasingly exercised over the university sector, with a concomitant loss of its independence. In the UK, this now extends to course provision. A Subject Benchmarking exercise carried out by the QAA is designed to ensure that threshold standards of provision and of student performance are met by each university and by individual disciplines across the range of institutions. Thus the agency claims to provide 'external assurance of quality and standards' (www.qaa.ac.uk). Some, however, see such quality assurance as assuring anything but quality and instead seeking to control the curriculum and pedagogy; these critics believe the current trends merely move the universities further down the 'managerialist' road that ultimately ends in a higher education system for all practical purposes controlled by external agencies. In this connection, philosophers of education Nigel Blake and his colleagues remark:

> It strikes us as too ironic for words that we should find ourselves invited by functionaries ... and politicians to stop thinking imaginatively and innovatively about education − to stop thinking about the very institution whose job it is to sustain and reproduce a thinking society.
>
> (Blake et al., 1998: 19)

Standardisation

Such moves to assure comparable standards nationally almost inevitably produce the kinds of standardising effect we remarked on earlier. Common measures of quality are required across the higher education curriculum, for example, even though like is not being compared to like and the standards adopted are almost everywhere derived from the temporal/social end of the disciplinary spectrum rather than the cognitive − from a discourse of practical competence characteristic mainly of applied scientific, technological and vocational subjects − and with an eye to students' employability. Hence the South African policy of Outcomes-Based Education for all. And hence the UK requirement to plan teaching in terms of the students' 'competence' to *perform* a range of 'learning outcomes' and their acquisition of certain key and 'transferable' *skills*, including information technology. We shall see shortly how inappropriate this discourse is for a discipline such as Literature, situated towards the cognitive end of the spectrum.

Centralised funding

First, though, we should observe that at the same time as budgets for teaching paid directly to the universities by governments in many countries are cut, *greater* resource is being allocated to centrally-inspired and governed teaching bodies – that is, spending which governments rather than the universities control. In Australia, for example, the national Carrick Institute for Learning and Teaching in Higher Education was launched in August 2004 (www.autc.gov.au/institute.htm), administering a national Teaching Development Grants scheme and 'Australian Awards for University Teaching'. There are plans to underline its authority by conferment of the title 'The Australian Institute for Learning and Teaching in Higher Education', or some such.

Likewise, in the UK a number of programmes were in 2004 subsumed under the Higher Education Academy (at www.heacademy.ac.uk), which also administers an awards programme for teachers. Large sums are now being invested in 74 Centres of Excellence in Teaching and Learning (CETLs) selected by a centrally-managed competition – £200–500,000 per annum for five years for each Centre's projects and a one-off capital sum in the millions – very few of them, incidentally, servicing the Humanities and none English Literature. In both countries the rhetoric is one of 'modernisation' and 'innovation', though again critics see this kind of centralising development as a further encroachment on the universities' and on academics' autonomy.

Matters are organised differently in the USA, where the Carnegie Foundation for the Advancement of Teaching, a 'national center for research and policy studies about teaching and learning' (www.carnegiefoundation.org), is independent and has a much longer history. The Foundation hosts a large number of programmes and offshoots, for instance the Carnegie Academy for the Scholarship of Teaching and Learning (CASTL), which is a major player in the rapidly developing and influential 'Scholarship of Teaching and Learning' movement (see Chapter 7). It also hosts a Knowledge Media Laboratory and it, too, runs a 'US Professors of the Year' awards programme. While it may seem churlish to question any celebration of teaching, one wonders whether, ironically, awards such as these might not in fact achieve the opposite of the desired effect (i.e. parity of esteem between teaching and discipline-based research), by corralling teaching and so further divorcing it from research?

Classroom control

Sweeping change extends not only to university accountability and funding but also to such previously entirely internal and autonomous matters as curriculum decision-making and on deep into classroom practice itself – in the UK, mainly via the Subject Benchmarking programme referred to earlier. And we are all e-universities now, constantly exhorted to apply the rapidly developing electronic technologies in our teaching in the belief that these technologies are both modernising and cost cutting, and lest *our* university should become eclipsed in the globalising educational marketplace. Teachers become students again as we learn to use the technologies and, even as established academics, must undergo (re)training in the business of teaching itself. In short, almost everywhere higher education is being transformed into something like an industry that makes 'courseware' and offers services around the world for which its 'clients' must pay – and a rather impoverished industry at that, with more and more of its workers doing predetermined externally controlled jobs on a contractual basis for relatively little remuneration.

But, if all these changes impose what sometimes seems to us a great burden, what of our students? How might fee-paying, mounting debt and the related need for part-time work affect their studies and their well-being? How should we respond to the extra demands on their energies, even during term-time? What, these days, do they 'need' from us as teachers? Such questions will crop up again, but seeking an answer to the last of them – what students might need from us – raises a prior, more fundamental question we will address now: what does it *mean* to study and 'learn' Literature?

The student agenda

Obviously, at bottom studying Literature means studying literary works – a curriculum involving some mix of courses/modules and texts of the kinds outlined earlier, often involving elements of the student's personal choice. Leaving aside the contested question of

which texts in particular, *all* literary works are of course representations: of the activities, ideas, beliefs, imaginings and cultural practices
of individuals and groups, in our own and other societies, over time.
As such, the literary text is always something that 'stands for' or
represents the conditions of time and place in which it was created, and
all the knowledge, ideas, beliefs and intentions that went into its
making – for we cannot, of course, gain access to these things in a direct
way. The text's meanings and significance stand in need of analysis,
interpretation and evaluation. This entails the *making* of *meaning*.
Meaning does not reside 'in' the text, as it were ready to jump out at us,
but is made in the active process of encounter between object and
inquirer (Gadamer, 1989), text and reader. The reader questions the
text and the text 'questions' the reader. Processes of analysis-interpretation-evaluation are central to the study of Literature, then; they are
the means through which we produce knowledge in our discipline.

Text and process

It follows from this that students must learn how to read texts closely.
They must engage actively in the quasi-technical process of *textual
analysis*, involving knowledge of the 'rules' governing the composition
of different text genres and sub-genres, their conventional subject
matters, purposes and formal elements, applying to them the relevant
analytical concepts. They must also learn how to make appropriate
interpretation of the text's meanings, arising out of that formal,
analytical study and including knowledge and understanding of the
socio-historical circumstances of the text's inception and reception,
along with the interplay of these contexts. Also implied here is
consideration of the text's (possibly changing) status over time, or acts
of *appraisal* involving the exercise of evaluative judgement. These
processes are of course contentious, subject to theories about why and
how we do them – theories which themselves change over time and
are part of the contexts that students must come to understand. They
also have to learn how to express persuasively in speech and writing
the ideas they read and think about, within the terms and conventions
of literary discourse (of illustrated argumentation supported by textual
and other evidence).

These central processes of textual analysis-interpretation-evaluation
and of communication are of course dynamic, interlinked and overlapping. It is not as if one analyses a text in detail, then moves on to
interpret its meanings and, finally, appraises the values it represents

and its value to us here and now. Students must come to understand that these are not sequential stages towards the painstaking construction of some mental edifice that is subsequently committed to paper or expressed in speech, but different aspects of a hermeneutic process. What happens is much more like a 'circling around' the text: reading and questioning, pulling back to consider the text as a whole, jotting down notes, reading on, re-reading and so on, back and forth, shifting the focus of one's attention and revising interim interpretations and judgements along the way. 'Questions always bring out the undetermined possibilities of a thing', says Gadamer (1989: 383), and 'no one knows in advance what will "come out" of a conversation'. The process is open-ended; the reader risks being changed by it.

Discursive knowledge

Along the way, the students are learning what *kind* of discipline Literature is, coming to understand that our knowledge is constituted in its very discursive process. They must understand that it is through language that we both negotiate and share our meanings with others and, therefore, that our knowledge is socially constructed within human language, history and culture, and so open to negotiation and change. They must understand that there are no fixed hierarchical structures of knowledge, no obvious causal explanations and no undisputable truths of any significance anywhere to be found; that rival discourses struggle for ascendancy within the discipline (witness in some places a recent redefinition of the discipline as 'Literatures in English'), constituting new entities and critical standpoints, such as 'gender'. (Of course, these observations do *not* mean that as regards textual interpretation 'anything goes'. As we just saw, appropriate interpretation of meaning is shaped and bounded – by the text's genre and form, and by the full range of circumstances of its inception and its reception including the theoretical-critical considerations brought to bear on it.) So, incidentally, more shame on us if we wage war over such change when after all it is in the nature of things. Indeed, without such creative tension the discipline would not be a *living* tradition of thought and practice.

Critical engagement

Our students learn that 'criticism' is both the method and the outcome of their study (Scholes, 1985), that when they attempt to analyse the formal elements of a text, interpret its meanings and evaluate its significance they necessarily take a critical stance in relation to it and, when they communicate their ideas to others, what they produce (their own text) is 'criticism'. Critical engagement is what study of humanities disciplines both entails and teaches. Students of Literature do not learn the skills involved – of analysis, interpretation, evaluation, synthesis, argumentation, written and verbal communication – as 'skills', in a vacuum, but in the course of their literary study and as mutually influencing and informing abilities that are necessarily bound up in the very *process* of that study. Clearly, this kind of learning involves much more than the acquisition of 'skills' (in the sense usually meant).

In summary, the study of Literature is hermeneutic, intertextual, participatory, value-laden, context-dependent and relatively indeterminate. As its participants learn to make theoretically informed, appropriate interpretations and judgements, by engaging with the primary and the secondary texts produced by their predecessors, by making their own inquiries and producing their own texts, so they engage in *critical* processes. As such, this kind of education offers insights into cultures of the past and of the ways in which, through our discourse, past and present, we negotiate and share meanings – insight that may increase and even transform people's understanding of themselves, their society and their place in it. Clearly, learning such as this can have no end-point and few predetermined, objective 'outcomes' (in the sense usually meant).

This, then, is the students' agenda: to learn in these ways and to learn well. And it is of course the literature teacher's job to help them do so. In the next chapter we address the question of appropriate pedagogy head on, posing the question: What is 'good' teaching?

INTRINSIC JUSTIFICATION

In referring just now to the potentially transformational effects of the study of Literature, we do not mean to suggest that this is the *purpose* of a higher education in the discipline. Certainly we have argued in favour of an approach to teaching Literature, a framing pedagogy, that foregrounds connections between literature and the human condition, but this argument was based on empirical truths about our physical and social existence. By contrast, to say that a higher education in

Literature should be undertaken for the sake of personal transformation would be to offer a normative, extrinsic justification for it that, like others of its kind (*for* wealth creation, social reform . . .) would serve only to divide the academic community even more. And to that objection we might add another, one of internal contradiction. For what about students who would resist the transformational endeavour? Might not they see insistence on it as the goal of literary education as condescending, or impertinent, or even (deep irony) authoritarian? ('We have ways of making you transform yourself . . .') And wouldn't there then be a tendency to pathologise those students who refused to be co-opted? What we *are* saying is that such transformation is implicit in the very processes of critical engagement involved in the study of Literature, and may well ensue.

Critical humanism?

So, might an intrinsic justification of this kind, a sort of marriage between hermeneutics and pedagogics,[4] be more appealing to the community – enabling some kind of federation among us, a 'speaking with one voice'? Perhaps coupled with a fuller appreciation of the autonomy of the Humanities generally, and the difference of this academic domain from others?[5] What is essential for this case is that humanities educators reach agreement about what *are* the centrally important processes of their disciplines. Only then will we be in a position to insist on the value of our hermeneutic and pedagogic practices – to justify offering our students the wide range of experiential and interactive opportunities many of us have so far managed to, despite the difficulties involved. And, simultaneously, we might better resist inappropriate educational conceptions and pedagogic prescriptions from whatever external source. For as regards Literature, we have seen that when these injunctions inhibit the inherent 'literariness' of the educational project, to that extent the discipline is distorted. We may then go so far as to draw the value of Literature's inherent processes to the attention of our students. For it appears that they are after all marketable; many employers actually want people who can think clearly and make appropriate interpretations of meaning, are flexible, adaptable and can communicate well! But that is not to say that this is what the study of Literature is *for*. For the study of Literature is for the study of Literature.

Notes
1. Notable among them: Duguid (1984); Bérubé and Nelson (1995); Graff (1995); Ellis (1997); Jay (1997); Scholes (1998); Delbanco (1999). Looking back, the next generation of US literary scholars is, according to Insko (2003: 347), able to take a more sedate view of the 'canon debates', seeing them as 'a part of a much longer continuum'. Likewise, scholars in the UK, where the warring was generally less vituperative and damaging, who tended to focus on developments in literary theory and criticism during the period (for example, Widdowson, 1982; Eagleton, 1983; Guy and Small, 1993; Evans, 1993). In short, the intellectual history of the discipline, its purposes and curriculum, are highly contested.
2. Jerome Bruner (1996b: 101) argues that there are three 'primitive' modes of narrative – the intersubjective, the actional, the normative – and that they 'probably all have biological roots in the genome'. As modes of making sense or meaning (that is, as modes of knowledge), he continues, 'They certainly have elaborated support systems in the cultures that humanize us'.
3. 'English Department Home Pages Worldwide' includes courses offered in more than 1,300 departments. See the book's Bibliography: Websites.
4. Dubbed 'critical humanism' (Chambers, 2001; in the same volume also see Hardwick, and Parker). The small 'c' of 'critical' is deliberate. In using the term 'critical humanism' there is no intention to refer to or endorse the tenets of Critical Theory, Habermasian or otherwise.
5. Unexpectedly, some support for this point of view is to be found among social psychologists, such as Feldman and Kalmar (1996). Elaborating an argument launched by Bruner (1986) they point to two distinct modes of thought, the Galilean and the Aristotelian. The Galilean addresses itself to non-intentional objects, affords causal explanations and understanding of what a thing *is like*, whereas the Aristotelian addresses intentional objects, offers teleological explanations and understanding of what a thing *means*. Each is scientific in that each has its own coherence, the former by subsumption under a covering law and the latter from within the abstract patternings (or frame) of genres which 'trigger' appropriate interpretations of meaning.

Key references
Chambers, E. A. (ed.) (2001) *Contemporary Themes in Humanities Higher Education*. Dordrecht: Kluwer Academic Publishers.
Readings, W. (1996) *The University in Ruins*. Cambridge, MA: Harvard University Press.
SAQA (2000) *The National Qualification Framework and Curriculum Development*. Waterkloof: South African Qualifications Authority.

Websites
Carnegie Foundation for the Advancement of Teaching, USA, at www.carnegiefoundation.org
Department of Education, Science and Training, Australia, at www.dest.gov.au/highered
UK Quality Assurance Agency for Higher Education, at www.qaa.ac.uk

2

What is good teaching?

'TEACHING' AND 'GOOD TEACHING'

A question prior to 'What is *good* teaching?' is 'What is teaching?' What, indeed. As teachers we may find this bald question strangely difficult to answer. It's just what we do, in lectures, classes, seminars, workshops, tutorials, by telephone, in teaching texts, websites, online. We study literary texts and movements, theoretical and critical works, performances and so forth, and analyse and discuss them with our students; we try to help our students become better at expressing their ideas and feelings verbally, in writing, creatively; we mark and assess their work ... But, whatever we might reply, we are unlikely these days to say, simply, 'Well, we tell them what we know'. And this is in large part owing to an extraordinarily popular and pervasive force in higher education known as the 'Student Learning' movement. Indeed, so successfully has attention been shifted from teachers/teaching to learners/learning in recent times, at least in Britain and Australia, that it is almost shocking to see the question 'What is teaching?' asked at all. In so far as the movement has helped us think of teaching as a means to an end rather than an end in itself the effect has been salutary, for teaching is, of course, a means to an end – a complex of activities, strategies, mechanisms, invitations, stimuli and rhetorical ploys designed to help students learn and to become better learners.

The Student Learning movement

Begun in the 1970s, the Student Learning movement's origins are credited to the Swedish Göteborg school of academics and educational researchers – to work carried out by Ference Marton and his colleagues. (See, for example, the seminal book by Marton et al. (1984) *The Experience of Learning*, in which the work of the movement's originators is re-presented along with subsequent development of it by them and by researchers in the UK; and also Ramsden (1992) on the implications of the movement's precepts for the practice of teaching.) This group's work was underpinned by the belief that 'good learning' should be judged by *what* students learn – rather than how much they learn, the main criterion of the then more familiar input-output model of such research (as outlined in Entwistle and Ramsden, 1983: chapter 3) – in the context of the academic subject under study. And it claims that the *approach* a student adopts to study is closely related to the learning outcomes of it. The researchers came to distinguish between two significantly different approaches to study among their student-subjects: a surface-level approach, in which the student focuses on the text ('the sign'), relies mainly on memorisation and largely regurgitates what has been 'learned' in assignments and exams; and a deep-level approach, in which 'what is signified' is the focus for interpretation and greater understanding is the goal of study (Marton and Säljö, 1976a: 7–8). Further, the researchers found that the conceptions that students have of the study tasks before them and the level at which they process what they study produce either 'surface', atomised learning and a tendency to fail (or partly fail) courses, or 'deep', meaningful learning and greater academic success.

On this view of things, the teachers' job is of course mainly to foster a deep-level approach to study among their students, and to encourage the students to reflect on the ways in which they study and learn. This the teacher can do by devising appropriate study activities and, especially, assessment tasks, for

> Students adopt an approach determined by their expectations of what is required of them. While many students are apparently capable of using 'deep' or 'surface' strategies, it may be that the current demands of the examination system are interpreted by them as requiring mainly the recall of factual information to the detriment of deeper levels of understanding.
>
> (Marton and Säljö, 1976b: 125)

Generic versus discipline-based

The tendency to adopt a surface or deep approach to study, then, is not so much a settled disposition or quality of the student herself or himself; more, it depends upon the educational *context* – of the subject being studied, of teachers' expectations and teaching methods, and of the kind of assessment system in operation. (For recent, detailed accounts of the original research and its later development, and for critique, see, for example, Richardson, 2000; McLean, 2001; Chambers, 2002a; Haggis, 2003.)

Whatever one might conclude about the validity and quality of the Göteborg researchers' work, it is clear that they perceived strong links between three factors – the nature and content of the discipline under study, teaching and learning – connections that have been weakened progressively over time as detailed investigation of students' subject-based study has given way, in the wider movement, to inventory studies of large numbers of students' study approaches and practices irrespective of their discipline, and as 'teaching' has become synonymous with 'facilitating learning'. Indeed, 'the more the teacher talks the less the student learns' has become something of a mantra in the new profession of staff/faculty development.

And the original researchers' conclusions are diametrically opposed to the tendencies in higher education policy noted in Chapter 1, towards development of students' 'generic' or 'transferable' skills. Rather, they argue,

> . . . if we want to improve the way people set about learning, we should not think in terms of a general kind of training independent of the content of the academic subject . . . general learning skills (if there are any) should rather be regarded as intrinsic to the study of subject content.

Likewise,

> . . . general principles of teaching (if there are any) should be viewed as aspects of the teaching of certain specific contents.
>
> (Dahlgren and Marton, 1978: 26–7)

Amen to that. How we got from such a laudable attempt to dent the carapace of complacency surrounding what was offered in the name of higher education in the mid-twentieth century – by turning the research spotlight onto the recipients of our systems – to the present situation in which 'teaching' is almost a dirty word in a 'student-centred' world view is another story. But, to us, the prevalent knee-jerk reaction that teaching is inherently suspect is badly mistaken and, indeed, an anti-intellectual view of things.

Academic-disciplinary core

No doubt there is poor teaching to be found in our universities: an overemphasis on the formal lecture and on book learning, perhaps, and insufficient attention to ways of working that help students make sense of what they read, hear and see. But to denigrate and diminish the role of the teacher as teacher, or in extreme cases deny it altogether, is no solution. Still, academic disciplines are the 'core business' of the university – despite being scorned, in some quarters, as producing a Balkanisation of knowledge. That is because the various disciplines of knowledge and inquiry we see today have been developed over time as the (increasingly differentiated) ways we distinguish between, and mediate, different aspects of human experience, activity and imagination. Far from constraining us and our understanding of the world, as teachers or students, the disciplines render our world *knowable*. They represent the ways in which people have, so to speak, 'divided up' the world (to some extent artificially no doubt) so that between us we may attend to different aspects of it in detail and, together, come to understand it better in all its complexity. However, what is understood by 'discipline' and (interdisciplinary) 'field' of knowledge and inquiry is contested (a classic account is to be found in Hirst, 1974; also see Blake, 2000, on Habermas and Lyotard, and Peters, 1995). Discipline boundaries are of course permeable and often overlapping, and the way the disciplines are constituted is constantly changing as our circumstances and our understandings change – witness, for example, the emergence of such fields as Cultural, Environmental and Media Studies in recent times. The disciplines and fields are thus *living* traditions of thought and inquiry.

Academics are those of us in society who make it their business to get 'on the inside' of the disciplines and fields: to understand how we come to know (the underlying theoretical issues, appropriate methods of inquiry and the principles and practices involved); to acquire substantive knowledge of the field, along with the ability to speak and write expertly in terms of the relevant discourses; to help extend the limits of our knowledge and understanding. To suggest that people who know and understand all these things should not directly teach them to others who have opted to study them is an astounding proposition. It betrays a woeful underestimation of the complexity of disciplinary structures and the demands they make on us all, and quite unrealistic optimism regarding most students' intellectual capacity and stamina for inquiry. Left to themselves, and to each other, students may 'pick up' these things, but to say that they will do so much more slowly than if they were taught well is surely not a problematic assertion. So we believe that good teaching must also be a major focus of educational research and development in our universities.

'Learning' and education

Having said all that, there is a sense in which 'learning' does not depend upon teaching (good or otherwise), as the founders of the discipline of Philosophy of Education in Britain argued some time ago (Hirst and Peters, 1970). While of course we are learning things all the time, in a variety of contexts, the authors first demonstrate that indeed there is a logical relationship between learning and education – the particular form of learning we are talking about here. That is, in *education*, learning is understood:

- to have particular objects (people are setting out to learn some*thing*);
- to imply certain levels or standards of achievement; and
- generally, to be worthwhile/non-trivial: involving the acquisition of knowledge, understanding and skills that are seen as desirable and important or useful (even though people may disagree about what precisely is desirable, etc.).

But, they continue, there is no such *necessary* relationship between 'learning' and 'teaching'. All students, and perhaps especially those in higher education, may learn without being taught directly: from books, films, TV, CD-ROM, the Internet, and from discussion among themselves (whether face to face or in computer conference).

'Teaching'

That said, however, the authors go on to argue that when teachers are teaching, *and if they can be said to be teaching at all*, they must, at least, be aiming to create conditions in which learning is possible. Accordingly, they identify three logically necessary conditions for central cases of 'teaching' activities:

1. 'they must be conducted with the intention of bringing about learning';

2. 'they must indicate or exhibit what is to be learnt';
3. 'they must do this in a way which is intelligible to, and within the capacities of, the learners' (Hirst and Peters, 1970: 81).

'Teaching', then, takes both a direct object and an indirect object – educators teach *subjects* to *students*.

Signalling 'content'

Let's just grant the first condition – assume that as teachers we do intend to bring about learning, by whatever means. The second condition draws attention to the point underlined by the Göteborg researchers: that in education there must be a content to be learned. (It should be clear that our understanding of content is not of a 'factual nuggets' kind, amenable to multiple-choice testing; nor is it restricted to propositional knowledge, but includes theories, processes, related activities and skills, open-ended pursuits, and so on.) Furthermore, whatever the content it must be made manifest to the students, otherwise the 'teacher' is being self-indulgent or is engaged (even if unintentionally) in some form of manipulation – and it is indeed hard to see how students can learn well if they are not aware, to some extent at least, what it is they are supposed to be learning. But we do not take this to mean, for instance, that learning objectives or outcomes for classroom activities should always be fully explained to students at the start. This would become formulaic and annoying or boring. Rather, it is often a matter of the teacher *contextualising* a new topic or aspect of study – so that the students can see its relationship to other topics, see the point of it – and often this may be achieved by means of a relevant, thought-provoking question or activity that focuses their minds on some of the issues about to be raised (see, for instance, the initial 'Activity' in the Words module, in Chapter 5 under 'The principle of engagement'). So perhaps 'signalling what is to be learnt' is a better, more inclusive way of expressing this idea.

Intelligibility

As regards the third of the conditions, the extent to which teachers address the question of intelligibility is an important way of distinguishing good teaching from poor because the educational aims that teachers have rarely determine the precise content to be taught/learned or the particular teaching methods to be used (as we demonstrate in the next chapter, under 'Approaches to teaching academic writing') – both of which of course profoundly affect the nature and extent of the students' understanding. This is actually a liberating observation. What it means is that there is a *variety* of ways in which teachers can make their subject matter intelligible to students. No doubt some ways of structuring the content of courses and some teaching methods will be more appropriate than others, depending on the topic or aspect of study and the students in question, but nothing (that is *educational*, in the above definition) is ruled out in principle.

Educators are justified, then, in thinking widely and creatively about their teaching methods. Indeed they must, because for cases of 'good teaching' in higher education we would want to add two more conditions. First, that through their teaching educators should be aiming to engage and/or extend their students' interest in and enthusiasm for the subject. We could hardly regard someone as a good teacher if in the process the students were bored rigid or otherwise alienated. And second, in order to promote meaningful learning we would say teaching should be conducted in such a way that students are encouraged to think critically and independently about what they study: to 'think for themselves'.[1] In these connections, we would acknowledge the energising value (and, from the teacher's point of view, the scholarly value) of teachers forging a close relationship between their discipline-based research and their teaching. Enthusiasm for the discipline and the display of serious critical engagement with it can of course be highly infectious in the classroom. However, there is more to be said about the relationship between research and teaching, and that more will mainly be said in Chapter 7. Meantime, all the conditions of good teaching are summarised in Figure 2.1.

Aims:

- to bring about learning;
- to signal what is to be learnt;
- to be intelligible to the students and within their capacities;
- to engage and/or extend their enthusiasm for the subject;
- to encourage critical, independent thinking.

FIGURE 2.1   *Summary: good teaching in higher education.*

Disciplinary process

So, what are the implications of this rather abstract discussion for the teaching and learning of English Literature? It follows that if the students' abilities to undertake the processes fundamental to the discipline (of literary-textual analysis, of interpretation and evaluation, and of communication) are relatively undeveloped – and why, otherwise, would they occupy the role of 'student'? – good teaching demands two things:

- that students should be *made aware* of the central importance of these processes for their knowledge and understanding of Literature; and
- that these processes should be *taught*, explicitly, comprehensively and in ways that are intelligible, engaging and thought-provoking (as we try to demonstrate here and in the next chapter with respect to teaching close reading, theory and essay writing).

In the past, teachers may have assumed that beginning undergraduates were already (from their schooling) quite accomplished at reading literary texts, and have taken the view that, if not, they would soon pick it up. However, that pragmatic 'solution' no longer applies (if it ever did). Given the conditions in the modern academy noted in Chapter 1 – particularly the demographic changes in the student body and shifts in the structure and emphases of the curriculum – along with broader cultural changes that (we shall see in a moment) have tended to marginalise reading, such an assumption is increasingly likely to be false. We *cannot* assume that our students just know how to read a literary text, or understand what might be meant by genre (either in the literary sense or as regards academic ways of writing), or are able to structure an argument and provide appropriate and sufficient evidence in support of it. What is not so clear is how such teaching is to be accomplished, when our students are so heterogeneous, the curriculum is expanding and also increasingly fragmented by modularisation, and class contact time and resource for teaching are curtailed. But, at least, we can acknowledge that some shift of attention and resource from the later to the early stages of undergraduate education is strongly implied – something that will be familiar to teachers of adult students for whom the conventional higher education entry qualifications are often waived. We will look more closely at issues of curriculum and teaching method in Chapters 4 and 5 of the book.

For now, the focus is on the *nature* of this kind of teaching and, specifically, on teaching three of the processes previously identified as fundamental to our students' interests as students of Literature. That is, on students' learning:

1. how to read literary texts closely (understanding processes of textual analysis and interpretation);
2. how to evaluate what they read (in the modern academy, associated with understanding the role of literary theory and the practice of criticism);
3. how to communicate their knowledge, understandings, ideas and judgements in writing.

The first of these processes is discussed in what follows and the remaining two in the next chapter.

Our emphases in this first part of the book – on close reading, evaluation and writing – are further justified by evidence from a recent survey of practice in UK Literature departments conducted on behalf of the Higher Education Academy English Subject Centre (Halcrow Group et al., 2003). The survey found that:

● departments regard attention to students' 'Reading/interpretative skills' as the second-most important guiding consideration in designing Literature degree courses (p. 55);
● 'critical/literary theory' is the most widely taught *compulsory* course at Level 1 (p. 70);
● departments regard 'Close reading' and 'Theoretical approaches to literature' (respectively) as second and fourth in importance among their graduates – yet these same categories top the list of aspects of the students' knowledge that the departments are *least* satisfied with on graduation (p. 74);
● 'presentation of academic work' (referencing, bibliography, etc.) and 'essay-writing skills' are most often made *compulsory* elements of the Literature programme (p. 44);
● the essay 'written in non-exam conditions' is the most frequently employed method of student assessment (p. 38).

So these three aspects of a higher education in Literature are of the first importance and are also widely recognised as problematic.

Given that our focus here is practical – *how to* teach these things – we will sometimes demonstrate as well as talk about them. Here at the start of the book we are addressing ourselves especially to beginning and fairly new teachers, on the assumption that they may have relatively little experience of teaching.

AN APPROACH TO TEACHING CLOSE READING: TEXTUAL ANALYSIS AND INTERPRETATION

One of the most deadly defects of the teacherly optic nerve is the blindness that hides from us the fact that few of our students, even literature majors or specialists, are readers of literature to the same great extent that we, their teachers, are, and the problem with this blindness is that it can lead us to think that students are being lazy, difficult or unintelligent when they are really being only inexperienced. More and more of us live in an image world, an icon world, a movie and TV world, an Internet world, and even when we do still live in a word-and-print world we are more likely to see or hear words and print in soundbite form than in literary form.[2] Even students who are only ten years younger than their youngest teachers will have been raised in an Internet world that was not available to those teachers when they were that age. What does this mean for us as teachers? In truth, nobody knows what the full implications of our societies' move from a word-and-print to an image-and-icon world means – discussion of the topic is moving full bore – but there are some obvious implications for teachers of Literature.

At the least, it means that most literature students will not be voracious readers (see Figure 2.2). They may not even be what most teachers would call avid readers. Saying this is not intended to deprecate students' abilities or their motives for taking literature courses. It is an attempt to be realistic about the place of serious reading in today's society. A recent report from the USA (*Reading at Risk: A Survey of Literary Reading in America*) summarises the situation 'in a single sentence: literary reading in America is not only declining rapidly among all groups, but the rate of decline has accelerated, especially among the young' (National Endowment for the Arts, 2004: Preface, vii). Just as writers of essays or novels must know who their

In response to the question . . . *have you observed any changes in the profile of your students over the last five years which have affected their teaching and learning?*, the following features were most often reported:

- constricted range of reading/knowledge;
- decline in writing skills;
- engaged in paid employment/other commitments.

The report's authors remark: 'Comments on student writing skills tend to concentrate on basic literacy shortcomings, and on weakness in expression and organisation. The burden of opinion is that these weaknesses are on the increase . . .' A marked drop in the range of students' reading is consistently noted 'under the heading of a decline in preparedness. There is a significant indication of concern about the extent of students' reading or knowledge. . . . Less experience of complex literary texts [especially pre-twentieth-century texts], and difficulties with "academic discourse" were also noted'.

(Halcrow Group et al., 2003: 14)

FIGURE 2.2 *Changes in student profile: UK English Subject Centre survey, 2002.*

audience is, so teachers must have a feel for where their students are, what world(s) they live in, and this means that all of us, experienced and inexperienced teachers alike, need to take our students' comparatively lesser degree of saturation in prints and words into account when we teach literature. 'Taking into account' does not mean that we have to make excuses for students when they perform poorly, but it does mean that if we have no idea where *their* starting point is or what *their* context is, then we can wind up making both them and ourselves miserable by holding inappropriate expectations. Worse, we can misdiagnose, and thus never fix, the nature of both our problems and theirs.

'Automatic' perception

Attending closely to complex, multilayered and densely evocative details arranged in formal patterns – as in stories, novels and poems – is not a natural act. What is natural is saving the energy that perception requires by learning routines, shortcuts and automatic screening strategies. All of us are incredibly skilled at making large inductive leaps of perception based on minimal data: this is of course how caricature works. If, for example, we could not screen out most of the visual and auditory stimuli in a room where we are listening to a lecture or a concert we would go crazy trying to deal with all the (irrelevant) data: dots in the acoustical tiles on the ceiling, the pattern in the carpet and curtains, the smudges and flecks on the painted walls, the quality of light coming in the windows, the squeaking of other people's chairs, the sounds of their breathing . . . In order to get through the day, any day, we must learn how *not* to attend to details that we can sacrifice. Indeed, as contemporary life grows more and more complex people learn to take more and more shortcuts. This general pattern of perception – relying automatically on cues that we know so well we don't have to think about either the cues or the response – is a way of life for all of us, a habit of mind. However, the negative side of this habit is that we don't cultivate it selectively. We automatically tend to see the world as caricature, to cease to see the details of life that would, if we were paying better attention, enrich and vivify us. So teachers can hardly be surprised when students distracted by lack of experience, by families, by employment or by all of these at once do not have good skills for paying close attention to complex, nuanced, connotative, suggestive, formalised literary details worked out according to literary conventions that few of them have very much real experience or knowledge of in today's image-and-icon world.

Habitualisation

As a teacher and a professional reader you will have worked hard to develop your own skills of analysing and responding to literary cues at a very high level of intellectual acuity, and now you possibly remember little of the difficulty involved in that process Between your student days and now, you have learned to overcome, at least with respect to literary experience, the tendency toward automatic perception – what the Russian formalist Viktor Shklovsky calls 'habitualization' and which he took to be the enemy of art as well as life – and now you have discovered the joy of paying close attention. You know what it can teach you, how it develops your cognitive powers and how it can carry you to new places in your intellect, feelings and judgements. But only a few of your students know this, and those few know it only intuitively or experientially, not theoretically. Few of them will have actually thought about it, and hardly any of them will have reflected on how to cultivate this ability. To help our students learn the thrill of paying close attention, to think about its advantages and to cultivate it as an ongoing skill is one of the great opportunities available to us as teachers of literature. However, the students' inability to read texts closely, their inability merely to attend to *all* the words in some sensitive and thoughtful fashion, stands in their way and in ours. What can be done about it?

A case-book class on James Joyce's 'Araby'

In what follows we present something like a case-book example of close reading based on Joyce's short story (from *Dubliners*). We have taught this story many times and can report that, no matter how simple it may appear to you, our students almost always find it confusing. Now you know that if they read it closely, take it apart into small pieces and reconstruct it into its large patterns, it will become clearer to them. But knowing how to help them do this, while it is of the essence in teaching literature, is no easy thing. No one can learn a complicated set of skills by listening to an expert talk about doing it. And it will do no good simply to display the doing of it yourself. When we do this our students are in the state we are all in when we watch a highly skilled and fast computer whiz, for example, who thinks to be showing us how to do this or that but is in fact doing it for us, and going so fast in the meantime that we have no idea how the outcome was achieved. So the question is, how do we get our students actively involved in analysing the details of 'Araby' in class such that they acquire a sense *of their own* of how it works?

The class is not a real class, of course, and the vignette that follows is not a transcript. But if not real it is certainly realistic in the sense that it is a compilation of many classes we have taught over the years. The questions and answers are designed to illustrate problems encountered by both students and the novice teacher, and to suggest what teachers can do to make those encounters, some of them problems, productive and useful. Our remarks (i.e. those of the 'Authors') are interspersed. The story is included as Appendix 1 on the book's website (www.sagepub.co.uk/chambers.pdf), with the paragraphs numbered for ease of reference. The students were asked to read the story, at least twice, before coming to class.

The kind of class we are imagining here is a seminar group, a class of students ranging somewhere in size from 15 to 25, in which the teacher takes the lead and teaches: that is, it is not the kind of seminar in which a student presents a paper and leads discussion of the topic. However, the teacher is not lecturing – she or he expects the students to talk, not just listen. It is the kind of class in which you want students to lay their views, analyses and interpretations out on the table for public discussion. The teacher's immediate job is to ask the questions and devise the strategies that will get students to open up and become involved, and the long-range task is to help students become better at detailed reading. To paraphrase a famous movie title from the 1980s, the teacher is trying to teach 'close encounters of the literary kind', and, at the same time, a kind of 'discourse domain' focusing on literary interpretation. We will assume that the students in the class have been made aware of these as learning goals prior to the start of the session: that the teacher indeed intends to bring about learning and has signalled to the students what they should be trying to do (or what is to be learnt).

Teacher: So . . . what do you think of this story?

Students: No response. No eye contact. Much scrutiny of walls and shoe laces.

(*A spirit of stolid resistance fills the room. The teacher silently thinks, 'the students, conscious of fear within themselves, gaze at the walls with dark imperturbable faces'. Time stretches away like an empty field. Teacher begins to tense, palms to sweat.*)

Authors (*magisterial voices from the ether speaking in unison*): The problem here is real but not insurmountable. It is not true that your students have just gazed on Medusa's face. The problem, in fact, is not your students at all. The problem is that question you started with, 'What do you think of this story?' It's what you want to know of course, and it's what some of your students, believe it or not, are actually eager to tell you, but the question is so amorphous, so big and so loose, that it's intimidating. It sounds as if the student who dares to answer it is committing herself to say the *last* word about the story, not the *first* word, and, so, he or she – all of them – would just as soon, in a sudden attack of generosity, allow some other brave soul the honour of dying on his or her sword, thank you. Start over, trying a different question that is more focused and permits an answer that doesn't force the student to speak from his or her sensibility, which is what most of them feel insecure about anyway. Ask a question that allows the student to back up what he or she says with a reference to the text. This will provide the students some solid footing, and allow them to feel that risking an answer is not the same thing as risking a reputation. And in any case it's what you want to encourage.

Teacher: Well, of course there are many entryways into this story. Can you suggest why there might be so many references to blindness, darkness, shadows, obscured vision and the like? How do these references seem to work? What do they make you think of? Where do they lead you?

Students: More impassive silence. More scrutiny of walls and shoes. More tangible but invisible resistance.

(*Teacher begins to feel really sick at heart, begins to think of being on the golf course, or in the library, or on the rack: anywhere but here in this classroom.*)

Teacher to Authors: So much for magisterial voices from the ether. OK, I did what you suggested. You two have any more bright ideas? I suppose you're going to say this is my fault.

Authors: No, this is not all your fault, and finding fault is not a very helpful strategy for fixing things in any case. Start down that route and soon you'll be translating all teaching problems into issues of moral character: 'Am I a good enough person to be an effective teacher?', or 'Why don't my students have a greater sense of responsibility for their own learning?' You don't need to reform your character; you've just got to get better at asking questions. The problem this time is not that the question was unfocused and vague but that, probably (one never knows for sure, but experience says . . .), you piled too many good questions on top of each other. The logic that if one good question is good then four good questions are four times as good doesn't hold. The students are not sure *which* question you want answered and, since most of them can't remember all four questions at once anyway, you get, once again, silence. So try again – no need to get bitter over one class that doesn't start right. On some days you'll ask the perfect questions, like a musician with absolute pitch, and things still won't go right, so don't think any one class or course is the ultimate test of your ability. Now, pick your favourite of the questions you asked and start over.

Teacher to Authors (*assertively*): No, I want to ask another question instead.

Authors (*rolling their eyes*): OK, fine. Ask another question. You certainly don't need our permission.

Teacher: Got rather carried away with questions there, didn't I? Let's go on to another one. Tell me, anyone, who is saying the words of the final sentence in paragraph 5, and how do you *know* who's saying them: 'But my body was like a harp and her words and gestures were like fingers running upon the wires'?

Tricia (*tentatively*): Well, I was confused about that. It seems like the reader is seeing everything through the young boy's eyes, but this doesn't sound to me like something a kid would say. It's too poetic and high-flown, isn't it? So I wasn't sure who was doing the speaking here. Is it really the boy or someone else?

Teacher (*with almost too much enthusiasm*): Great. Very good comment, Tricia. There is something odd about the narrative technique here, isn't there? Can someone point to a passage where it seems clear that the young boy *is* doing the speaking?

Authors: Good stuff. Tricia didn't mention narrative technique as such, and although she didn't quite say there was something odd about it she did imply it, but you've managed to throw a usefully tighter noose around her insight *and* slip a technical term into the discussion so that it seems natural to use it and not just something to be memorised.

Paul: Yes, in paragraph 4 everything that is said could be the young boy narrating his own experience, at least until 'and yet her name was like a summons to all my foolish blood', and suddenly this doesn't sound like a young kid any longer. Kids don't talk about their 'foolish blood'. The narration seems to skip back and forth from one point of view to another.

Students: Nods of agreement around the room.

Teacher (*starting to relax now, feeling the flow; resisting the temptation to ask what 'foolish blood' actually means; sensing that that juicy question – regardless of how nice it would be to bite into – will take everyone off the track of learning something about narrative technique, 'and we're getting so close to the big point about narration in this story; gotta see it through'.*) Yes indeed. So whose point of view could this be? The only other characters in the story who even *know* the young boy are his aunt and uncle, but they're clearly not the narrators, so where does this other point of view come from? Is Joyce sticking these poetic bits in gratuitously, or are they connected somehow, and to whom?

> **Authors** (*whispering in the teacher's ear*): You're doing great; *they're* doing great, but resist the temptation to run on. Don't put together a laundry list of questions. Keep the discussion on track.

Beth: Well, I hadn't realised this until you asked that question, but now that I think about who the other speaker *couldn't* be, it's got to be the young boy, after all, doesn't it? Only he's different in some passages.

Sam (*sees something; doesn't wait for the teacher*): Yeah, he's different. He's *older*. It seems as if the narration is slipping back and forth between the young boy's point of view and himself as an older man, looking back.

Teacher (*immensely pleased*): Absolutely right! All of you, building on each other's answers, have put this puzzle together. The odd thing about the narrative technique in this story – and as you study more stories you will see that it's not really so odd – is that you've got two points of view coming from the same person at different ages in his life: first, the young boy actually going through the represented experiences and, second, the older man looking back, remembering his youthful experiences and commenting on his boyhood self as he remembers. Does this make sense? Can anyone find another passage where you see this happening?

Andrea: Sure. Look at paragraph 12. It begins with a point of view only the older man could have – 'What innumerable follies laid waste my waking and sleeping thoughts' blah blah – but then suddenly the little kid is speaking: 'I asked for leave to go to the bazaar on Saturday night. My aunt was surprised' and so on. I see it now. The two points of view get interwoven throughout the story.

Teacher: Exactly. And how does knowing this affect your view of the ending of the story? Does it change your view of the ending?

Esther: Yes, it does. When I first read the story I thought the ending was *way* overdone. Very melodramatic, an over-the-top kind of thing. But if that final sentence is the older guy putting an interpretation on the feelings of his younger self, then maybe it works.

Teacher: Yes, Esther, and *how* does it work? Do over-the-top feelings go with being older or with being younger?

Esther: Oh, with being younger I think. I mean, I guess there are a lot of emotional adults, but adolescent kids are brilliant at being overly emotional.

Teacher: Very keen. So someone tell me what he's got to be so emotional *about.*

> **Authors:** You're getting really good at this: single questions, tight focus, good tracking. Next you'll be wanting a teaching award.
>
> **Teacher to Authors:** Don't interrupt. I'm busy. No, I don't want a teaching award. I want this class to work round to seeing that the boy's temperament and attitudes are out of place in the dreary world of clichés and empty pieties and dull routines of Dublin life, and what that might mean. But I'm not sure how to get there. Time is passing and we haven't even *begun* to talk about the story's metaphors yet, or the overall plot.
>
> **Authors:** Laudably ambitious. Look, there's no rule about this but you never get everything done that you want to get done. As long as what you *are* getting done leads to actual skills and knowledge – even if it's not all the actual skills and knowledge you'd like – that's all right. You're doing something real here. You're actually teaching; the students are actually learning. This is what it's all about (and you can't expect it to go this well all the time). Even if you did get everything done that you've got in your mind, you'd suddenly discover there was a lot more you left out. Teaching is like politics: the art of the possible. Go for what you can do in the time you've got and let the rest take care of itself. If you help make real learners out of these students they'll be putting things together in new ways for the rest of their lives, and they may discover on their own the parts you didn't have time to explore with them.

Kevin: Well, I guess he could be an emotional kind of kid for psychological reasons. I mean, it appears that he's an orphan, and that his aunt and uncle don't know anything about raising kids, that he doesn't have anyone as a role model for growing up, and that he's just failed at doing something he promised for the girl he wants to impress. I guess I might be emotional.

Teacher: Right, Kevin, but can you see any evidence in the story that this particular young lad has a different kind of emotional life from the people around him even without the problems you've just pointed to? What do you make of such statements as, 'I imagined that I bore my chalice safely through a throng of foes', and 'The syllables of the word *Araby* . . . cast an Eastern enchantment over me'?

Students: Kevin subsides. Other students stare blankly.

(*There's a shift of mood in the room, a sudden evasiveness, and then . . . silence. The just now lively discussion slides smoothly under water like a submarine and disappears.*)

Teacher (*to self, then to the Authors*): Whoa! What happened there? What'd I say? Hey, you two, where are you when I need you?

Authors: What can we say? You used the 'good/but' construction.

Teacher: What in the world are you talking about? What's the 'good/but' construction? I thought you said there were no hard rules.

Authors: There aren't, but . . . – well, what do you take someone to mean when he or she uses the 'good/but' construction with you?

Teacher (*thinks a moment*): I take it to mean 'good but not-so-good', like pretending that a rictus is a smile.

Authors: Agreed. Kevin actually put forward an array of textual evidence in support of his claim about the young boy's emotionalism. You and we know there's more to it, and that it would be good to get this out on the table, but not at the expense of shutting down a productive discussion. You just got too far ahead of your class there. Survive and learn. This is not a class in how much more you know than the students. It's not their job to guess what's in your mind – what the 'right' answer is. It's a class in *teaching* textual analysis and interpretation, and you reacted to an inexperienced student who did a pretty impressive job of it with a 'good but not-so-good' response that suddenly shut down the whole class. Do you want a suggestion?

Teacher: No! . . . Yes, I suppose.

Authors: Try changing the pedagogical format. When a patient's heart suddenly stops beating, apply the electric paddles. Changing formats in mid-class can be like that. Experience tells us that you are not likely to resuscitate this discussion so instead of floundering for the rest of the hour try a peer-collaboration format. Break the class up into small groups of four or five students, and give them a topic – or perhaps different topics for each group – to discuss among themselves and then report back their findings to the class as a whole.

Teacher: I have an idea for pursuing that question and some others. There are twenty of us round the table, so let's divide up in five groups to discuss them. The first thing for each group to do is quickly decide who will speak for the group at the end of the session.

Group 1, you four round this end of the table, your assignment is to examine *style*, that is particular instances of heightened language in the story. Find some examples – metaphors, images, allusions, sentence rhythms, tone and so on – and discuss among yourselves what kind of purposes or effects these stylistic strokes accomplish.

Group 2 over here, your assignment is to examine *plot*, not as a matter of 'first this happens then that happens' but as a matter of overarching structure. If the story ends with a sense of finality, of resolution, how did it get there from its opening sense of instability, of something *about* to happen?

Group 3, your assignment is to pick up on the last question I asked. Take the two passages I asked about, see if there are any others like them, and try to extend Kevin's fine analysis of some of the reasons for the boy's highly wrought emotions at the end of the story.

Group 4, your assignment is to look at the references to social class in this story and to try and figure out how they contribute to the story's overall effect. There are not a lot of class references, and they're a bit subtle, but they're there.

Group 5, your assignment is to think about gender and sexual issues. Is there any gender significance to the fact that neither the boy nor Mangan's sister is ever given a name? To what extent does sex enter into the boy's 'confused adoration', as he calls it, of Mangan's sister? What stage of life do you think the young boy is at with regard to sexual development, and what does it have to do with anything?

I'll just jot these topics down on the whiteboard while you get yourselves organised . . .

You may be thinking that not much progress was made in this class on teaching close reading and interpretation of text. In a way, that's true. The class really only began to explore some aspects of the narrative form. (In this connection, McGann et al. (2001) discuss the somewhat unexpected problems their students have with reading fiction – issues that re-emerge in Chapter 5 under 'Reading'). But what the students are beginning to understand, in the context of the story 'Araby' and not in the abstract, is some of the ways in which the story 'works' and what is meant by 'narrative technique'. And, led by a teacher and in discussion with other students, they are coming to *understand* these things *for themselves*. They will need further sessions of this narrowly focused kind, exploring other stories and also texts that represent other literary genres.[3] All the time they will be building secure foundations of knowledge and understanding for their later, more independent and sophisticated studies. Meaningful learning such as this cannot be rushed and it certainly makes demands on teaching time. Paradoxically, this class shows both how little beginning students can be expected to achieve in one session and how much.

Pedagogic issues

As regards pedagogy, a number of issues were exemplified or raised in the course of the seminar: how important it is to lead classroom discussion along fruitful lines by asking tightly focused, text-based questions that beginning students are able to respond to and thereafter to keep the discussion 'on track'; to avoid making a discouraging 'Good, but ...' response to the students' contributions; to shift the focus of questioning if the hoped-for response is not made; to limit one's ambitions and so avoid despondency (neither blaming oneself unduly nor the students) if the discussion is not brilliant nor its scope as broad as planned; if discussion breaks down, to consider shifting the pedagogic format. All these strategies help ensure that the discussion is to the point, is intelligible to the students and is engaging. To this we would add the desirability of encouraging the students to respond to each other, as Sam did to Beth, so that (even at this early stage in their studies) the teacher takes a back seat at times when discussion is going well – that is, of promoting the idea that the students should be thinking for themselves. Apart from these matters, there are a few other points we might draw out from the class.

Engagement in discussion

You may have noticed that the teacher praised every student who spoke – indeed 'all' of them for helping solve the 'puzzle' – if rather belatedly in Kevin's case and sometimes perhaps over-enthusiastically. (There is undoubtedly a tendency for passages such as these to 'sound' rather condescending in print, as writers of distance-teaching material are well aware.) Obviously, teachers should not patronise their students – nor indeed show them up publicly in any way – but, whatever one's feelings about such praise-giving, the intention is undoubtedly good: to reassure the student speakers (and nodders) and to encourage all the students to join in the discussion. But can everyone join in, anything like equally, given class sizes and the constraints on class time? And does it really matter if some students speak only occasionally? Silence does not necessarily indicate disengagement or lack of understanding or even passivity. The quiet students may be following the discussion carefully and thinking hard – as nods of the head and changes in facial expression often testify – and they may perform just as well in their subsequent written work as their more garrulous (confident?) peers. Leaving these questions open for now, there is no doubt that if our aim is to involve every student actively then the small-group strategy with which the class ended is an effective way of doing it. Less confident students are usually a lot happier to speak in small peer groups; indeed, it is much harder for anyone to remain silent for whatever reason. And this is surely far preferable to the teacher picking out one particular student after another to answer questions – something that the novice teacher of this class didn't ever do.

Peer collaboration

The peer-collaboration format is presented sketchily here. But note that the teacher took a firm lead in identifying the topics for discussion and in assigning students to their various groups – on the basis of convenience, of where they happened to be sitting – which was necessary for getting this hastily introduced stratagem underway quickly. There are of course other ways of doing it. Also, the subsequent plenary period is not depicted in which the groups' spokespersons would make their reports and the teacher sum up. However, we should note here the importance of the teacher allocating equal reporting-back periods to the groups and of keeping in reserve sufficient time to pull the whole discussion together. In summarising, the teacher fulfils the crucial functions of confirming for the whole group the learning gains that have been made and continuing the process (begun in response to the first contribution to the class by Tricia) of 'translating' what the students have said into terms that are closer to the target literary-analytical discourse. In a sense the teacher 'models' this academic discourse – demonstrates it in speech – and at the same time expresses in her or his conduct of the class the scholarly values enshrined in it: a desire to get at the 'truth', patient attention to detail, treating other people (as independent centres of consciousness) and their views with respect, and so on. Many of the issues raised here are discussed further in Chapter 5 of the book, on methods of teaching.

Finally, you will have noticed that in the discussion no reference was made to literary theory or criticism: no formal reference to 'genre', 'character', 'focalisation', etc., and no explication of the mimetic theoretical orientation or other theories in general or particular. This was deliberate; the next chapter includes discussion of literary theory and criticism in the context of pedagogy. But of course theoretical-critical considerations are also bound up in processes of text analysis.

POSTSCRIPT

In this chapter we discussed what it means 'to teach' and, subsequently, conceptions of 'good' teaching. And we tried to demonstrate how some of those principles might be applied in practice within our discipline – especially (by means of the 'Araby' vignette) setting out to teach beginning students close reading of text and interpretation of textual meanings. Many of the issues raised will of course recur throughout the book. But early on in the book processes of 'reading' seem a particularly appropriate emphasis, in view of our previous discussion of the nature of Literature as a discipline, of the forces currently acting on higher education and their effects on the contemporary student body, and of evidence that this aspect of undergraduate education is problematic drawn from a recent survey of UK Literature departments.

In short, we have argued that processes of textual analysis-interpretation-evaluation and communication are fundamental to students' interests as students of Literature. And we argued that as a consequence of recent demographic and other changes within the academy, along with significant shifts in the wider culture, teachers cannot make assumptions about beginning students' previous knowledge and experience of literature. Thus, we concluded, all the centrally important processes of the discipline must be *taught* explicitly. Accordingly, in the next chapter we turn to preliminary discussion of the remaining processes: the complex and highly contested questions of textual evaluation and the place of literary theory and criticism in the teaching of Literature, and the teaching of writing.

Notes

1. Here we are referring to 'critical thinking' in general: that is, taking a critical stance to any 'text' (including the teacher's) and forming one's own judgements of it – such matters as whether the argument is well reasoned, supported with convincing evidence/apparently unbiased, sufficiently comprehensive and so on, and also whether the reader agrees with the authors' assumptions, beliefs and claims (see Moore, 2004). Specifically literary-critical processes are discussed throughout the book.

2. For analyses of the major, and as yet not fully understood, cultural shifts that the world is now undergoing from being print- to media-based, see such works as: Wendell Berry (1983) *Standing by Words*; Sven Birkerts (1994) *Gutenburg Elegies* and (1996) *Tolstoy's Dictaphone: Technology and the Muse*; Bill McKibben (1992) *The Age of Missing Information*; Mark Crispin Miller (1998) *Boxed In*; and Neil Postman (1982) *The Disappearance of Childhood* and (1985) *Amusing Ourselves to Death*.

3. Detailed analysis of a poem, for beginning students, is to be found in Chambers and Northedge (1997) *The Arts Good Study Guide*, Chapter 6. The chapter also explores some applications of literary theory to the poem in a preliminary way. Highly recommended books on close reading are Scholes (2001) and Lentricchia and DuBois (2003). And the essays in the section 'From the Classroom' in the journal *Pedagogy* (Duke University Press) are richly suggestive, offering a variety of up-to-date examples of classroom practice; similarly the 'Case Studies' in *Arts and Humanities in Higher Education* (Sage). An especially rich source of ideas about group discussion processes is Ben Knights' book *From Reader to Reader* (1992).

Key references

Halcrow Group with Gawthrope, J. and Martin, P. (2003) *A Report to the LTSN English Subject Centre: Survey of the English Curriculum and Teaching in UK Higher Education*. Royal Holloway, University of London: LTSN English Subject Centre (Report Series No. 8).

Marton, F., Hounsell, D. and Entwistle, N. (eds) (1984) *The Experience of Learning*. Edinburgh: Scottish Academic Press.

Ramsden, P. (1992) *Learning to Teach in Higher Education*. London: Routledge.

Websites

Website for this book, *Teaching and Learning English Literature*, at www.sagepub.co.uk/chambers.pdf

3

Teaching literary theory and teaching writing

'POSITIONING' LITERARY THEORY

As the value of theory stock began to rise dramatically about thirty years ago – in a bull market that still persists – many teachers of literature back then (and some still today) were highly suspicious of it in the classroom. Occasionally, the more excitable among them were given to pounding the table like Dickensian characters, asserting loudly (thump thump) that they weren't going to stand for any of this blasted 'theory nonsense' in *their* literature classes, where they performed the time-honoured, probably divinely appointed job of teaching students 'just to read the words on the page'. We've come a long way since then. No one believes in 'innocent' readings any more, or theory-free readings either. And no one thinks any longer that just the words on the page are transparent with regard to anything, whether semantics, gender, politics, ethnicity or any other issue that might (or might not) be explicitly referred to in any particular work of literature 'under interrogation' – a courtroom or jail house metaphor that says volumes about contemporary approaches to literary analysis. Given the long history of literature and the extremely recent 'moment' of theory's ascendancy, it is astonishing that theory could have become so important in such a short time. A brief look at the history of literary study in the academy (with apologies for the sketchiness of the look) should help us position theory appropriately.

Intellectual traditions

Academic study of literature has its roots in four intellectual and academic traditions – philology, classics, rhetoric, belles-lettres – and owes many of its analytical techniques to these traditions.

Philology

From philology, literary study inherited highly developed techniques for concentrating powerfully on all the possible meanings and significance of individual words. Philology as a discipline provided the model of a methodology for interpreting individual words at three important levels: their semantic territory, their etymological history, and the semantic layers made up by their etymological history. Philology also taught literary study how to fit the word, with all its unpacked baggage, back into the context of the passage from which it came.

Classics

Classics provided literary study with two things, as we saw in Chapter 1: literary works to be studied (a curriculum for Literature) and the model of a pedagogy for teaching literature. It was a pedagogy of professorial lecture combined with student recitation, that is each student in turn translating a given passage. In classics classes the translation was literal (Greek and Latin words rendered into English words); in later literature classes taught in the vernacular the translation became 'interpretation', but often of a literal sort based on word-by-word paraphrasing ('What Milton is saying in these lines is . . .') to establish to the teacher's satisfaction that the student 'got' the meaning of the passage.

Rhetoric

Rhetoric, the ancient discipline of the arts of persuasion, provided literary study with a large number of concepts, analytical categories and methodological strategies that were easily transferred from the analysis of speeches to the analysis of literary works. Rhetoric has a 2,500 year history during which it has developed ways of analysing the ethos – the characteristic spirit and beliefs – of speakers (easily transferred to the analysis of literary narrators and even the analysis of literary authors); analysing the speakers' ethical, emotional and intellectual effects (easily transferred to a concern for a literary work's effects on readers); and analysing a vast array of figures of speech (which required no transfer techniques at all but could be incorporated in their entirety into literary analysis).

Belles-lettres

Finally, the tradition of belles-lettres included not only literary works that were treasured and studied but also the fine writing about these treasured texts produced by well-educated readers, whose own refinements of sensibility and literary talent often rivalled the sensibility and talent of the writers in whose praise they wrote. Belles-lettristic writing about literature developed the model of a thoughtful person sitting down with a literary work of life-long acquaintance and writing his or her reactions to that work, often in an impressionistic way but also in a way informed by additional reading that was both wide and deep, intelligence that was flexible and far ranging, thoughtfulness that tended to concentrate on moral issues central to the universal task of making a life, and an analytical sensibility that was not professional in orientation but nevertheless powerfully attentive to literary details, nuances, tones and linguistic suggestiveness of all sorts. Horace, Cicero, Petrarch, Philip Sidney, Dryden, Samuel Johnson, Montaigne, William Hazlitt, Charles Lamb, Matthew Arnold, Virginia Woolf, F. R. Leavis, Edmund Wilson, C. S. Lewis, Lionel Trilling – these are some of the writers who in the belles-lettristic tradition helped develop the model of a particular kind of literary responsiveness that became an important strand in the intellectual, professional and historical development of the discipline of English Literature.

When these four models of linguistic and literary study were pulled together to form the intellectual foundation for the first departments of English Literature near the end of the nineteenth century, it was to be expected (and was, indeed, the case) that the departments at first found their interests and their methodologies deeply tinctured by the intellectual roots from which they drew. However, the very fact that the departments were founded as academic enclaves unto themselves meant that inevitably the study of literature would begin to professionalise, subdivide and specialise itself on the model of the other academic disciplines for which subdivision, specialisation and professionalisation had already proved a spectacular means of both making and measuring intellectual progress. These were also ways of making careers; it became incumbent on academics to make themselves successful because literary study in the modern research university became a way of *making* a living, not just a habit or a manner *of* living.

Specialisation

The importance of literary theory today is in large part the consequence of a straight path of development along lines of specialisation, subdivision and professionalisation that began nearly a hundred years ago. What specialisation and professionalisation had already accomplished in the Sciences and other academic disciplines they have also accomplished in the discipline of Literature: an upward ratcheting of sophisticated analytical methods, vastly higher standards than in the past for uses of argument and evidence, the development of ever more specialised terms and concepts, the development of ever smaller domains of inquiry accompanied by deeper and deeper studies within those narrowed domains, the development of professional peer review of new ideas and of appropriately oriented journals for the constant display of new notions. In short, 'progress', when progress is defined as that which advances the intellectual professionalisation of the discipline.

Theory, then, is a way of specialising the study of literature such that only professionals can do it (in the sense of making a career of it). It is also the case that certain large historical and political developments liberated literary study from its historical roots and not only hastened its professionalisation but made that professionalisation easier to accomplish and, moreover, imparted to contemporary criticism some of its special attitudes and concerns. Scientific positivism, for example, emerging at the end of the nineteenth century, helped throw the older, belles-lettristic study of literature into question. But the loss of credibility that old-fashioned literary study suffered on this front was nothing to the credibility it lost after the carnage of the First and Second World Wars, and then the world's horror as the facts about the Holocaust emerged. For one consequence of the historic dislocations, catastrophic losses of life and moral disgust provoked by these events was a profound disillusionment with all the forces that seemed responsible for making a world in which such horrors were possible. Literary study seemed to be one of those forces, and a special kind of fury was turned toward traditional forms of literary study because they had been largely reverential, or at least uncritical, of what had long been called 'great literature'. Postwar critics such as George Steiner and Elie Wiesel have spent the last fifty years impressing on us that literary study, despite all its traditional promises about refining readers' sensibilities and teaching people how to become decent human beings, had been profoundly feeble in the face of the fierce nationalisms, ethnic genocides and territorial aggressions that marked so much of the twentieth century (and in this connection also see Duguid, 1984).

The theoretical turn

On the positive side, the specialisation of literary study by means of theory released an outpouring of intellectual energy, a wide array of theoretical perspectives that hitherto had been masked by literary study's traditional (biographical, philological and 'intellectual background') paradigms. The first of the theoretical perspectives to gain ascendancy was New Criticism, commonly called 'close reading', an approach primarily worked out in Anglo-American universities, which began to be developed in the second decade of the twentieth century, enjoyed its heyday in the 1940s and 1950s, coasted on the power of its inertia during the 1950s and 1960s, and was ultimately replaced by new theoretical influences emanating from French intellectual initiatives in philosophy (deconstruction) and anthropology (structuralism). Following the demise of New Criticism – dominant for so long partly because of its teachability and thus perpetuated by succeeding generations of scholars – a range of approaches was fired into hot flame in what is known in the profession as 'the theoretical turn': phenomenological; psychoanalytic; feminist; Marxist, historical and political; structural; deconstruction; queer theory; race and ethnic criticism; a recent resurgence in ethical criticism ... – and see Chapter 1 under 'The academic agenda' on the corresponding breadth of the modern curriculum. Whether theory has produced as much light as heat is a question that will be answered quite differently by various constituencies in the Humanities and Arts, but there is little doubt that the theoretical turn has not only generated intense intellectual energy but has also reshaped more than one of the disciplines. (On different interpretations of the intellectual history of Literature as a discipline see the references in Chapter 1, note 1; also, see Knights (2005) for an illuminating account of the theoretical shifts that took place in the 1930s and 1980s and their impact on pedagogy and students' identities.)

Literary theory, then, became a way of doing two things. It became a way of ceasing to offer old-fashioned exhortations about the value of literature as such, thus removing Literature as a target of attack by those disillusioned with traditional studies of all sorts. It also became a way, starting around 1970, of both appropriating and expressing that disillusionment itself. In other words, the attacks on Literature, the accusation that it had been complicit in all of the world's forms of oppression – gender oppression, colonialism, racism, ethnic stereotyping, bourgeois glorification, etc. – was a set of accusations that literary theorists since 1970 (as opposed to many of those who considered themselves traditional literature teachers) themselves embraced and found ways in different theoretical perspectives to advance. The energy released by these new approaches has either swept all forms of opposition before it – remember the 'culture wars'? – or has forced any would-be opposition to accommodate itself somehow to the theoretical turn the discipline has taken (see Gregory, 1997). As a magazine cigarette ad targeted at women used to say, 'We've come a long way, baby!' What the implications are of this long way we've come, for teachers and students of Literature, is the question at issue here.

APPROACHING THE TEACHING OF THEORY AND CRITICISM

A common response to the 'position' of theory just outlined is to see its aggressive ascendancy as a phase in the development of the discipline: that with greater understanding of the conditions of its genesis (both historical and professional), with some distance from those conditions and in the light of contemporary circumstances we may come to take a more dispassionate view of things. Indeed, something like this seems to be expressed by those who insist that as teachers our interest should be in the *range* of theoretical perspectives that can be brought to bear on literature, rather than in adherence to any particular theoretical approach or theory. On this view, a literary theory provides directions for an interpretative approach to the text that, like all such perspectives, allows some things to be seen and certain kinds of questions to be asked, while others are obscured from view but may come into focus through the lens of a different theory. At bottom, the argument goes, what undergraduates need to understand is that *all* literary interpretations and judgements derive from certain presuppositions: that even as simple a judgement as 'the ending of this novel (short story, film, TV play) is so unrealistic' is underpinned by theoretical suppositions about the imitative function of art, and what might seem to students a spontaneous response ('That's disgusting!') goes back to ethical theories of art as old as Plato. ('Just reading the words on the page' is, as we all now realise, a theory in itself – or at least a view based on a theory about the denotational transparency of semantic meanings – and one that should be treated *as* a theory in the classroom.) In short, it is the teacher's job to help students become aware of their critical presuppositions and practices.

So the question is, not *whether* we should teach literary theory and criticism – that's the long way we've come – but how much/what theory should we teach? And when, and how, should it be taught? The answers to these questions undoubtedly vary between different cultures and their educational traditions.

Culture-based differences

In the USA, for instance, theory instruction since the mid-1960s has mostly been experienced in graduate, not undergraduate, classes. It is not the case that theory hasn't entered the undergraduate classroom at all, but it is the case that teachers of undergraduates are much less sure what to do with it than graduate-school teachers – how much theory to teach, when to introduce it, how technical to become, and so on. Undergraduate programmes of education in the USA, moreover, are influenced strongly by the liberal arts aims of what many American institutions call 'core' requirements. The core curriculum in most universities often takes a traditional approach to literature as the approach most congenial to a liberal arts orientation, which is not deeply compatible with the professionalisation implied by theory instruction. In graduate school, by contrast, the more theory you can give your students the better, and the supporting argument looks like a simple syllogism: graduate school is professional training in the discipline; the discipline is agog with love of theory; therefore you can't teach too much theory. If there is more to the story than this, most people in graduate schools, teachers and students alike, are not interested in it.

But when the typical teacher of undergraduates walks in and faces a class of students, it is certainly the case that most of the students, including the English majors, will not be steering for careers in academe but for careers in business, government, corporations and various forms of public service. Within this teaching context it is much less clear whether literature instruction ought to be shaved to make room for theory instruction, and the basic issue of what students will find more valuable over the years – learning about literature or learning about criticism – pushes many teachers who loved theory in their own graduate training to wonder whether they should yield the time it takes to teach it in their undergraduate classrooms. In short, literature teachers may wonder what *purposes* literary theory serves in undergraduate education. If choice must be made, it may be seen as

The evidence from this survey is that in UK English departments 'Critical/Literary theory is the most widely taught compulsory course' – in the case of all other courses 'the number of optional courses is greater than the number of compulsory courses' (p. 70). For specialist Literature students, this kind of course was compulsory in 62 per cent of the departments at Level 1, and in 34 per cent of departments at Level 2 and above (p. 47).

The survey also collected data about how popular with students all courses were when offered as options. In only six of the departments was Critical/Literary theory reported as being 'very popular' with students – well behind courses in Shakespeare, Women's writing, American literature and most of the post-medieval period courses (p. 57).

More respondents were dissatisfied with their students' knowledge of 'theoretical approaches to literature' on graduation than any other aspect of their learning – closely followed by dissatisfaction with their 'close reading' (p. 74).

(Halcrow Group et al., 2003)

FIGURE 3.1   *Courses in theory/criticism: UK English Subject Centre survey, 2002.*

preferable to teach the classic texts (Plato, Aristotle, Sidney, Dryden, Arnold, Eliot) because contemporary criticism, while necessary for academic professionals in the discipline, will not be useful to all the students not on the academic track. The classic texts, however, are liberally educational and are thus important for a students' general understanding of self, others and art. In any case theory is more often worked into the range of courses offered, as part of the discourse (the way the teacher of 'Araby', for instance, introduced the concept of 'narrative technique' into the discussion) rather than seen as a set of tools only opened up for special jobs on special occasions – apart perhaps from an elective course such as 'History of Literary Criticism'.

The situation in Australia, continental Europe and the UK is somewhat different. There, 'learning about literature' is seen as necessarily involving 'learning about criticism' and, hence, about literary theory – regardless of students' future career intentions. Reading and criticism are not generally regarded as separable activities: literary theory is pursued as a study of the problems that are inevitably thrown up by serious reading and discussion of literature, and is therefore seen as informing all parts of the curriculum (see Figure 3.1). Often it will be accessed through the work of particular theorists and critics in relation to certain literary works, within a course on, say, the Romantic Poets (for instance, see the sample syllabuses in Appendix 3(b) and (c) on the book's website: www.sagepub.co.uk/chambers.pdf). But literary theory is increasingly offered as a separate area of study in the undergraduate curriculum (often compulsorily, as a core study even at First level), in a course on the history of literary criticism – encompassing the approaches, theories and methods of influential critics and critical movements both classic and modern – or in a 'theory only' course (see the Higher Education Academy English Subject Centre website 'Seminars in Theory and Practice: English Subject Centre Working Paper', at http://www.english.heacademy.ac.uk/events/archive/seminars/index.htm: accessed February 2003). Even in the latter type of course, practice varies. One theory course may offer an introduction to Formalism, Poststructuralism, Marxism, New Historicism and Post-colonialism, while another explores concepts and themes such as text and context, discourse, the subject, representation, ideology, the unconscious, gender and race, drawing on the work of a range of theorists and critics.

But although in general teachers in Europe may be less concerned about what purposes literary theory serves in undergraduate educa-tion, they may be as doubtful as their North American counterparts about how best to *teach* works of literary theory and criticism. And, undoubtedly, these texts take some teaching. Often, this is the least well taught of any aspect of literary studies and the part of the curriculum that is among the least congenial to students. Many undergraduates find theoretical and critical texts just very difficult to understand, first because these discourses are profoundly unfamiliar to them and, since such texts are not normally written for students at all but for academic peers, also because the particular texts they study tend to be abstract and/or technical. Added to such intrinsic difficulty, students often have very little idea what to *do* with the theories once they have (to whatever degree) understood them: how to apply theoretical-critical ideas to literary texts. So, the student 'researching' a paper may end up citing critics working from very different theoretical perspectives as if they had the same or similar aims and purposes. They simply don't recognise that the feminist critic who takes Mark Twain to task for 'reinscribing patriarchy' is conducting a quite different critical discourse from the humanist critic who honours Twain for his 'moral vision' in showing Huck Finn's developing conscience. Another main difficulty for teachers, then, is how to teach students to apply appropriately the theories and critical texts they study to the literary works they study. Such application, too, needs to be *taught*. The question is, how is this kind of teaching to be tackled?

TEACHING THEORY AND CRITICISM

When we recall the conditions of 'good' teaching discussed in Chapter 2 – that the teacher intends to bring about learning (i.e. understanding); indicates or exhibits what is to be learnt; does so in ways that are intelligible to, and within the capacities of, the learners; engages and/or extends students' interest and enthusiasm for the subject – it seems that teaching theory and criticism represents the worst-case scenario! As regards content, courses in theory or with a theoretical/critical emphasis need to be planned especially carefully, with an eye to the theoretical orientations and texts to be taught or to the selection of critical texts and literary works and the balance between them. A complicating factor is that in these courses, in the UK often taught by a number of academics or by a team, teachers tend to disagree about which approaches and texts to include because, as we have seen, within the profession such matters are contentious. Furthermore, the method of teaching will need careful consideration. Indeed, 'good teaching' may require that a range of methods is employed: students' independent reading of theoretical/critical texts; the lecture (mainly for explication of the theory, exploring some of its central concepts and terms at an appropriate level of difficulty); seminar/classroom or online discussion (towards deeper understanding and especially for the application of theory, offering the stimulation of working with others and encouraging independent thought); and writing workshops addressing the particular difficulties involved in writing essays incorporating critical perspectives. (On these difficulties see Smallwood (2002), in which the author also argues the case for 'a new approach' to teaching criticism in undergraduate literature and cultural studies courses, and an earlier paper (Smallwood, 1997) on the various meanings of 'theory' itself. Hopkins (2001) and Barry (2003) are books for students.)

Thinking about how to tackle all this here, expeditiously and unpretentiously, we will first explore some of these problematic issues and canvass a range of possible teaching solutions, and then propose an overarching or 'framing' approach to teaching theory and criticism that seems to us to address at least some of the students' main difficulties.

Teaching theoretical and critical texts

Acknowledging the difficulty

If the majority of our beginning students have not read any, or many, theoretical/critical works before – and there is evidence to suggest that, in the UK at least, probably this is the case (see Smith's survey (2004), in which around only a quarter of students felt 'well prepared' for this kind of reading) – then we should surely just accept that they will find it difficult. They are likely to be unfamiliar with even the most basic conventions of theoretical-critical discourse: unaware of who is 'speaking' to whom, why and about what. And they may well be distracted, and depressed, by the frequent references in such writings to further theoretical positions or critics and to literary works they have never even heard of, let alone read. So it may be helpful to introduce theoretical-critical writing as a specific text genre, accompanied by some explicit discussion of the conventions at work and of how to approach and read these texts: that is, emphasising the importance of reading slowly, to grasp ideas, of *not expecting* to understand 'all at once'; of the value of supplying one's own concrete instances and examples to aid understanding while reading; and of re-reading. Indeed, in terms of genre this is a lot more like reading a philosophical than a literary work. To begin with, it will be helpful if the teacher actually models this process for the students – showing them, by talking them through (out loud in class, on tape for independent study or in writing online) the way she goes about the task of reading and understanding a representative text or section of text; and especially how she negotiates a way through 'unfamiliar' references of all kinds, always keeping her eye on the main line of argument as it develops. Then, at least, the students will begin to understand what *kind* of text they are faced with, may have more appropriate expectations of it and will have some clue as to how to go about the job of reading, assimilating and applying it.

Against this is the view that to present 'theory' as something new to the students, however gently, may be counterproductive, mainly giving rise to (even greater) trepidation. Rather, the teacher might work from the basis of students' existing knowledge and experience so that they begin to grasp a theoretical concept in the context of literary examples they themselves generate, before they discover the theory's 'name' and provenance. For instance, students may be asked to think of a poem they like and know well, and then to try to explain what it is about the poem that especially appeals to them. Depending on the characteristics they identify (of form, mood or whatever), in the ensuing discussion the teacher may move towards identifying the students' (theoretical) interest as mainly formal, expressive and so on (see the discussion of 'When I Have Fears That I May Cease to Be' in Appendix 2 on the book's website: www.sagepub.co.uk/chambers. pdf). This could well be a helpful approach, and certainly emphasises how important the students' *understanding* is from the outset, but it looks as if it might take quite some time to get the enterprise off the ground. In any case, it seems to us that these approaches to the problem of intrinsic difficulty are not mutually exclusive and may profitably be combined. Working from 'where the students are' is almost always a productive strategy initially, but moving fairly swiftly towards the idea of literary-critical writing as a genre need not inspire great terror – quite the reverse if the message is a calming one: this is just another genre, not an impenetrable mystery, and its 'rules' can be learned and understood. However, employing any such strategy to good effect depends upon the teacher first having acknowledged the difficulties involved in this kind of study, and her or himself understanding what they are.

'Preparing' to understand

Setting a theoretical/critical text or extract for students to study independently prior to a lecture or seminar devoted to it is valuable in that it gives the students the opportunity to see what they can do for themselves. If, as one would expect, they become more competent over time then that inspires confidence and probably also boosts their enthusiasm for this kind of study. Even if such independent work is a bit too much of a challenge to begin with, it at least enables the students to identify some questions they will need to raise, safe in the knowledge that they will likely be able to rectify any gross misapprehensions or get some discussion of their difficulties in the course of the ensuing lecture or seminar. When setting a text for independent study it is helpful also to pose a few questions that the students should strive to answer as/after they read. This tends to focus the mind, and makes reading an active process (of seeking out some answers) rather than a somewhat aimless 'comprehension exercise'. Well chosen questions can make the task of reading easier too, by helping students to focus on the essentials of the argument and so avoid getting completely lost in its thickets and byways.

'Engaging' to understand

Seminars or class discussions can be especially engaging of students' attention, and interesting, provided of course that they are well focused (as we saw in the 'Araby' vignette in Chapter 2). In particular, they may encourage the students to explore the theories they have been reading about as they hear the way other students, learners like themselves, interpret and use the new concepts in their thinking and as, in the process, they find their own understandings challenged, extended or refined. Later on, they might be encouraged to enter into explicit, more structured argument with each other. They might 'debate' a topic or text (either self-chosen or teacher-appointed) from different theoretical standpoints, with the seminar group/class divided into two (or more) groups for the purpose and the debate conducted more or less formally. This strategy can also be used to help students practise *applying* different theoretical approaches to a given literary work. Whatever form such argumentation takes, it can help students to explore theoretical concepts in greater depth and to develop their own critical 'voices'. And oral presentations, seminar performance and associated work can be assessed just as evidence of knowledge and understanding in written assignments can be assessed (see Chapter 6) – perhaps providing a further incentive for the students to take this aspect of their studies seriously.

The conversion syndrome

The ultimate aim of all this teaching will be to engender in students themselves a critical stance to what they study and so discourage what might be called the 'conversion syndrome'. Here, rapturously confused and anxious students happen upon some theoretical or critical work they manage to understand without too much difficulty, and immediately become zealots or dogmatists of that particular approach – often not because they are really convinced of its superiority, but because at least they feel they can discuss it without appearing foolish. Another bad effect of poor teaching of theoretical/critical texts is that the students feel so resentfully confused they become cynical about theory and criticism altogether. Or, perhaps worst of all, they end up feeling deeply inadequate, when really they have not been taught enough to begin to make sense of what they are expected to read and apply.

Teaching the application of literary theory

In the type of course in which theory is taught alongside literary works, with a focus on its application to those works, a major difficulty is achieving some satisfactory balance between, on the one hand, study of theoretical and critical texts and, on the other, reading literary works – and both kinds of activity are time-consuming, if for different reasons. At the extreme, the theory-loving teacher lets theory take over, become more important than the literature, become very technical, and gives students the impression that literary study is not literary study at all but critical study instead, thus ensuring that all but a very few students tune out. Even when a teacher is on his or her guard against such overkill, in view of the time needed for reading and understanding the theoretical/critical texts themselves, application of critical concepts to literary works may anyway tend to be squeezed out.

One theoretical orientation, many literary texts?

A 'solution' to this dilemma is to narrow down the theoretical approaches studied in the course so that theoretical/critical works within *one* orientation only may be explored in seminars before being discussed in relation to a range of literary works. But, say the teacher decided to restrict himself to teaching the 'expressive' theoretical orientation, focusing on relationships between text and author, there would still be a number of theories and a host of critics to choose among – including all of biographical criticism, psychological (psychoanalytical and Jungian) criticism based on theories about the creative process, some feminist approaches and even some Lacanian psychology. What to include?

In any event, the students may get the impression that the chosen orientation is the one favoured and espoused by the teacher (and, indeed, it may be). If, furthermore, the teacher applies that approach without having positioned it intellectually among alternative or competing orientations then what the students experience, lacking any larger picture, is criticism as prejudice – indeed, as a series of prejudices they learn as they migrate from one teacher to another. The student may become a convert of the chosen approach or reject it, but what she will *not* become is thoughtful and critical about either the strengths or the limitations of any of them.

Many theoretical orientations, one literary text?

Alternatively, a range of theoretical orientations might be studied and each one applied to the *same* literary work – which would certainly reduce the time the students need to spend reading. But it will also reduce the extent of their reading of literature, without which they often lack any sense of how theory may possibly apply. People studying theory who have not read much literature tend to *stock* rather than assimilate their knowledge of theory. Thus, in reading a Shakespeare play or sonnet, a Burgess novel or a Restoration comedy, the student is likely to send messages to his mental warehouse calling for a certain tonnage of feminist or Marxist or formalist edicts from the available stock, which he dumps like concrete slurry into a big hole of literary inexperience where, alas, the crude opinions tend to harden into non-negotiable utterances that are solid, massive, ugly and depressing, like Moscow apartment blocks built in the Soviet era. Some of the problems of the conversion syndrome, then – dogmatism and zealotry – that we identified earlier as occurring if theory is *not* taught can also occur as a *consequence* of theory's being taught. It looks like you're damned if you do and you're damned if you don't. At this point, however, we'll step into the breach to propose a way of approaching the teaching of literary theory and criticism that we think takes care of at least some of these difficulties.

'Framing' the study of theories and criticism

We have just seen the dangers involved in trying to teach literary theory without attending to a range of theoretical approaches. And we've seen the difficulties of trying to teach students whose knowledge of literature is quite limited how to apply the theories and criticism they study to a breadth of literary works. Both activities are made more problematic because time for teaching (and study) is short, so we are aware that our framing suggestion must not add to the curriculum unduly if it is to be practicable and helpful. In brief, what we propose is that teachers might introduce their students to a simplified 'map' of theoretical *orientations* to literature so that, from early in their studies, the students have some idea from what direction the various critics they study are 'coming at' the literary text, which is positioned in the middle of the map.

The map presented in Figure 3.2 is our map. If you take up the map idea you may well want to construct your own, and because your own,

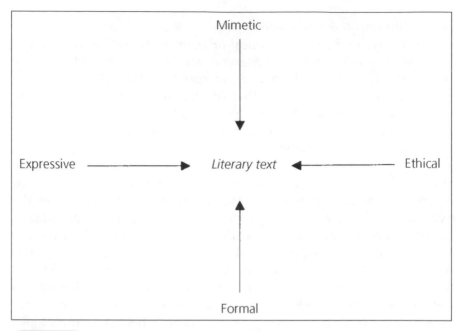

FIGURE 3.2 *A map of theoretical orientations.*

better, map. You will notice that an orientation that would *not* place the literary text at the centre of any map is missing here; 'deconstruction' may also need to be taught. We suggest that introduction to the theoretical orientations should be conducted at a fairly elementary level; it should be seen as a bare-bones foundation for the wider and more detailed study the students will undertake as their education proceeds. Later on the map will no doubt be discarded for a more sophisticated representation, perhaps of the student's own making.

Initially, the attempt is to explore with students the 'interests' of each broad theoretical orientation, so that they can begin to understand its 'point of view' on the text. In each case, this understanding may be enhanced by the students' reading of quite short extracts the teacher selects from some representative theorists and from critics who work within that orientation. From there, the teacher may move into the regular syllabus, setting theoretical/critical readings and applying them to particular literary works – but always returning to the (evolving) map to make sure that the students know the provenance of the readings before getting stuck into them. Progressively, the strengths and limitations of the various theoretical orientations may be discussed explicitly, and in the context of the light they shed on works of literature (that is, in the context of their application). In such a way the students may be helped to see the different interests, strengths and limitations of particular theoretical orientations, and all of them to some extent, and will be correspondingly less likely to become either disciples of one or another approach or sceptics about theory in general.

It remains to be seen how such a framing map might actually be taught. By a foundational bare-bones account we mean something like the 'tutorial discussion' of the theoretical orientations and their application that takes place between a few students and a teacher, to be found in Appendix 2 on the book's website (www.sagepub.co.uk/chambers.pdf).

In the tutorial the teacher makes 'possible responses' to the student's questions and remarks because, by its nature, small-group tutorial discussion can be more relaxed and free-flowing than larger, whole-class sessions such as we saw enacted in Chapter 2. This, we think, makes the tutorial an appropriate teaching format for exploratory work over difficult terrain with relatively inexperienced students (even if it is harder to employ in these days of large classes and dwindling resource for teaching). The implication of the teacher's 'possible' response is of course that such a conversation might take a number of directions. But notice that, as before, the teacher is clearly in control of the way this conversation develops – for example, in moving it on from discussion of one orientation to the next so that during the session all the orientations at least get an airing. We'll assume that the notion of the map and its purposes have been introduced in a lecture, and join the group as the teacher begins to explore the Expressive orientation. As you read, you may be just as interested in the dynamics of the small group and the teacher's role in the discussion as you are in the content of the session.

As before, the tutor aims to teach well: to engage the students in a discussion that is intelligible to them, interesting and thought provoking – although whether she or he achieves this is once more for you to judge.

Some implications

As we said, your map may be different from ours. For instance, we did not go on to discuss the orientation that would not fit on the map precisely because it does not make the assumption of a stable literary text. You may or you may not want to include discussion of deconstruction: according to Bleich (2001: 127), possibly not, since these days 'Critics do not "deconstruct" literature any longer, and most, in fact, don't know why they would want to undertake such a project at all'. But what at least you might do is try this 'framing' approach, and see if it works for you and your students. We ourselves have found that when undergraduates understand the genesis of different kinds of critical statement about literature, then critical discourse begins to sound less like static and more like, well . . . discourse. And more importantly, a form of discourse they can enter, engage with meaningfully and, increasingly, participate in.

A final point. We remarked that you might be as interested in thinking about the dynamics of the small group and the teacher's role in the discussion as in thinking about the map of theoretical orientations and the content of the tutorial. What is noticeable in this respect is that the teacher undoubtedly does most of the talking. Also, question and answer usually flow between the teacher and one or another of the students; the students rarely question and respond to each other. Perhaps you were thinking that the teacher's style was too didactic and that she or he should have taken a more 'student-centred' approach to the tutorial? We ourselves would say that the teacher's style was justified by the introductory nature of the discussion, by the students' relative ignorance of the subject matter and by their understandable reticence, at least until they had the text of the Keats poem in front of them. In introducing the poem, the teacher both made the discussion more focused and began to show how theory can be applied to the literary text. We would also point out that the teacher's manner was informal yet unpatronising, and that in his or her questioning of the students she or he often tried to 'guide' them towards or to elicit an appropriate example or response which could then be confirmed – a strategy designed to build confidence. Having said all that, these questions of the teacher's style and of her or his relationship to students are of course much debated. They are among the issues that will be addressed in the second part of the book.

APPROACHES TO TEACHING ACADEMIC WRITING

Following classroom discussion of a short story such as 'Araby', students might well be asked to write an essay on some aspect of it, or possibly on several short stories: for example, 'How does the treatment of either gender, or sexuality, contribute to the success of any one or two of the short stories you have studied on this module?' (see Appendix 3(a) under 'Coursework Essays' on the book's website). Although the types of assignment that are set in Literature courses are now quite varied, as we will see (Chapter 6), writing is still the main focus. This not only reflects the situation of the academy generally, based as it is on the written mode as the means of codifying knowledge (enabling analysis of and reflection on it) and of dissemination,[1] but also the situation of Literature and other text-based disciplines and fields in particular (e.g. History, Philosophy, Sociology, European Studies . . .) in which the essay is still the favoured form of writing. Accordingly, this is our focus here.

The essay

Above all, the essay form allows students the 'space' to construct an *argument* (see Mitchell and Andrews, 2000: 9, and in particular the Introduction on the case for seeing 'the dialogic principle at the core of argument (Bakhtin, 1981)' and on 'learning to argue'). That is, an argument that expresses interpretative points of view, using the appropriate theoretical and analytical concepts and terms – and space to illustrate that argument and offer evidence in support of it.[2] When the teacher marks and comments on the essay, that argument forms the basis of a 'dialogue' between teacher and student. Essay writing, then, is a main way in which students *learn* Literature, not just a way of demonstrating their knowledge and skill and having them graded; as Taylor et al. put it (1988: 2), writing demands 'the creation of meaning and the expression of understanding'. It follows from this that teaching students to write about literary texts and topics *is* teaching them Literature – which, in turn, seems to suggest that it is an important part of the Literature teacher's job to teach students to write. Indeed in the UK, three-quarters of English departments do teach 'Essay-writing skills' at Level 1, and around half do so at Level 2 and beyond (Halcrow Group at al., 2003: 44).

One objection, however, might be that there are aspects of essay writing that are generic and can be taught by others than literature teachers – as indeed is the case in many universities world-wide, where 'academic support' units offer all students a drop-in service and/or a dedicated website,[3] and may also offer courses on writing (such as composition classes in the USA) as well as study skills more widely. In this context, the focus is normally on the conventions of 'the academic' way of writing as an identifiable and distinct form. While in such courses worked examples of writing may be taken from a range of disciplines and fields (though rarely from Literature it seems), these examples are most often used to illustrate general features of academic writing such as voice, objectivity, structuring, referencing, etc. This kind of teaching may be very helpful to students who have little or no knowledge of the academy and we certainly do not mean to denigrate it, but arguably it hardly touches the deeper purposes of writing in the discipline or the particularities of the discipline's practices.

Models of academic writing

Broadly, there are three main conceptions of academic writing in currency (Lea and Street, 1998): 'skills', 'academic socialisation' and 'academic literacies' models.

Skills

On this model, writing is regarded mainly as a technical and instrumental skill or set of skills in which individual students may be more or less deficient. Teaching aims to fix the students' 'problems', often through advice about structuring the essay into stages (introduction, main body, conclusion), for example, and attention to grammar, spelling and other 'surface' features of writing: as Crowther et al. (2001: 4) have argued, 'the policy discourse within the UK and the wider world is premised on a basic skills model that prioritises the surface features of literacy and language'. These skills are assumed to be fairly unproblematically 'transferable' to the students' disciplinary studies.

Academic socialisation

By contrast, in this model (drawing on the work of the Student Learning movement referred to at the start of the chapter), writing is seen as a medium through which students represent their knowledge and understanding. Here the focus is on 'inducting' students into the new academic culture, with an emphasis on their orientation to study, their understanding of what it means to 'learn' and their interpretation of assignment tasks. As in the study skills model, however, the aim is that students should align their understandings and adapt their practices to those of the academy and the discipline (in both cases understood as monolithic); little attention is paid to the varieties of writing required even within a single discipline, to contestation within the discipline, to writing as a *social* practice, to uncertainties students may feel about their identity as writers, or to issues of power and authority in the student–teacher–institution matrix.

Academic literacies

All these matters are foregrounded in the academic literacies model, which will be our focus in what follows. In taking this model as our focus we do not mean to overlook or underestimate all the excellent work done in the long-standing tradition of composition teaching in the US. However, approaches to teaching writing that are closer to the academic literacies model appear to be increasingly adopted within that tradition too (see, for example, Bizell, 1982; Bleich, 2001; Crowley, 1999): that is, the work of 'outer-directed theorists' who, drawing on Linguistics, literary theory and Philosophy, are concerned with the social context of writing and the influence of particular discourse communities (as opposed to that of 'inner-directed theorists' working within the framework of cognitive psychological models of the, decontextualised, individual student). Similarly, in the 1980s in Australia, Halliday's work in applied linguistics became very influential (e.g. Halliday, 1985), and Ballard and Clanchy (1988), drawing on Anthropology, focused on relationships between language and culture. In South Africa, in the midst of fundamental changes in society and critical reconceptualisation of the purposes and nature of student writing in the academy, see the work of, for example, Angelil-Carter (1998) and Thesen (2001). Socio-cultural conceptions of writing such as these may be especially congenial to teachers of Literature.

However, the academic literacies model does not stand apart from or in opposition to the study skills or academic socialisation models:

> *Rather, we would like to think that each model successively encapsulates the other, so that the academic socialisation perspective takes account of study skills but includes them in the broader context of the acculturation processes . . ., and likewise the academic literacies approach encapsulates the academic socialisation model, building on the insights developed there as well as the study skills view. The academic literacies model, then,*

incorporates both of the other models into a more encompassing understanding of the nature of student writing within institutional practices, power relations and identities . . .

(Lea and Street, 1998: 158)

Quite a claim. It rests on the authors' ethnographic research into writing practices, informed by theoretical understanding drawn from functional linguistics and cultural anthropology. Their paper, 'Student Writing in Higher Education: An academic literacies approach', to which this discussion mainly refers, is based on research in two types of university in England ('old', research-based and 'new', post-1992 ex-polytechnics), involving interviews with students and their teachers, classroom observation and scrutiny of a range of students' written work along with their teachers' comments on it.

ACADEMIC LITERACIES

The concept of academic literacies as a framework for understanding writing (and reading) practices is based on the assumption that, broadly, students will not learn to write well in the academic context unless they understand the nature and purposes of such writing. More specifically, students learn to write in particular contexts, of discipline or field (teachers and institution), and both the nature of knowledge and writing conventions *differ* between the various disciplines. Further, within a discipline, writing does not only reflect or mediate knowledge but, more fundamentally, constructs it: writing involves making meaning – and, as we are reminded by Bleich (2001: 120), among others, 'language [is] meaningful only within the interpersonal and collective contexts of its use': that is, its use among people who are 'alive, functioning, changing and interacting'. Through writing, then, students learn not only about the discipline, they also learn to become members of, or 'legitimate participants' in, the disciplinary 'community' (Lave and Wenger, 1991, 1999). And this endeavour has implications for a student's personal and social identity – identities that are also influenced of course by his or her educational background, ethnicity, cultural expectations and gender (Ivanič, 1998; Lillis, 2001).

So, in the academic literacies view, students will need some understanding of the nature of the discipline (as a 'community of speakers and writers') in order to write meaningfully and in accordance with the discipline's particular requirements and conventions.

However, Lea and Street argue, the community's writing practices are far from transparent, more often understood tacitly by teachers than made explicit to students. On this point, the researchers note that although many teachers identified the concepts of 'structure' and 'argument' as key elements in a successful piece of student writing, they were not always able to explain just 'how a particular piece of writing "lacked" structure' (p. 162). The authors conclude that 'underlying, often disciplinary, assumptions about the nature of knowledge affect the meaning given to the terms "structure" and "argument" ' – and so, incidentally, even these concepts are not generic and simply transferable between disciplines. They continue:

> We suggest that, in practice, what makes a piece of student writing 'appropriate' has more to do with issues of epistemology than with the surface features of form to which staff often have recourse when describing their students' writing

– and, indeed, when commenting on it to the students. Thus, while a student's difficulty may actually be lack of familiarity with the subject matter, in her or his comments the teacher may be directing the student's attention to surface writing problems: a prime case of miscommunication between teacher and taught. And as a result, the student may (mistakenly) think that these problems are remediable through 'generic' study skills work.

Furthermore, even within the single discipline academic writing practices are far from homogeneous. Rather, they are contested – just as conceptions of Literature as a discipline are contested. Thus the succession of teachers that students encounter as they progress from course to course may have rather different conceptions of successful writing in the discipline, and their expectations may differ. Yet each of these teachers is in a position of 'authority' with respect to disciplinary practices. This no doubt gives rise to even greater confusion among students. Teachers themselves are also constrained by institutional or departmental policies, often designed to meet the requirements of external quality assurance and other agencies. Lea and Street provide a telling example of this, arguing that the effects of multidisciplinarity and modularisation on students only compound the difficulties they face as they attempt to 'switch' between the demands of one disciplinary setting and set of teachers to another. (See Chapter 6 for further discussion of this and of issues of power and authority in the context of student assessment, including as regards plagiarism.) The authors' critique of writing practices in the disciplines is compelling; what they do not attempt, however, is to draw out the implications of their research for teachers.

WRITING PEDAGOGY

Let's say that one of our main pedagogic aims early on in the students' higher education in Literature is to teach them to write a 'good' essay. There are of course a number of ways in which we might go about this, including discussion about the purposes of essay writing based on the students' existing experience; direct instruction (e.g. about structuring essays); setting practice exercises on various aspects of writing; critiquing sample essays, and so on. That is, as we saw earlier, our aim (of teaching students to write well) does not of itself determine the precise content of our teaching, the methods of teaching we will use or when we might use them. In this case, such matters will depend on our conception of writing which, in turn, rests on our understanding of the context of its use (the discipline). If our conception of writing is of a socio-cultural, broadly academic literacies kind, then a main concern will be the students' understanding of the particular context of the academic discipline Literature, located as it is within the academy, which is likely to privilege some teaching methods and content over others. Starting out with direct instruction about 'correct' surface features of language or the academic voice that should be adopted is unlikely to meet the case, for example, while certain more heuristic methods may well be preferred.

Heuristic exercises

Certainly educators in this tradition value students' exploring, with them and with peers, their past experiences of writing. They might then proceed to discussion of the differences between those forms of writing and the forms required in the new situation of discipline and academy. For instance, they are likely to set exercises in which students are asked to identify different 'types' of writing from a set of given extracts, and to articulate the differences of form, structure and language feature on which their discriminations are (whether they know it or not) based – with, in this case, particular attention to the essay type. The students might also be asked to 'mark' and comment on given, anonymised, student essays. All such activities are likely to precede constructive writing exercises in the new academic context. *Teaching Academic Writing* (Coffin et al., 2003) includes a series of such exercises that teachers may adapt to their purposes and, similarly, *Writing at University: A Guide for Students* (Crème and Lea, 1977; second edition, 2003) and *The Arts Good Study Guide* (Chambers and Northedge, 1997) – books that, although written for students, have been plundered by teachers for ideas and materials to use with their students. Also see Evans (1995) for uses of workshops, syndicates, etc., and other practical matters.

These educators, then, 'conceptualise successful teaching and learning as "scaffolded" activity, whereby lecturers actively support and guide students' participation in knowledge-making practices (Bruner, 1983; Vygotsky, 1978)':

> *In the process of scaffolding, a more advanced 'expert' or 'teacher' is seen as helping a less-experienced student to learn to do a particular task so that the learner can replicate the process alone at some point in the future. For successful scaffolding to take place, lecturers need to know where the student is starting from and aiming for in the process of learning. A key aspect of this scaffolding ... is raising students' awareness of the conventions within which they are expected to write and then helping students to add these conventions to their linguistic and rhetorical repertoires.*
>
> (Coffin et al., 2003: 12)

Constructive writing exercises

Following the kind of 'awareness raising' gained through heuristic exercises such as those just outlined, Coffin et al. (2003: 34) recommend a *process* approach to constructive writing (and see Murray, 1987). That is, like Mitchell and Andrews (2000) on arguing, they regard the *doing* of writing as the appropriate focus. Although a number of 'stages' of the essay-writing process are identified, they are regarded as iterative: the stages are overlapping and may occur in various orders. Nevertheless, students may be taught and asked to practise each of the stages as separate activities in an overall process of writing an essay, the final outcome or product (see Figure 3.3). Once an essay has been produced the student can then learn from the teacher's comments on it and ensuing discussion about it ('feedback' from teacher to student is discussed in Chapter 6).

- *Pre-writing* – understanding the ideas of others, generating ideas, collecting information: note-making, brainstorming (accessing tacit knowledge), 'journaling', freewriting (see Elbow, 1998).
- *Planning* – organising and focusing ideas: mindmapping or clustering (graphic organising techniques), listing, outline planning.
- *Drafting* – writing initial drafts: focusing on the development, organisation and elaboration of ideas (i.e. a focus on making meaning).
- *Reflecting* – letting work sit, thinking, coming back to it later.
- *Peer or tutor reviewing* – feedback from others (peer-reviewers will need guidance in how to offer helpful feedback), whether offered in class or informally.
- *Revising/additional research, idea generation* – acting on feedback; further developing and clarifying ideas, structuring the text.
- *Editing and proofreading* – focusing attention on the surface features of the text, including linguistic accuracy, layout, footnotes and references; polishing.

(Adapted from Coffin et al., 2003: 33–43)

FIGURE 3.3   *Process approach: stages of essay writing.*

In reality, all of these stages might not be needed in a given writing task. For instance, if the essay topic were text-based and the text(s) had been the subject of discussion in seminars then brainstorming might not be necessary; if the assignment were summative and a main component of the grade for the course, peer review might be discouraged. However, all of the stages can be taught – in discussion (classes, seminars) and perhaps especially in dedicated writing work-shops. Practice constructive-writing sessions are very often designated 'workshops', drawing attention to the fact that they involve activity of various kinds: that students and teacher roll up their sleeves and get down to work. As work proceeds, the activities may become more sophisticated, for example addressing meta-discursive matters such as signposting text structure (exploring ways of signalling agreement or qualification, recapping and summarising).

Making it real

As all we have said here suggests, constructive writing exercises such as these are valuable to the extent that they are 'real' tasks, appro-priately contextualised: that is, grounded in understanding of the disciplinary context in which they are set, its requirements and conventions, typical of the writing tasks encountered in that context, and timely – preferably related to actual assignments the students are undertaking so that they are motivated to engage fully with the activities. These requirements may seem to rule out any 'generic' teaching of writing and identify teachers of Literature as fully responsible for the students' learning. That is indeed the extreme position which – even if the preferred one – may simply be impracticable. However, it may well be possible for members of student-support staff to work with discipline specialists, at times perhaps together in the same classroom and at other times separately, to a carefully orchestrated schedule that exploits the particular strengths of both parties.

POSTSCRIPT

In this chapter we have seen how two of the most important aspects of our students' education in Literature – understanding the role of literary theory and essay writing – may be taught. This is in addition to the teaching of close reading exemplified in Chapter 2. All three processes are regarded as problematic; teachers, in the UK at least, are most concerned about their students' understanding of them or ability to perform them upon graduation.

In the process we have tried to model two of the most common teaching methods employed by literature teachers – the class or seminar and the tutorial – and we have discussed the main features of the writing workshop. This first part of the book was addressed mainly to new or beginning teachers. In the rest of the book, we examine some of the broader issues and recent thinking surrounding curriculum and course design, methods of teaching, means of student assessment and course evaluation. We hope these discussions will interest all teachers of Literature.

Notes

1. These days it is sometimes argued that the dominance of the written mode is being challenged by the 'multimodality' offered by electronic technologies, CD-ROMs, etc. (see, for example, Kress, 1998, 2003; Snyder, 2002). However, most uses of these technologies in the Humanities still rely on written forms – for example, computer conferencing (even if a hybrid form that incorporates some features of speech), resource-based study (e.g. text databases), 'interactive' text and text 'searching'.

2. In a very interesting paper on genre and the materiality of language Bleich (2001) suggests that since 'argument' is understood as contestation, in which the aim is to 'win', this is not the appropriate way to conceive of what should

go on. We are not taking a common-sense definition of argument here, however, but discussing more specific, academic, understandings of the term. (Nevertheless, Bleich's own argument is really quite persuasive.)

3. See, for example, the website offered by the University of Southern Queensland, Australia: http://www.usq.edu.au/opacs/learningsupport/stafflearnsupport/default.htm (accessed October 2004); and the online Writing Essays Guide offered by Sheffield Hallam University, UK: http://www.shu.ac.uk/schools/cs/english/essayguide/enter.htm (accessed March 2004).

Key references

Coffin, C., Curry, M. J., Goodman, S., Hewings, A., Lillis, T. M. and Swann, J. (2003) *Teaching Academic Writing: A Toolkit for Higher Education*. London and New York: Routledge.

Knights, Ben (2005) 'Intelligence and interrogation: the identity of the English student', *Arts and Humanities in Higher Education*, 4(1): 33–52.

Lea, M. R. and Street, B. V. (1998) 'Student writing in higher education: an academic literacies approach', *Studies in Higher Education*, 23(2): 157–72.

Websites

HEA English Subject Centre, 'Seminars in Theory and Practice: English Subject Centre Working Paper', at: http://www.english.heacademy.ac.uk/events/archive/seminars/index.htm

Study skills/writing website, University of Southern Queensland: http://www.usq.edu.au/opacs/learningsupport/stafflearnsupport/default.htm

Writing Essays Guide, Sheffield Hallam University, UK: http://www.shu.ac.uk/schools/cs/english/essayguide/enter.htm

4

Planning for teaching: curriculum and course design

'MODELLING' CURRICULUM DESIGN

We saw in Chapter 3 the way English Literature emerged as a new discipline out of existing literary and intellectual traditions (philology, classics, rhetoric and belles-lettres) which supplied it with both contents and pedagogy. And we saw how those roots have shaped the discipline's development over time, along with certain forces acting upon it from within the wider academy (such as long-term trends towards specialisation and professionalisation) and from socio-political changes and events in the world beyond. It was argued there that the outcome of these combined forces has been the 'theoretical turn' the discipline has taken since around 1970, expressed today in a much wider curriculum and in a range of theoretical orientations. Also, conceptions of teaching and teaching-learning practices have been as profoundly affected in recent times. All these changes prompt us to re-examine some fundamental questions: 'What should I be teaching, and why?', and 'How should I be teaching?' These questions arise whenever there is the possibility of change or of choice. Indeed, can we call ourselves educators at all unless we address them seriously?

The first questions, which concern our *purposes* and *aims* as educators, mainly impact upon the curriculum and the contents of courses, the topics of this chapter. (The second question concerns *methods* of teaching-learning, the media to be used, the activities students are asked to engage in and the ways we will assess their work and progress. These matters are discussed in the following chapters.) We begin by considering the prevalent, rational or classical, model of developing curricula and courses of study, with which you may be familiar. It requires that teachers first determine their curriculum aims and teaching-learning objectives – from which all else is said to flow.

The 'rational', product-oriented curriculum model

In this model the curriculum is defined broadly, as *a programme of study in a particular subject area that is explicitly organised so that the students of it may achieve certain desired learning aims and objectives* – rather than the narrower common-sense notion of the 'content' of what is taught. Planning the curriculum means first identifying the overarching aims of the programme of study: in practice, this means that as teachers we answer the 'what should I be teaching, and why?' questions for ourselves in the light of our knowledge and experience of literary study, our understanding of the discipline's nature and purposes, our interpretation of the canon, knowledge of our particular students, and our practical circumstances.

From such *overarching programme aims*, in linear fashion:

- teachers begin to derive particular, achievable teaching-learning objectives, which mark out the courses or modules that will make up the programme;
- in turn, these objectives suggest appropriate contents for the courses, and each syllabus is defined accordingly;
- the teaching strategies and media of delivery that will best enable students to meet the learning objectives are then identified, along with the methods of student assessment that will confirm for teachers and the students (and, ultimately, prospective employers) that those objectives have been met;
- during teaching and afterwards teachers evaluate the programme – turn researcher and try to find out how the planned curriculum works in practice (do the courses make up a coherent 'whole', expressing programme aims in the ways intended? are the teaching-learning objectives appropriate and achievable? are all the elements of each course well designed in relation to its objectives? are the syllabuses fruitful, the courses stimulating and interesting to the students? are the teaching-learning methods employed effective, the methods of student assessment appropriate and fair?);

● progressively, teachers feed back the findings of evaluation into the design process and make appropriate adjustments to any or all aspects of the programme.

So such a stage-by-stage, linear model of curriculum development ultimately takes the form of an imaginary circle, with periodic feedback informing an ongoing process of adjustment or redesign. And, as we shall see, in all these 'stages' of the design teachers must take into account the requirements of the wider society and university, and of course the student body.

Creative course design

That, then, is the 'rational' model of what teachers do when designing the curriculum – no doubt an accurate label as regards its reasonableness[1] but perhaps a rather technical and less than inspiring view of things? For instance, for many teachers the stage described as 'defining the syllabus' is the creative heart of the process, not only drawing on their expert knowledge of literature and their understanding of their students but also on their particular literary passions. Such knowledge and understanding, combined with the teacher's value judgements and enthusiasms, can result in courses that are novel and exciting for teachers and students alike. And so individual teachers have surely contributed to widening the literary canon and to the introduction of the new types of course and emphasis we remarked on earlier – perhaps especially those of us teaching students from a range of ethnic backgrounds or who have little previous experience of education in the discipline, and when we have the opportunity to teach in our specialist areas of knowledge and can integrate up-to-date research. In these situations we may feel particularly challenged by the curricular possibilities and excited and satisfied by the courses we develop.

In what follows we must cling on to the notion of the teacher as expert and the process of curriculum and course design as a creative one, as we explore the thickets of 'regulation' that as teachers we are now subject to. This is especially so in the UK where government and its agencies have gone further than elsewhere towards prescribing academics' activities, and for this reason the focus in the chapter is mainly on UK 'requirements'. But, as we have seen with regard to centralising tendencies everywhere, it is a path down which most of us seem to be heading.

In the bulk of the chapter our focus will be on planning courses or modules of study – syllabuses rather than the entire curriculum – on pragmatic grounds: that, as teachers, we are most likely to find ourselves responsible for planning and teaching individual courses or modules of study. But there is another reason for this emphasis too. VanZanten Gallagher (2001: 54) has proposed that the literary canon is 'a loose, baggy monster, a fluid movement of ebbs and flows, ins and outs – imaginary, therefore, as opposed to concrete'. What is concrete, she argues, is the syllabus: the list of works that are frequently taught in the classroom, 'a list that is empirically verifiable' which she calls the 'pedagogical canon'. Citing Guillory (1993: 28), she concurs with the view that:

> *An individual's judgement that a work is great does nothing in itself to preserve that work, unless that judgement is made in a certain institutional context, a setting in which it is possible to insure the* reproduction *of the work, its continual reintroduction to generations of readers.*

The literary canon, then, 'emerges from the operations of pedagogical canons' – rather than the other way round, as is the conventional understanding. That is, through their syllabuses teachers 'produce' the literary canon rather than simply applying the (imaginary) canon in their courses. She concludes that, therefore, 'The more important question, from the pedagogical point of view, is how we decide what goes into the construction of our syllabi' (VanZanten Gallagher, 2001: 56).

Appendix 3

Shortly we will be looking at some 'sample' course designs, presented in Appendix 3 on the book's website (www.sagepub.co.uk/chambers.pdf). These are outline descriptions of three modules within the English Literature curriculum of an anonymous UK university – one at each of the three levels (or years) of undergraduate study. Note that the documents have been lightly edited; in particular, reading lists are not included in full.

A cursory glance will show that these documents, designed for student consumption at the start of the courses, follow a similar pattern. That is, any objectives of the course are discussed and issues of course content (syllabus), timetable, methods of teaching-learning and student assessment are usually explained thereafter. But the differences among them are perhaps even more interesting. It will be helpful to read through the documents quite quickly at this point.

THE CURRICULUM

The higher education English Literature curriculum, like any curriculum, arises out of demands made by the wider society, out of the history of people's attempts to understand a particular aspect of our experience (here, the discipline Literature), and out of the needs of the student body. The curriculum is therefore not invariable: as these constituents change so the curriculum changes.

In Chapter 1 we saw the extent to which many governments now seek to influence the form and content of all higher education curricula. For example, throughout much of the West a preoccupation with national wealth creation in the modern, globalised economy has prompted a policy of massively increasing student numbers and focusing on the students' acquisition of marketable 'skills'. We also saw how the student body has changed, becoming markedly more heterogeneous and including many more mature and part-time students. In Chapters 1 and 3 we saw how changes in academics' and critics' views of the nature of Literature and the value of literary study have led to expansion of the 'traditional' curriculum: in particular extending the canon, including a wide range of literary theory and new types of course (e.g. theme-based, regional literatures, postmodern perspectives . . .). And in Chapter 2 we saw how a paradigm shift (via the Student Learning movement) has occurred among educationalists regarding the focus of their work, from teachers and teaching to students and their learning, the effects of which are reverberating around the academy as we write. So, we may well ask, where does all this leave the people who teach the curriculum?[2]

Demands on the curriculum

Each set of demands is of course difficult to negotiate. The first of them, the demands made by the wider society, entails our engagement with (at least) the university's committee and other structures that normally act as mediators of the policies of government and its agencies. And such external demands are often seen as constraining, not least when resource for teaching is cut, or as an unwelcome intrusion because inappropriate to the discipline and distorting, or because trying to meet the demands takes up time that could otherwise be devoted to teaching literature, to research and to writing. The second set of demands, arising from within the discipline, is always difficult too, given uncertainties surrounding shifting definitions of the discipline's purposes, scope and emphases, along with constraints on class time. But the last set of demands is perhaps especially problematic: how are teachers to know what their students' needs are, especially today when we are faced with a large, heterogeneous body of people? And, in any case, what exactly is meant by 'need' in this context?

Students' needs

When people talk about their need for food and sleep, for a bed to sleep in or for warmth, or for love and security, we know what they mean. They are referring to their biological, basic and psychological needs, respectively; and they are not needs that, as teachers, we can normally meet. (But perhaps teachers can and should take into account certain of students' psychological needs, such as the need to feel accepted and valued as a student (rather than 'put down' or overlooked), to feel stimulated (rather than reduced to boredom) – and in current circumstances perhaps we should also try to take account of the effects of part-time work on the hours students may give to productive study?) By contrast, 'need' in the higher education context surely refers to something much more specific – to something required to fulfil a purpose or role that people have chosen for themselves.

Perhaps we can say that these people, students, may need to have matters explained to them carefully, they will need access to books and paper, to learn to use a word-processor, access the Internet . . . So far so good – we can in principle simply offer or provide such opportunities. But these are all things that students are likely to know they need. What about things that people who have chosen to study Literature do *not* know they need, or can only glimpse, in advance of that study? That is, precisely what they will need to read, do and learn in the process. As we saw in Chapter 2, all *education* must (logically, must) have 'particular objects (people are setting out to learn some*thing*)', involving the acquisition of knowledge, understanding and skills that are seen as desirable and important or useful, to a certain level or standard (Hirst and Peters, 1970: 81). Who, then, is to be responsible for determining the students' needs, *as students of Literature*, with respect to acquiring knowledge (etc.) of literary objects that is important, to the standards required? Of course, the people who do know what's involved: subject-expert teachers.

Cognitive, disciplinary core

Ultimately, then, it is teachers who are responsible for applying the demands of the wider society to the curriculum, for teaching their discipline and for determining their students' needs as students. Teachers, precisely because of their subject expertise, must be the pre-eminent determiners of the curriculum – though they may well discuss aims and objectives with students, and include large elements of student choice in the programme design (such as the 'Elective' course in Appendix 3(c), the option to write a dissertation on an agreed subject in place of studying a set course, to choose among texts to be studied within courses or to undertake project work). Such qualification notwithstanding, among other things that hang upon this conclusion is reaffirmation that *the core of the academy is cognitive and disciplinary*.

We can test out this proposition by applying it to a 'hard case': to a discipline or field at the social/temporal, applied rather than the cognitive end of the spectrum (see Kelly, 2001, in Chapter 1). For instance, a formal university course in Caring for the Elderly, while a practical field, would draw on a range of bodies of thought – the discipline of Sociology in exploration of the concept 'institutional-isation', on Psychology in discussion of needs (e.g. for 'personal space'), on Philosophy (ethics) as regards people's 'rights' (to privacy for example), and so forth. By contrast, on-the-job training in caring for the elderly would not take this form. In higher education, then, even such fields as these are at bottom cognitive and discipline-based.

CURRICULUM AIMS

It follows from this conclusion that in higher education curriculum aims and course objectives are chiefly cognitive, deriving from consideration of the nature of the discipline or field in question. As regards our subject, learning Literature is possible only to the extent that students acquire the network of shared concepts that make literary experience available and the public forms of discourse that make it discussable. Higher education, then, is centrally concerned with *public modes* of knowledge, understanding and experience. This does not mean that's all it is about. But it means that teachers must keep at the forefront of their minds those processes that are central to the discipline itself, from which they may derive appropriately cognitive aims and objectives for their teaching. In Chapter 2 we identified processes of textual analysis-interpretation-evaluation, and of communication, as central to the discipline of Literature.

Cognitive aims

If these processes are understood to be our focus, certain cognitive aims follow on. Broadly speaking, we propose that as teachers of Literature we should *at least* aim to offer our students opportunities to:

- learn to read a range of primary texts and text genres appropriately – in breadth and depth – engaging in associated processes of textual analysis, interpretation and evaluation;
- engage with the concepts and networks of ideas that characterise literary discourse, and learn to think in terms of them;
- grasp the assumptions and purposes that underlie debates (theoretical-critical) within the discipline along with the beliefs and values that inform them;
- understand the way argument is conducted within literary discourse, what counts as evidence and how it is used;
- learn to speak and write within the conventions that apply;
- take an independent, critical stance to study.

Also, it is most important that students should come to understand *why* the knowledge and cognitive skills that make up this list are important. Often their importance is simply assumed and is not discussed with the students. But explanations of this kind are not arcane and need not be impossibly abstract; when they are advanced, the teacher's job becomes easier because the students' sense of 'what's at stake' in literary study becomes clearer.

Cognitive skills, and values

In developmental terms, for example, the cognitive skills taught by literary study address one of the most distinctive features that make human beings what they are: the possession of natural language. When students are given reason and opportunity to consider that in the absence of language their humanity would lie mostly locked up and inaccessible even to themselves, they recognise that working at the development of this capacity is to work at the fulfilment of an existential need that is real and demanding. In social terms, the cognitive skills taught by literary study address the development of the one skill upon which more human failure and success is built than any other: the skill of using language – and responding to others' use of language – with precision, vividness, clarity, power, grace, wit and, most importantly, with success. The skills of language that lead to these kinds of powerful use can only be acquired by people who immerse themselves in the medium of language. And no programme of study addresses the need for language creatures to expand and empower their language ability more than literary study. (In this connection, see a thought-provoking article by the philosopher Robin Barrow, 2004.)

It is also important to remember that our purposes are not exhausted by curriculum aims such as those just outlined. Many teachers would frame their aims in the context of long-term benefits to students that are not primarily related to disciplinary content or skills: intellectual and ethical outcomes such as to become more open-minded, introspective, intellectually flexible, creative and curious, to become better problem solvers, to imagine more vividly and in more detail, to become more tolerant of differences, more sensitive to moral principles and to show greater concern for others, to find joy in learning for its own sake. These curriculum 'aims' impact upon the person and the *quality* of a life. They are not so much taught directly as modelled by teachers; they are the features of mind and character that students remember about their teachers often well beyond the years of their higher education – the teachers' enthusiasm for the subject, their fairness, their sensitivity to others, their intellectual playfulness – or not.

But whether or not you agree that the list of cognitive aims just offered is indeed appropriate to the teaching/study of Literature, a point to note is that these aims are different from instrumental ones such as acquiring time management or information technology skills. Those other skills, however desirable, may be developed only *as* students acquire the knowledge, understanding and practices that are central to the study of Literature. That is, as teachers, we must *grasp the structure or pattern of relationships between curriculum aims* so that we may focus our efforts appropriately.

SUBJECT BENCHMARKING

Traditionally, curriculum aims have been established by the head of the literature department or through departmental discussion, and objectives for courses of study very often by the individuals responsible for teaching them. Latterly all such matters have tended to be more collaborative, with teachers often working in teams and increasingly taking into account students' views and preferences. However, now in the UK, the curriculum aims that students are expected to meet (or the 'learning outcomes' they are expected to demonstrate), whatever their discipline or field, are defined externally to institutions and faculties/departments in a Subject Benchmark Statement published by the Quality Assurance Agency for Higher Education (QAA), a government agency. The Statement for English is described as 'the first attempt to make explicit the general academic characteristics and standards of an honours degree in this subject area', and was devised by the QAA in collaboration with 'a group of subject specialists drawn from and acting on behalf of the subject community' (QAA, 2000: 1; see Figure 4.1).

In effect – the final sentence of the Statement's purposes notwithstanding – unless a literature department can show congruence between the definitions and standards identified in the Benchmark Statement and its curriculum, its courses will not be rated highly in

---

Subject Benchmark statements provide a means for the academic community to describe the nature and characteristics of programmes in a specific subject. They also represent general expectations about the standards for the award of qualifications at a given level and articulate the attributes and capabilities that those possessing such qualifications should be able to demonstrate . . .

[They] are used for a variety of purposes. Primarily, they are an important external source of reference for higher education institutions when new programmes are being designed and developed in a subject area. They provide general guidance for articulating the learning outcomes associated with the programme but *are not a specification of a detailed curriculum* in the subject. Benchmark statements provide for variety and flexibility in the design of programmes and encourage innovation within an agreed overall framework . . . [They] also provide support to institutions in pursuit of internal quality assurance. They enable the learning outcomes specified for a particular programme to be reviewed and evaluated against agreed general expectations about standards. Finally, subject benchmark statements are *one of a number of external sources of information that are drawn upon for the purposes of academic review* [the Agency's arrangements for external assurance of quality and standards] and for making judgements about threshold standards being met.

(QAA, 2000: 1–2, emphases added)

FIGURE 4.1 *Purposes of subject benchmarking.*

- knowledge of literature [which] should include a substantial number of authors and texts from different periods of literary history. For Single Honours literature students this should include knowledge of writing from periods before 1800 . . .;
- knowledge and understanding of the distinctive character of texts written in the principal literary genres, fiction, poetry and drama, and of other kinds of writing and communication;
- experience of the range of literatures in English . . .;
- appreciation of the power of imagination in literary creation;
- awareness of the role of critical traditions in shaping literary history;
- knowledge of linguistic, literary, cultural and socio-historical contexts in which literature is written and read;
- knowledge of useful and precise critical terminology and, where appropriate, linguistic and stylistic terminology;
- awareness of the range and variety of approaches to literary study, which may include creative practice, performance, and extensive specialisation in critical and/or linguistic theory;
- awareness of how literature and language produce and reflect cultural change and difference;
- recognition of the multi-faceted nature of the discipline, and of its complex relationship to other disciplines and forms of knowledge.

(QAA, 2000: 4–5)

Note: The Statement includes English language. The specific requirements for these graduates are omitted from this list and from the 'skills' list that follows.

FIGURE 4.2 *Subject knowledge.*

external academic review. A high score in the review gives access to certain funds and a prominent place in the 'tables of performance' of English departments that are subsequently compiled for public consumption.

Knowledge

The Benchmark Statement for English identifies the knowledge graduates 'who have studied English as a significant component of their degree' should be able to demonstrate, as shown in Figure 4.2.

Clearly, the list in Figure 4.2 is an attempt to sketch the contours of the curriculum in English Literature: what, broadly, should be 'covered' over the years of undergraduate study. So, how do you measure up? Does your department's curriculum include all the subject knowledge required: a 'substantial number of texts' from different periods (some of them pre-1800) and a range of genres,

including 'the range' of literatures in English, all adequately contextualised (in language, culture and social history), and theorised, and
related to other disciplines? What about critical traditions and literary
history, cultural change and difference, performance, imagination in
literary creation? Perhaps it does indeed encompass all or most of
these things.

What immediately strikes us about these specifications, however, is
their vagueness (even though the compilers have prepared us for the
fact that this is not to be a 'detailed' curriculum). Nothing at all is said
here about the contents of the curriculum – *which* authors and texts
'from different periods' (which periods?) might be taught/studied and
when. The contested question of the canon is completely sidestepped.
Likewise, the list does not suggest any particular approach to the
teaching of literary theory and criticism, nor express a view on the
extent to which they should be taught, even though this aspect of the
curriculum is widely known to be problematic. Rather, this kind of
study is framed within tradition and history ('the role of critical
traditions in shaping literary history'), and as one possible 'specialist'
approach to literary study along with 'creative practice' and 'performance'. Leaving aside the facts that, as we have seen, most UK literature
departments do not frame theoretical study in this way and do not
make study of it 'specialist' but compulsory, it looks as if all these
questions of purpose and value are to be matters for individual
institutions and their teaching staffs to determine and express through
their course syllabuses.

Such a degree of generality has no doubt made the Subject
Knowledge list, indeed the whole benchmarking enterprise, more
acceptable to the community of literature teachers in the UK – teachers
who are always characterised as 'diverse in their approaches to study'.
In the *Subject Overview Report – English* (QAA, 1995), external reviewers (assessors) of some 72 per cent of English departments in
England and Northern Ireland summed up as follows:

> *Different emphases can be given to knowledge of literature ... very
> different approaches to the English curriculum ... [ranging from] the
> teaching of established canons of literature to an emphasis on exploring
> the relationship of texts and contemporary social issues ... The variety
> encountered extends to related subjects such as film, drama, creative
> writing ... the literatures of other English-speaking countries and
> cultural studies.*

All well and good no doubt. But how is this diverse body of teachers to ensure that their graduates demonstrate sufficient 'awareness . . .', 'appreciation . . .', 'experience . . .' and so on, when what the Statement offers is in effect a list of topic headings – and headings, moreover, that have no criteria attached to them? What, after all, is to count as *sufficient* awareness, etc.? Indeed, one wonders quite how the external reviewers of English provision can make their judgements and assessments on the basis of the subject knowledge requirements listed here, and the next (skills) list, without their own perceptions of purpose and value entering into the equation.

Normal provision

Despite the diversity in approach that characterises the discipline, the English Subject Centre survey of 2002 provides a snapshot of 'normal' provision in the UK, shedding light on actual curriculum values and practices in English departments.

First, it transpires that the considerations which guide the design of the undergraduate curriculum 'to a large extent' are (in descending order):

- Coverage of literary periods
- Reading/interpretive skills
- Specialist interests of staff
- Giving student choice
- Coverage of literary history
- Genre study
- Theoretical issues.

(Halcrow Group et al., 2003: 55)

Perhaps the only surprise here is that 'Theoretical issues' comes so far down the list when, as we saw in Chapter 3, elsewhere in the report theoretical-critical courses and teaching emerge as far more significant. Indeed, this kind of course is the only exception to the rule that in literature departments 'the number of optional courses [on offer] is greater than the number of compulsory courses' (p. 70). Rather a puzzle. Are we perhaps to understand that, while teachers regard it as essential for their students to study literary theory, they do not accord it the same great prominence as a guide in their own planning of the curriculum?

The survey also explored in some depth the kinds of course that departments designate compulsory and those that are optional or

Courses most commonly offered as:	
(a) Compulsory	**(b) Optional/elective**
1. Critical/Literary theory	1. Late 20th century and contemporary
2. Shakespeare	2. Modernist
3. Renaissance	3. Renaissance
4. Medieval	4. Medieval/Victorian/Shakespeare
5. Victorian	5. Women's writing
6. Modernist	6. Mid-20th century/Shakespeare/Romantic/ 18th century/20th century American/Film/ Creative writing

Adapted from Halcrow Group et al., 2003: 56.

FIGURE 4.3 *UK English Subject Centre survey, 2002.*

elective – and, of the (majority) optional courses, which are most popular with students as judged by enrolment numbers. The summary chart in Figure 4.3 shows the courses most frequently found in each category.

Clearly, the courses most commonly provided in UK literature departments are (still) period- and style-based, with Shakespeare as the only single-author course identified (though no doubt the traditional canon is well represented within many of the courses). However, note that 'Critical/Literary theory' is confirmed as the most commonly designated compulsory course, and that Women's writing features strongly among optional course provision along with probably even more recent extensions to the curriculum such as creative writing and film.

The most popular of the optional courses (among those deemed 'very popular') are as follows:

1. Late 20th century and contemporary
2. Shakespeare/Women's writing
3. Modernist/20th century American

4. Victorian/Creative writing
5. Film
6. Mid-20th century/Colonial and Postcolonial.

What is immediately striking about this list (p. 57 of the report) is the popularity among students of the newest kinds of course. In addition to those referred to above, colonial and postcolonial literature is not very commonly provided but, where it is, is highly valued. It is also striking that no literature before about the 1830s is represented, with the exception of Shakespeare (still hanging in there). Obviously, students prefer recent and contemporary literature, American as well as British, and Women's writing, over all the other courses offered of whatever type. These findings would seem to support our earlier conclusions about the wider social forces impacting upon students' reading habits and, especially, their desire for study that is meaningfully relevant to their lives.

The curriculum as represented here appears to be a compromise between those aspects of study that literature academics regard as essential (coverage of literary periods/history, theory and criticism) and the newer fields that their fee-paying and increasingly mobile students want to study. We do not mean to suggest that academics are being dragged along by their students kicking and screaming – many will have a primary interest in the newer fields – but it certainly seems that (as we remarked at the start of the book) the constitution of the discipline is changing as boundaries between it and adjacent fields weaken. Although an earlier prediction that Literature would be subsumed by Cultural Studies (e.g. Easthope, 1991) does not seem to be coming to pass, there is compelling evidence here of a discipline in the process of (if not revolution) marked, and mainly demand-led, change. At the moment, though, the curriculum seems genuinely a compromise: as we have seen, academics are not budging on the issue of the importance of theoretical-critical study even though it is not popular with students.

Skills

Further, the Subject Benchmark document identifies the subject-specific skills that 'are intended to provide a broad framework for *articulating the outcomes* of individual programmes' (emphasis added), a 'range of complementary literary, linguistic and critical skills' (see

- critical skills in the close reading and analysis of texts;
- ability to articulate knowledge and understanding of texts, concepts and theories relating to English studies;
- sensitivity to generic conventions and to the shaping effects upon communication of circumstances, authorship, textual production and intended audience;
- responsiveness to the central role of language in the creation of meaning and sensitivity to the affective power of language;
- rhetorical skills of effective communication and argument, both oral and written;
- command of a broad range of vocabulary and an appropriate critical terminology;
- bibliographic skills appropriate to the discipline, including accurate citation of sources and consistent use of conventions in the presentation of scholarly work;
- awareness of how different social and cultural contexts affect the nature of language and meaning;
- understanding of how cultural norms and assumptions influence questions of judgement;
- comprehension of the complex nature of literary languages, and an awareness of the relevant research by which they may be better understood.

(QAA, 2000: 5)

FIGURE 4.4 *Key subject-specific skills.*

Figure 4.4). Notice that while this list emphasises the importance of language to students of literature, no mention is made here or elsewhere in the document of the intellectual and ethical kinds of understanding and reasoning we referred to earlier – open-mindedness, intellectual flexibility, tolerance, love of learning, and so on – which should surely find some place in the characterisation of an *education* in Literature?

External reviewers of literature courses would again regard these 'learning outcomes' as demonstrable and would expect to see them assessed in some way. But this list is perhaps a rather different matter for the community, since most teachers of literature are not accustomed to think of themselves as teaching skills per se.[3] Exceptions to this include writing and presentation skills, which were reported as Year 1 compulsory elements in 70 per cent of the UK English departments surveyed in 2002 and in most cases were taught by the English department itself (Halcrow Group et al., 2003: 44). Interestingly, the report also records that the departments surveyed were *least* satisfied with the level of knowledge their graduate students had acquired in presentational and writing skills, in 'confidence to effect change', in creativity/originality and in research and communication skills, in that order (p. 76). And we notice, in passing, that the list of skills in this survey is considerably broader than that presented in the benchmark document.

Nonetheless, as we look down the benchmark list (and leaving aside the rather odd definition of sensitivity, awareness, understanding and comprehension as 'skills') it is clear that the actual skills identified are indeed subject-specific, part and parcel of studying Literature. That is, they concern 'knowing how to' do the things involved in the discipline; they are its genuine practices. But, while your courses no doubt provide opportunities for students to exercise these skills, do you deliberately aim to develop them progressively over the years of undergraduate study – that is, do you attend to another of the QAA's requirements, for 'progression'? And could you demonstrate this? We'll look at a few real courses to see how some of these things might be accomplished in practice.

COURSE DESIGN ISSUES

Appendix 3 on the book's website presents descriptive outlines of three modules of the English Literature curriculum at a UK university, one at each of Levels (Years) 1–3. They are offered as a stimulus to reflection on your own and your department's practice of course design and, in particular, of constructing syllabuses. At the end of the chapter the issues involved are summarised in the form of questions, designed to help you analyse an existing course or think about a course you may be setting out to design or redesign.

Three case studies

Studying literature: 1901–1945
Appendix 3(a) presents the outline of a period-based module – as we have seen, a staple of literary studies – for students in the second half of their first year at university. Looking at the first three sections, and the last (brief Conclusion), we can see that these are designed to inform the students about the aims and objectives of the module and its contents or syllabus. The opening sentence of the Introduction clearly sets the module in the context of degree-level studies: with respect to progression, as one in a series of courses the students will study. Further, the next two sentences look back to the course studied

in Semester 1, explain how this module builds on it and so help the students identify the progress they are making.

The module's objectives are expressed in broad terms of what the students are expected to achieve – by implication, beyond what they have achieved before ('increase ...', 'further practise ...', 'extend ...'). Specifically, they are encouraged to:

- *increase your ability to read carefully and critically;*
- *further practise your responses to literature, orally and in writing;*
- *extend your confidence in engaging with a text;*
- *advance your competence as researchers;*
- *further your understanding of relationships between an age and the literature it produces;*
- *through study of novels, short stories and poetry, address a range of generic as well as subject-based issues.*

The final section of the document expresses some of the teachers' values: that it is the students' responsibility to *work hard* to achieve these things, and the hope that they will be *interested* and *stimulated* by the course.

The students also discover how they may achieve these objectives: by participating in seminars (where they will 'express their views' sincerely and 'listen to the views of others'; while they will work independently to prepare for seminars, during them they will also work together in small groups); by completing work such as an oral presentation (which will also help to 'clarify and structure [their] thoughts'); by means of a written (in fact, word-processed) essay, in which appropriate referencing of source material is required; and in an unseen end-of-course examination. There will also be a series of lectures, the details of which are not presented in the document except to say that the first lecture will inform the students about making oral presentations. Finally, the students are assured that their teacher is very willing to offer help and advice, and they are told when and where she or he will be available to them. They *must* consult their teacher about the subject and progress of their oral presentation in advance: apart from ensuring a safety net, this indicates that the students have some choice in the matter of what they focus attention on.

In the Course Texts and Seminars sections of the document we discover the 'stuff' of the module: the course syllabus and the way it is structured. The seminar timetable shows exactly what will need to be read and considered by when – and, indeed, the promised generic variety seems represented here in a syllabus that looks likely to promote the students' 'understanding of relationships between an age and the literature it produces'.

Literature 1830–1901: the Victorians

This module, outlined in Appendix 3(b), is similarly a popular period course, this time for students in the first semester of their second year – i.e. this is a module they might study immediately after the one we have just been examining. So what we may expect to find here is progression from one course to the next. Indeed, it is clear at a glance that more is expected of the second-year students. First, in this 12-week module they must study three (rather than two) novels in depth, lengthy ones at that. And they are asked to read the poetry of Tennyson and Browning widely: the Week 4 Introduction to Victorian poetry 'includes' the poems listed but, by implication, is not restricted to them. Also, in this course it is 'vital' that the students read widely among secondary sources for the period 'as contextual knowledge is essential to a good understanding of the literature'. A Bibliography is included, comprising 21 'general books' and 53 titles related to the novelists and poets featured in the course, along with journals and electronic resources. The students are exhorted to 'Be selective and discriminating and don't let critics swamp your views'. Also, they are expected to bring outcomes of their study to seminars ('a page of notes') and to produce a '500-word commentary', a rationale, to accompany the oral presentation.

Although some advice is given regarding these activities, the assumption seems to be that the students have now acquired the necessary skills to accomplish them to some sufficient degree. It is also interesting to note that there is no Introduction to this module outline in which the objectives of the course are communicated (though, as before, we are able to glean a few from the document as a whole). We may assume that, by this stage, the teachers expect their students to have 'internalised' such matters as what the point of studying literature is and what they are setting out to achieve.

Utopias and dystopias: science fiction

Likewise, in the third course description in Appendix 3(c) there is no explicit discussion of course objectives. And again, we see evidence of (further) progression. This is a Level 3 'Elective' course, which in itself suggests the opportunity to exercise much more choice than before (although in this and many UK universities such opportunities are available in Year 2 if not from the start). It is also unlike the other courses we have looked at in that it is a genre-based module, in which the focus is on particular themes ('fictional engagement with time and space, imagination and fantasy'). And it appears to be more challenging intellectually, in that it attends to 'context' in a much broader sense ('historical, political, sexual and spiritual') – and not just because the Introduction refers explicitly to 'the critical challenge'. This time, study is based on five set books, but it is clear that much wider reading of both primary and secondary texts is expected. A General Reading list (17 titles) and Specific Titles (24) here *precede* the Course Outline, and, rather than classes based on study of each set text in turn, the weekly topics are a lot broader in scope. They must be prepared *as topics* for discussion (e.g. Week 2: 'Utopia: Narrative Form/Structure'; Week 10: 'Ideas of Humanity in SF/ Fantasy Texts'). And there is much more emphasis in this document on getting out into libraries and exploring journals to research the course themes: 'It is thus essential . . . that you research topics indicated in the programme in a library'; '. . . do you own investigation . . .'; 'So **research**: use indexes and bibliographies'.

QAA requirements

Looking back to the Benchmark Statement lists, it is of course not possible to judge how well the English 'Subject Knowledge' requirements are met in this university on the basis of only three of its courses. But you will see that many if not most of the 'Key subject-specific skills' listed are (explicitly or, often, implicitly) taught. However, demonstrating that this is the case – to the QAA's satisfaction, for the benefit of the students – would almost certainly require more explicit and detailed explanation in the documents, especially as regards the objectives of the modules at Levels 2 and 3 and 'progression' from one course/level to the next. The QAA's *Subject Overview Report – English* (QAA, 1995: Summary) says as much – and, indeed, much more. Having noted that 'overall aims, and more specifically the learning objectives of specific course components, were not fully rationalised or articulated for the benefit of students', in paragraphs 16 and 17 of Figure 4.5 we see that clarity regarding

15. Excellence in teaching and learning was characterised by: **careful planning and formulation of well-defined objectives** . . .; the clear exposition of new material; an innovative selection of challenging texts or data, in many cases drawing on up-to-date scholarly material or the teacher's own research; well-focused elicitation, based on careful listening; students displaying confidence and self-expression, often associated with a critique of the product of self-directed work; the fostering of genuinely open debate about the nature of the subject and current debates within it; and the setting of well-judged recommendations for further reading or follow-up assignments. Flair, enthusiasm and the lecturers' ability to inspire students also featured strongly.

16. . . . Other features of excellence include the **links between the particular class and the curriculum as a whole** . . . also . . . the students' quality of experience in undertaking studies with a high degree of independence, supported by excellent tutorial guidance and well-designed course material.

17. . . . **The main recurring need was to articulate more clearly to students the particular part the class played in meeting the course objectives**.

18. Other aspects in observed classes judged to require improvement included a lack of rigour and intellectual challenge, **an absence of overall structure or a failure to clarify key points of learning**, or a tendency for some students to lose interest.

(QAA, 1995. Available at: www.qaa.ac.uk – accessed 12 March 2004. Emphases added.)

FIGURE 4.5 *Subject Overview Report – English: Summary . . .*

objectives (or, 'learning outcomes') is also required at the level of the individual class. Although in our anonymous university these and other matters will probably have been discussed with students during teaching sessions, the text in Figure 4.5 shows that this is not enough.

Similar issues are highlighted in the concluding section of the report: 'Many providers need to articulate more clearly for the benefit of students the relationship between subject aims, methods of learning, criteria and methods of assessment, and intended learning objectives.' Since the mid-1990s, when the report was compiled, specification of 'learning outcomes' that students must demonstrate has replaced all talk of 'intended learning objectives'. And, as we saw in Chapter 2, reference to 'learning' (as opposed to 'teaching') is now ubiquitous. Nevertheless, what the report draws teachers' attention to is the need to achieve congruence between curriculum aims and the objectives and design of individual courses – a matter to which we will return.

'Other' skills

Meanwhile, this is not the end of the story. In UK higher education, students of all subjects must also acquire general (often, confusingly for us, dubbed 'generic') skills, such as those of information technology, teamwork and time management. The complete list of 'Generic and graduate skills' is presented in Appendix 5 on the book's website. You will see that all but three (possibly four) of the points are in fact expressly taught in and through the discipline. The genuinely 'other' skills are: the third point, 'employability'; the last two, 'IT skills' and 'time-management and organisational skills'; and the ninth, 'team work' (although that is more debatable). These skills, we argued earlier, are different in kind and properly may be taught only *as* students pursue their study of Literature.

IT skills

Of these other skills, we saw that IT skills are indeed addressed in the sample course outlines, in the requirements for students to use CD-ROMs and to access databases and websites on the Internet for research purposes and to word-process their essays. In common with other UK universities, this one has a Media Centre (or some such) where students may use equipment of various kinds, always including a bank of computers, and where they can seek technical help from members of staff dedicated to running it. Library staff (here located in Learning Resources) are available to offer their help too. However, in the English Subject Overview Report (QAA, 1995) acquisition of IT skills is described as 'an area in need of development' in many universities. In 2002 the English Subject Centre discovered that 70 per cent of the English departments surveyed regarded their use of IT in teaching as 'underdeveloped' or 'early stages' – although by 2005 the great majority hoped to see it 'well established' (49 per cent) or 'innovative' (25 per cent) (Halcrow Group et al., 2003: 26).

Teamwork

Teamwork also has its place in these (and most) literature courses, as students work in twos and threes to plan and deliver oral presentations and engage in small-group work during seminars. Although teamwork of these kinds does not strictly speaking flow from consideration of the overarching aims of the English curriculum, discussion of ideas among peers certainly does – and from early on in the discipline's history UK university departments have practised (at least) whole-group seminar discussion. As we shall see in the next chapter, small-group work has been gaining significant ground in the last decade or so and mainly for reasons intrinsic to the discipline.

Time-management and organisational skills

Acquisition of these skills is a similar case in point – they are things students have always had to grapple with when trying to meet the demands of the syllabus: making choices among a wealth of primary and secondary reading, organising themselves to deliver the required work, making time for writing essays, preparing for seminars, and so forth. They are, rightly, things that students learn to do as they study literature courses. But it is only quite recently (and patchily) that these skills have been identified as such, and presented to students as important because they are 'marketable' aspects of their higher education.

The capacity to adapt and transfer the critical methods of the discipline to a variety of working environments

The last of the skills, this is probably the most contentious within a mainly cognitive discipline such as Literature. Some academics regard it as well beyond their remit and/or their ability to offer. Indeed, patchy provision is highlighted in the Subject Overview Report (QAA, 1995: Conclusions):

> m. Whilst almost all English providers include preparation for employment in their aims and objectives, in practice such aims are seldom articulated in the form of specific learning objectives, and their value is frequently understated . . .

We might ourselves be tempted to conclude that 'almost all . . . providers include preparation for employment in their aims and objectives' largely because the QAA requires it (but see Yorke and Knight, 2004). Nevertheless, the report confirms that 'employers . . . valued highly the skills acquired by students' (§38), and we may take it that the skills they are thought to value most are those listed in Appendix 5. Or, alternatively, we may prefer to attend to the Dearing Report's conclusion that 'The single most important capacity employers seek in those with higher education qualifications is intellectual capabilities of a high order' (National Committee of Inquiry into Higher Education, 1997).

PROGRESSION

As we have seen, the QAA also requires and assesses evidence of progression over the years of undergraduate study (and of differentiation between levels of study). However, in the Benchmark Statement there is little or no discussion of what precisely is meant by this. What we gleaned from the reviewers' Subject Overview Report is that teachers must make the relationships between their courses plain and clear to students. We are also given to understand that the ultimate goal of progression is 'independent study', and that achieving it is enhanced by '. . . better tutorial support in the first stages, special attention to the identified needs of non-standard entrants and mature students, and increasing, controlled, progression to independent study' (§22).

Choice

In the three sample modules, we saw that students' progression is addressed to some extent and that one measure of it is the increased choice the students are offered over the years of undergraduate study, as regards both what they study and how. Offering such choice is common practice in UK English departments; according to the QAA reviewers, in 1994–5 'approximately 80 per cent of the providers offer a degree of flexibility and choice to their students, either by using unitised or modular structures, or by designing courses with optional studies'. There is every reason to suppose that the proportion is now if anything greater – the 2002 English Subject Centre survey lists 45 different optional courses (Halcrow Group et al., 2003: 70). In that same survey we have seen that 'Giving student choice' was fourth in the list of guiding considerations in course planning among the respondents (p. 55). And in the three sample modules we saw that, over time, students are required to make increasingly independent judgements about their reading. But is this all that can be said on the subject of progression, let alone the measures of it?

'Spiral' curriculum

In this connection, an educationalist we might turn to for some inspiration is Jerome Bruner, who in the 1960s first conceived of the curriculum as a 'spiral'. More recently, he characterised 'the idea' as follows:

> . . . *that in teaching a subject you begin with an 'intuitive' account that is well within the reach of a student, and then circle back later to a more formal or highly structured account, until, with however many more recyclings are necessary, the learner has mastered the topic or subject in its full generative power.*

He continues:

> . . . *'Readiness is not only born but made.' The general proposition rests on the still deeper truth that any domain of knowledge can be constructed at varying levels of abstractness or complexity. That is to say, domains of knowledge are* made, not found: *they can be constructed simply or complexly, abstractly or concretely. And it can easily be demonstrated within certain interesting limits that a so-called 'higher level' way of characterizing a domain of knowledge encompasses, replaces, and renders more powerful and precise a 'lower-level' characterization.*

(Bruner, 1996a: 119)

Perhaps we can think more productively about progression in these cognitive terms, which give some content to the notion of independent study as the ultimate goal of a university education.[4] That is, the aim is to enable students to think in the 'higher level' – abstract, complex and generative – manner Bruner describes. It maybe seems obvious that achieving this depends on first introducing ideas in an intuitive, concrete, simpler manner and then quite deliberately revisiting these same ideas at some later stage(s) 'in a more formal or highly structured account'; such progression would clearly need careful planning, quite possibly over a number of levels/years of study. But, as we shall see in Chapter 5, obvious though this 'idea' of Bruner's may seem, it is powerful and far-reaching. And, maybe, the ultimate aim is really meta-cognition? – not just 'mastering the topic' or the doing of things but, in the process, knowing what one is doing and why.

Specialisation vs multidisciplinarity

Course design is not only affected by the level of the course in question but also by the degree of specialisation in the subject offered to or chosen by students. In 1995 the subject assessors found that:

Approximately half the institutions visited provide English in some form of modular structure ... The most extreme form ..., where students have an entirely free choice in devising their programme after the first year, is only operated in about 10 per cent of the visited providers. Where this is the case, the assessors often raised questions about coherence and progression in the curriculum as well as the quality of the processes for students to make informed choices. The normal pattern is some form of core or prescribed structure, with a varying number of options.

(QAA, 1995)

In 2000 the conclusions of the English benchmark Statement were similar; around half of the (then *c.* 40,000) students studying Literature at university were doing so in specialist single honours degree programmes, the other half as part of combined or joint honours degrees, or as 'a central subject in ... modular schemes in the Humanities'. The document continues:

Combined and Joint Honours students are rarely taught or assessed separately from their peers in Single Honours at the level of course or module. This benchmarking statement therefore applies to all students taking a significant proportion of English courses as part of their degree programme.

(QAA, 2000: 3)

Presumably, the students who are not in the single honours programme simply study fewer of the Literature courses the university offers. Students in a combined honours programme, for example, can expect to spend around half the time studying English as specialists in the subject – and those in joint and modular programmes, a smaller proportion still. So, thinking back to the QAA's lists of 'Subject knowledge' and 'Key subject-specific skills' requirements (and without knowing quite what is meant in the Statement by taking 'a significant proportion' of English courses), these students surely cannot be expected to acquire the same breadth or depth of knowledge and understanding as their specialist peers. And is it really the case that they will be acquiring knowledge, understanding and skill that is similar, if not the same, in kind? Are we comparing like with like here?

Multidisciplinarity

Usually, the strength of specialised study is that it allows sustained, systematic attention to be given to a class of objects (in the case of

Literature, mainly texts) and to progressive mastery of the associated interrelated concepts, patterns of reasoning and expression over time. Those who study a combined/joint honours or modular programme, in which courses in Literature are mixed with those in another or other subjects, must of course divide their attention between those subjects – inevitably, their education in Literature is less sustained and less systematic.

On the other hand, we know that development of knowledge and understanding in one discipline may be impossible or hampered without elements of knowledge and understanding in another: this is perhaps true of Literature and History. (In the UK, the English Subject Centre survey (Halcrow Group et al., 2003: 53) reports that almost 80 per cent of Literature departments offer opportunities for 'interdisciplinary [?] study' and that the combination most often chosen by students is Literature with History, followed by media/film/television studies.) But, even so, History (like Literature) retains its validity and unique character as a discipline. This suggests that we can properly understand the interrelationship between the two disciplines only if we first recognise the basic differences between them. Then we may go on to see in what respects they may be related. The main problem for students in multidisciplinary programmes is how to develop an adequate grasp of elements within two (or more) quite different types of experience and knowledge without sustained, systematic attention to them individually.

And these programmes present difficulties for teachers too. Either they must strive, in interdisciplinary fashion, to integrate their knowledge of different subjects; or they must learn to work collaboratively with colleagues from other disciplinary traditions – not alongside, but with them, otherwise students will face the further problem of studying a programme that is at best fragmentary and, at worst, unintelligible. Those of us who teach in combined, joint or modular degree programmes, then, face the extra challenge of designing courses that pay sufficient attention to disciplinary integrity and difference within a multidisciplinary framework that is coherent and offers progression. Leaving aside the question of what 'sufficient attention' might be, even if we were to achieve all this spectacularly well – design perfectly balanced multidisciplinary programmes – the question remains: should we apply the *same* criteria of judgement to these students' achievements as we apply to the single-honours (specialist) student of the disciplines concerned?

This is not at all to suggest that for these students our standards should be lower; rather it raises the question: are these students' knowledge, understanding and skills *different from* the specialist students'? If, like us, you are inclined to answer 'yes' – with no implication of inferiority or superiority – then, simply, there can be no justification for treating all the students as if they were the same. As we saw, the English Benchmark Statement does just that (except to say that non-specialist students are not required to study writing pre-1800); and, in doing so, it offers no guidance to the many teachers who must grapple with such difficult issues. It might be helpful to indicate which among the many requirements in the lists may be expected to apply, or apply to whatever extent, to students who spend, say, 50–60 per cent and 30–40 per cent of their time studying Literature. (If you teach such students, perhaps have a go at it yourself?) Other implications of this question, to do with student assessment, are discussed in Chapter 6.

MODELS OF CURRICULUM DESIGN REVISITED

We saw earlier that a major thrust of the Subject Overview Report for English (QAA, 1995) is to draw attention to the need for congruence between curriculum/programme aims and the objectives and design of individual courses of study. That is, a need for planning conceived as a coherent process is emphasised, in which the various parts (courses: their objectives and contents, and teaching-learning and assessment methods) are brought into what might be termed 'constructive alignment' with the overarching aims of the discipline and programme. What we are concerned with here, then, is relational patterns.

A process-oriented curriculum model

As we saw, when designing courses our jumping-off point is cognitive – the discipline is our central concern. Practically speaking, we start with subject-curriculum aims which are designed to express our purposes and our values as educators, from which we derive more specific teaching/learning objectives and begin to delineate a number of courses, at different levels, that will offer opportunities for our particular students progressively to acquire the desired knowledge, understanding, experience, abilities and values – toggling back and forth between overarching curriculum aims and the details of the developing courses as we proceed – and in the process taking account of the requirements of the other interested parties.

We conclude, then, that an *iterative* process such as this, of alignment between curriculum aims and (the various components of) courses, perhaps captures the sense of dynamic relationships – of a process that is creative and participatory – rather better than the more linear and mechanistic procedure implied in the 'rational' curriculum development model. We would say, too, that in this more creative conception of the process the central role of teachers – as experts in the discipline and professional educators – is fully acknowledged, not only as regards their role in determining educational aims, objectives and syllabuses but also the other aspects of course design we have yet to explore: appropriate methods of teaching, of student assessment and of evaluation.

Activity?

If you are setting out to design or redesign a course/module or would like to analyse the structure of an existing course, bear in mind these *interconnected* questions:

- The discipline is your starting point: what overarching curriculum/programme aims shape this course?
- What are the objectives (or, if you prefer, learning outcomes) of the course, in terms of what [knowledge/understandings/abilities/values/skills . . .]?
- What type of course is it [e.g. period, genre, theme based . . .]?
- what is its 'value' and status [length/credits awarded . . .; first, second level, etc.; compulsory/optional . . .]?
- Who is the course for [specialist literature students/combined or joint honours/ multidisciplinary]? How would you characterise the 'student body'?
- This is just one of a number of literature courses students must 'progress' through: where does it 'fit' in your department's offerings [curriculum aims expressed/level/type/status], and what is its relationship to (central concepts/practices in) courses students may study before and after? How does it differ from courses offered at other levels?
- Which texts make up the syllabus and how is the course structured? Are the students offered choice in the matter of what they study?
- How does the course meet any 'external' requirements that apply, from government and its agencies and from the wider university?

POSTSCRIPT

Finally, we should briefly make our own position as clear as we can. We have been concerned to argue here for a view of higher education curriculum design that locates the subject to be taught and studied at the centre – which, we further argue, entails a central role in course design for the expert teacher. We have argued this case by proceeding from the broad question examined in Chapters 1 and 2, 'what is a higher education in Literature?', and in this chapter from discussion of students' needs. However, we are aware that the idea of 'negotiating' the curriculum with students is currently in favour among educationalists. Some go further, promoting a 'learner-centredness' that seems to deny teaching and the teacher much of a role at all. In that context, we would emphasise that our argument has *not* been an attempt to promote a teacher- (rather than student-) centred ideology. These must be matters of genuine, reasoned debate, not genuflection. As we remark in Chapter 1, it is perfectly legitimate, indeed desirable, that students have purposes and objectives of their own in choosing a higher education in any subject.[5] And on the question of students' choice regarding *what* is studied, we have suggested in a number of places in this chapter that the exercise of such choice is desirable on educational grounds. The question of students' needs is raised again and the notion of student-centredness addressed directly in the next chapter, where we believe these matters more clearly (or at least, less controversially) belong.

Notes

1. Maybe too reasonable in view of the extent of *tacit* or 'hidden' knowledge that teachers need to bring to the surface in the process of design and make explicit to students in course descriptions and in their teaching – the many assumptions that lie 'behind' the course requirements: see the classic text, *The Hidden Curriculum*, Snyder (1971).
2. This is not an innocent question. 'Delivering' the curriculum is currently the fashionable term in some parts of the world, but it is misleading. However the curriculum is delivered (whether by text, TV, computer, a person in a classroom), it is mainly *teachers* who shape it: who make the necessary prior cognitive and value judgements about what is to be taught/learned. Students may well have a role to play, but, it will be argued, these matters cannot be mainly their responsibility. And we must surely question the metaphor of delivering knowledge to students, as if it is an object they can 'possess'. The metaphor is reductive in that it begs the whole question of the students' learning, of what it means 'to learn'.

3. However, a focus on *methodology* – on how texts are taught and studied, rather than on what is taught and studied – is not new (e.g. Scholes, 1985). And recently, in the context of lack of consensus regarding the purposes of literary study, a 'reshaping of literary identity' by foregrounding *pedagogy* is proposed: that is, a new focus on 'the context and the means through which knowledge is produced' (McCurrie, 2004: 44).

4. Vygotsky's notion of 'scaffolding' is analogous and relevant here. As we saw in Chapter 2, the idea is that students need guidance and support in the early stages of their development if they are to become more expert and autonomous. As they proceed along the path of development, less and less support is needed or should be offered by the teacher – whether in the face-to-face or online setting. This may apply to the design of study tasks (from the teacher spelling out what needs to be done to students themselves identifying the 'problem' and possible solutions); to acquiring resources (from the teacher making appropriate resources available to the students identifying what they need and finding it); and to social support (from the teacher closely supervising group work to students working together independently or, as individuals, undertaking research-based study).

5. An argument about this might also derive from consideration of what we mean by 'higher education'. Or it might be based on the notion of 'adulthood' and its implications for higher education – see, for instance, Paterson (1979) for a thoroughgoing examination of the issues. The age of majority in the UK is 18 years, so almost all students in higher education are deemed adult.

Key references

Brookfield, S. D. (1986) *Understanding and Facilitating Adult Learning*. Buckingham: Open University Press, Chapter 9.

Bruner, J. (1996) *The Culture of Education*. Cambridge, MA: Harvard University Press.

Eisner, E. W. (1976) 'Educational connoisseurship and criticism: their form and functions in educational evaluation', *Journal of Aesthetic Education*, 10(3–4): 135–50.

Websites

QAA (1995) *QO 12/95 Subject Overview Report – English*. Higher Education Funding Council for England, Quality Assessment of English 1994–95. Available at: http://www.qaa.ac.uk/revreps/subjrev/All/qo_12_95.htm

QAA (2000) *Subject Benchmark Statement – English*. Gloucester: Quality Assurance Agency for Higher Education. Available at: www.qaa.ac.uk

5

Methods of teaching

'GOOD TEACHING' REVISITED

In Chapter 4 we explored aspects of a planning cycle for teaching, addressing the questions *'what* should I be teaching, and *why?'* By the end of the discussion, the notion of a 'rational' model of curriculum and course design had been replaced by a more dynamic – creative and participatory – understanding of how courses in Literature might be developed: an iterative process of alignment between subject/curriculum aims, course objectives and contents that not only takes into account the requirements of the discipline but also of students of Literature, the university and the wider society. This chapter addresses the question *'how* should I be teaching?' and discusses another major aspect of course planning: the methods and media of teaching-learning to be used, and the study activities teachers ask their students to engage in.

As a preliminary, we should first briefly return to the elements of 'good teaching' discussed in Chapter 2. There, with educational philosophers Hirst and Peters (1970), we argued that as teachers – and for what we do to count as 'teaching' at all – we must, at least, be aiming to create conditions in which learning is possible. That is, teachers must engage in activities with the intention of bringing about learning and which signal what is to be learned, and teach in ways that are intelligible to and within the capacities of the learners. And we argued that for 'good' teaching we must also aim to engage and/or extend students' interest in and enthusiasm for the subjects of study, and encourage them to think independently and critically about what they study (see Figure 2.1). These conditions, then, are the jumping-off point for our consideration of methods of teaching Literature.

Second, in asking the question 'how should I be teaching?' we should always bear in mind the less formal issues touched on in previous chapters, such as the persona the teacher adopts in class and its impact on students' trust in his or her skill and commitment; the impact on students of the teacher's pedagogic style (a preference for lecturing, for questioning and guided discussion, open seminar or tutorial discussion, and so on); the teacher's abilities as a guide, mentor and model (as opposed to a remote expert), helping to engage students in the issues; the teacher's skill at explanations that work for particular student audiences, and at making reference to existential, social and topical matters that connect course content to the world of students' lives. We remind you of these matters here lest in what follows they should become swamped by the many more formal considerations of teaching.

Educational aims and teaching methods

Calls for one kind of curriculum organisation or another are often confused with calls for the introduction of new types of teaching and learning activity, perhaps especially electronic forms these days. But, really, questions about the ends and contents of the curriculum (which we explored in Chapter 4) should be kept distinct in teachers' minds from questions about which teaching-learning methods they might use, for two reasons. First, we argued in Chapter 2 that educational aims and the contents of courses do not *determine* methods of teaching, and went on to demonstrate this in the section 'Writing pedagogy' in Chapter 3. In principle, no method (that is educational) is ruled out; we have seen that the means by which teachers can engage students in the subject matter and help make it intelligible and interesting are many and varied.

However, second, teaching-learning methods, being educational, themselves embody and express educational aims. They have a double significance: means to curriculum ends *and* educational in their own right. For example, adopting methods that encourage students to think independently and critically will serve one of the literature teacher's main curriculum aims – to promote the kind of study in which greater understanding of meaning and significance is the goal – while, at the same time, being able to 'think for oneself' is clearly an educational end in itself. In effect, certain teaching methods *are* ruled out by such an aim. Clearly it could not be achieved by methods that disregard the students' critical autonomy: for example, an exclusive focus on right/wrong answers or the use of drill. Repetitious exercises cannot encourage independent, critical thinking (furthermore, drill is not of itself educational, even if it might be justified in some circumstances and on other grounds). And methods that are inherently ethically objectionable would certainly be ruled out; any method that is biased in some way, for instance, or which involves moral or emotional pressures or a manipulative withholding of information and ideas.

So, ideally, the teaching methods we employ will be *both* appropriate to Literature curriculum aims and educational in their own right. The classroom discussion of 'Araby' in Chapter 2 is an instance of this. Among other things, the vignette was designed to illustrate that literary concepts are not built hierarchically; that, for example, there is no one 'right' way in to the story but, rather, many possible ways in, all of them valid (although not necessarily equally fruitful in particular cases). In our discipline, concepts are fluid, made and remade in relationship to other concepts and intimately bound up with beliefs and values within social discourse. Critical thinking involves problem-atising, *not* taking things at face value, and also creativity – sensing difficulties and gaps, 'something askew' in understanding, imagining alternative possibilities and making guesses (Garrison, 1991: 291). It follows, then, that the *way* students learn to study literature is fundamentally important. And this of course has profound implications for the teacher's pedagogic practice.

Most obviously, it is both inappropriate and counterproductive to teach texts in a manner that suggests they may be known 'correctly' or 'incorrectly', once and for all. Current external demands for containment, quantification, efficiency and observable, measurable outcomes of learning in all higher education – in short, performativity[1] – simply miss the point when applied to a discipline characterised by abstract, complex mental discriminations and richly dynamic relationships between processes of analysis, interpretation and evaluation. As we argued in Chapter 2, the Literature teacher's prime responsibility is to induct students into the distinctive purposes, objects of study and text-genres, methods of inquiry, central concepts and networks of ideas, conventional uses of evidence and modes of written and verbal expression that characterise the discipline – that is, the particularities of literary-critical discourse. In Chapter 4 (under 'Cognitive aims'), these responsibilities were translated into overarching aims of the teaching-learning of literature. And we argued that these aims, concerning the acquisition of certain knowledge, abilities and values, should be 'framed' by an understanding of why they are important:

connected to the existential and social purposes that make them *worth* acquiring.

In short, we should aim to offer our students the opportunity to engage in literary-critical discourse *as participants in a significant socio-cultural process*. On that understanding of our task, the question before us is 'how best can it be achieved?'

TEACHING BEGINNING STUDENTS: SOCIO-CULTURAL PEDAGOGIC PRINCIPLES

It will be helpful to begin by deriving from what has been said so far some fundamental *pedagogic principles* that can act as guides to the teacher's thoughts and actions – especially as regards the crucial early stages of students' higher education. Apart from the fact that beginnings just are fundamental, we also have in mind the facts about our student populations: that, in the UK for example, 'The majority of English programmes in almost all institutions are attracting proportions of mature students in excess of 30 per cent' – many of them under-qualified returners-to-study – and 'significant numbers of international students' (QAA, 1995). Of course it is not sufficient simply to note such demographic change. It is vital that teachers think through its implications for their teaching practices.

In Chapter 1, we suggested one such implication – that some shift of emphasis and resource will need to be made (in the clear absence of any increase in resources for teaching) from the later to the earlier stages of higher education. We also suggested there that, crucially, beginning students of Literature should be engaged in the *processes* that are central to the discipline – reading (the discursive processes of textual analysis-interpretation-evaluation) and communication (speaking and writing appropriately) – and engaged in ways that promote their participation as independent, critical centres of consciousness. Also taking account of the precepts of good teaching, we suggest here that the interconnected pedagogic principles of *engagement, intelligibility* and *participation* can offer us the right kind of guidance.

In discussing these principles we'll take as an example a module of the distance-taught UK Open University (UKOU) course, Living Arts, entitled Words (Robb, 1994). The Words module is both introductory and exemplifies these principles; because UKOU students are not required to have any academic qualifications on enrolment in the undergraduate programme their teachers have been forced to rethink approaches to introductory teaching. We also chose this module on grounds of convenience – unlike the ephemeral nature of what goes on face-to-face in the classroom, in distance education teaching is often via printed text that is published and available for public scrutiny, and for us to examine here.

The Principle of Engagement

This principle posits that introductory courses, intended as a prelude to years of further study, must arouse students' interest in the study of Literature/sustain their initial enthusiasm and aim to increase it. Furthermore, 'engagement' implies a process of connecting with, or latching onto, something that already exists (people's knowledge, experience, understanding, preconception, skill, desire) and harnessing it, ready to take off in appropriate directions. It may seem that teachers must therefore have some reliable knowledge of their students' backgrounds, in particular their current knowledge and experience of literature, their enthusiasms and their expectations of higher education. But this poses problems, in distance education especially, when teachers are faced with large classes or when reaching out to new or hitherto under-represented student groups. So, how is it possible to teach in ways that engage *all* our students?

In Words this is largely achieved by re-conceptualising the process of engagement. The module begins with brief discussion of the range of pastimes now available to people in their homes, and goes on to show (from newspaper reports of recent surveys) that nevertheless reading for pleasure is on the increase in the UK. This raises certain questions:

> Why it is that reading is still so popular, when the newer forms of entertainment . . . such as television, video and computers, offer such colourful and exciting alternatives? Why . . . should anyone choose to go to the trouble and effort of reading a book?

The students are then asked to explore these questions through the following 'Activity'.

Think of a TV programme that you watched and enjoyed recently – one that told a story, such as an episode from a drama series or soap opera, or a TV film.

Think also of a story that you've read, whether in a book or a magazine . . .

Spend a few minutes thinking about the *main differences* between the two experiences . . . and then jot down your thoughts. You may find it helpful to use these questions as a guide:

1. Did you read the story/watch the programme in one go, or spread it out over a number of occasions?
2. Where were you when you were reading/watching?
3. How much work do you feel you were made to do in each case?
4. Was the experience a private one, or one that you shared with other people?
5. Which of the two experiences was more enjoyable?

(Words: 8)

Each of the numbered questions is then taken up and discussed, and the students are also asked to listen to part of a cassette-tape in which a group of people discuss their experiences and judgements (all of which of course translates readily to small- or whole-group classroom discussion). Aspects of this discussion lead students into the next section of the teaching text, entitled 'Writing and imagination', in which they are asked to read a short story about a woman's conflict with her young child as she shops in a supermarket. In the process, their study of 'what happens when we read and how writing "works"' (p. 6) is launched.

So, this introduction to Literature does not begin with a potted history of Eng. Lit., with discussion of the major literary genres or literary-critical movements. Nor is it grounded in the belief that teachers must have knowledge of individual students' previous experience of such things or even of their preparedness for study generally. Rather, it starts by asking the students to reflect on what they actually do and experience while doing – it engages the students' attention by connecting with their thoughts, beliefs and feelings – with the intention of bringing their ideas about the roles of imaginative writing in the contemporary context to the forefront of their minds. It aims to *focus* their minds appropriately, on the subject to be studied, and get them *thinking constructively* about it from the start; thus, the general concerns of the subject are active in their minds. In doing this, the activities create a conceptual 'framework for understanding' and the making of meaning. As Bruner (1996a: 13) avers: 'The meaning of any fact, proposition or encounter is relative to the . . . frame of reference in terms of which it is construed'. This has particular force when applied to propositional knowledge, the kind mainly encountered in higher education, which by its nature is decontextualised, abstract and rule-based, and so is especially challenging for beginning students. As teachers, all too often we *assume* that the context or framework for understanding what we are setting out to teach is already understood (Northedge, 2003: 172).

Such frameworks may be established in a variety of ways (by presenting students with a case study or a few photographs for analysis, for example, or with a vignette, scenario or story) but any activities such as those just described provide starting points for study which may be developed in what follows. They are designed to explore the knowledge, experience and preconceptions that students are likely to *share* at the outset, by virtue of their membership of a broadly common cultural group. No matter what their personal, gender, class, age or ethnic differences may be, all the students of Words are inhabitants of contemporary British-European society; they experience and are influenced by current cultural preoccupations and forms, especially through the ubiquitous mass media, and already participate in a wide range of 'everyday' discourses about them. The teacher's aim is to plan and conduct 'excursions' from these familiar discourses into the target, specialist discourse (Northedge, 2003: 175).

In other words, these introductory strategies arise out of a *socio-cultural* conception of engagement, which suggests reliable and appropriate jumping-off points for the teaching-learning enterprise – just as the authors of the literary texts the students read themselves rely on this kind of engagement with their broad audiences. An approach to teaching such as this therefore has the same kind of validity as the works of literature being studied; both the literary works and the teaching materials appeal to the same notional 'reading public'. It is thus an approach that is intrinsically appropriate to the teaching of Literature.

The principle of intelligibility

At the same time, this socio-cultural conception of engagement accords with the principle of intelligibility, which assumes that if students are actively to engage in processes of textual analysis-interpretation-evaluation – to be active 'makers of meaning' – then what they are taught must be intelligible to them *from the start*. Further, if the students' everyday experiences and understandings, invoked at the outset, are to be brought into ever closer relationship with the concerns, processes and terms of the academic, literary-analytical discourse to which they seek introduction, then those frameworks for understanding must be *sustained*. Strands of meaning must run through our teaching, frequently connecting with students' everyday experience and concerns. In this context, UKOU teachers have found the notion of the 'teaching narrative' a fruitful one. That is, introductory teaching is conducted through a series of concrete activities contained within a developing 'story'.

> *Story helps to construct conditions of intersubjectivity . . . In contrast to the sharing of rule-based propositional meaning, which can easily break down, stories reliably generate stable shared meaning. This makes them excellent vehicles in teaching . . .*
>
> (Northedge, 2003: 174)

In other words, intelligibility demands that teachers show and demonstrate rather than always explain matters propositionally. Teachers tend first to explain a proposition or theory and then offer an example, and students rarely understand that initial explanation. Intelligibility demands the reverse of this procedure: teaching *from* example *to* explanation. Definitions come last, not first, because understanding them is a high-level ability.

The storyline of the *Words* module, which encompasses both *subject content and study process*, is based on a few core questions put as simply as possible near the start (indeed, meeting Hirst and Peters' injunction to 'exhibit what is to be learnt'). Questions imply 'answers' and so offer directional impetus to teachers when plotting the teaching narrative.

Core questions

1. What can imaginative writing do?
2. How do fiction and poetry 'work'?
3. Is there a 'right' way to read a novel, story or poem?
4. How do some novels, stories and poems come to be seen as better than others?

(Words: 17)

Each major section of the teaching text focuses on one question only and, in turn, builds on the work done in previous sections. Accordingly, attention is focused also on *connections* between sections of text and relationships *between* main teaching points – that is, the flow of meaning is sustained – along the way towards some resolution of the issues (if only provisional). Each section ends with a short 'Section Summary' which provides an 'answer' to the question addressed there. So, students may easily locate and refer to these summaries in order to remind themselves how the story is developing. Within each section, fairly frequent 'Key Points' boxes remind the students of the main issues as they are developed. For example, the Key Points which round off the opening section of Words are as follows.

> ## Key points
>
> Changes in technology have transformed both the range and nature of the leisure activities available to us.
>   Despite this, reading is still an extremely popular activity. In fact, more people are reading books than ever before.
>   Reading offers different kinds of enjoyment from watching television. While television and films use images and sounds to appeal to our senses, writing uses words to appeal to the imagination.
>
> (Words: 12)

These devices enable students to follow the meaning of the teaching text as they go along and to access parts of it at will, and so more easily keep in mind relationships between the parts and the whole – rather than experiencing their study as a series of episodes or fragments, 'one damn thing after another'. In the introductory stages, some 'redundancy' is entirely necessary (underscoring of main (key) points, summaries, repetition of unfamiliar terms) within a generally discursive, though direct, mode of address. Furthermore, intelligibility demands that, to begin with, technical terms and abstractions are kept to a minimum, introduced only gradually and always explored at the point of introduction. In effect, 'the teacher is able to "lend" students the capacity to frame meanings they cannot yet produce independently' (Northedge, 2003: 172) by initiating and supporting a vigorous flow of meaning.

Comparison between the transparency of the Key Points for Section 1 of the module (above), and the relative conceptual and linguistic complexity of those for the final section, below, demonstrates how much this pedagogic approach enables beginning students to achieve in a short time.

Key points

One of the ways in which critical opinion can influence the status of a text is by classifying it, for example as either 'popular' or 'serious'.

The public reputation or status of a text can influence our private judgements about it.

The reputation of a text can change over time, as changing ideas and tastes make it possible to reappraise its status.

(Words: 99)

The principle of participation

The principles of engagement and intelligibility both encourage the students' participation. But, in particular, it is promoted through the series of Activities referred to earlier, which drives the teaching narrative and is designed to keep students actively engaged in their studies. In the first few sections of the Words module, for example, Activities take the form of the one cited above – a specific task (watching a TV programme, etc.), followed by a number of questions that provide some direction for the students' thinking. Some of these strands of meaning are then developed in subsequent sections of the teaching – in this case, those connected with writing's appeal to the imagination. The tasks themselves almost always involve reading a story or poem (characteristic objects of study/text genres); through a series of related questions, students are offered a *staged* approach to their reading, and analysis and interpretation of it. In ensuing discussion of these activities, the teacher-writer anticipates the students' likely responses and recasts these responses in terms closer to those of the 'target', academic, discourse (a process that we saw at work in the classroom in the 'Araby' vignette). In these ways, the students' thinking and growing understanding is channelled in fruitful directions.

Activities are always concrete tasks, put as precisely as possible, so that students may indeed make some constructive sense of them. But in later parts of the module less 'scaffolding' is provided and, through the activities, students are taken closer to the heart of contemporary literary-critical concerns and categories. For instance, having read a poem (*If Life's a Lousy Picture, Why Not Leave Before the End* by Roger McGough, which plays on the theme of the Hollywood Western), students are presented with this scenario:

> Imagine for a moment that you had spent all your life in another country which had no cinema or television. However, you can speak English and have some experience of reading poetry. What do you think you would make of this poem? Would there be parts of it that you wouldn't understand?
>
> (Words: 62)

The author then explores what historical and cultural knowledge the reader would need in order to understand reference to a 'deserted kinema' with 'torches extinguished' and 'cornish ripples locked away',[2] along with such word play as:

> *The tornoff tickets chucked*
> *in the tornoff shotbin*

(p. 63)

This particular instance leads into more general discussion of the assumptions writers make about their readers' shared frameworks of knowledge and experience. A further Activity asks students to guess how a story will develop after reading only the opening paragraph, which leads to discussion of how we distinguish between literary genres and understand the expectations they raise in us as readers – abilities we acquire from familiarity with literature itself. In other words, by the end of this introductory module students are led to some understanding of the contemporary, and sophisticated, concept of 'intertextuality'.

Process

Study skills

Throughout, the students are asked to write down their ideas in response to these exercises, not just think about them, at first as jotted notes; later on they are asked to compose paragraph-length responses and, towards the end of the module, they are given guidance in how to make a case in essay form using appropriate evidence in support of their argument. Although such skills are an integral part of the subject matter of study, and are always taught in this 'situated' manner, aspects of them are picked out for special emphasis in occasional Study Skills boxes. Students are also required to read parts of a set book on study skills progressively, alongside their work on the module text.

As with other exercises, these study skills activities arise out of the students' actual experience. When they reach the end of Section 1 of the module, for example, a box entitled 'Getting Organised' asks them to work out how long they had spent studying the section, which parts were the most time-consuming and why they think this was so – with assistance from the relevant part of the study skills book. On the basis of that understanding, the students are then asked to skim-read Section 2 and try to organise themselves and their time in advance of studying it. Later on, following a section of analysis and then comparison of two short stories, guidance is given on how to make notes that summarise the similarities/differences in structure and treatment the students had been asked to identify in previous activities. Other boxes deal in similar fashion with such matters as 'Interpretation and Evidence', 'Understanding Ideas', 'Discussing Ideas' and 'Writing' – all of them centrally important study processes. Note that students are not simply 'told about' these skills and processes; they always *practise* them, to some extent, before being asked to reflect on them.

Metacognition

Through activities of this kind students are encouraged to think about how they go about their studies at appropriate moments, and their attention is drawn to some of the key processes involved in it. In other words, they are helped to understand what they are doing, and why, while they are doing it – on the assumption that people cannot participate in something mindfully unless they have some understanding of what that thing is and what they might be aiming for. They are thus introduced, at an early stage, to the idea of *reflecting* on their own studying and learning. That is, they are encouraged to engage in metacognitive activity. This takes us beyond Bruner's idea of a 'spiral' of learning (of progression from a relatively simple and concrete characterisation of the domain of knowledge to higher – abstract, complex and generative – levels (Chapter 4)) to the perception that the higher levels, or 'mastery', of the discipline also entail increasing metacognitive understanding of its purposes and processes. To be knowledgeable, then, is not just a matter of being able to participate in the specialist discourse of a knowledge community but also of being aware both that this *is* what one is doing and of *what* it is that one is doing.

Teacher- versus *student-centredness revisited*

It will be apparent from this discussion that in the early stages of higher education it is not helpful for teachers to think in terms of individual students' prior knowledge or experience and, on that basis, to teach incrementally in accordance with precise, predetermined instructional objectives or outcomes. Nor is it helpful, we believe, to imagine that the only other recourse is to student-centredness: to negotiated aims and curricula, self-reflection and 'discovery'. For this is the opposite face of the same, individualistic, coin – in its different way, just as anti-intellectual and asocial. Rather, students are here conceived as members of societies and language groups – as *encultured*, subject to the historical and cultural influences that both constrain and enable us all; and also as *mindful* – thinking, feeling beings who have interests, intentions and aspirations. Again, just like the authors they read. Likewise, Literature (as all academic disciplines) is a product of history and culture, and also a communicative process constantly in the making. Such beliefs are what underpin a socio-cultural conception of higher education.

It will also be apparent that in the context of a discursive, dialogic discipline such as Literature, talk about teacher- *or* student-centredness is misleading. In dialogue, the notion of a 'central' participant is inappropriate – the whole point of dialogue is that it doesn't centre on one person. But if we must talk in these terms, then in a socio-cultural conception of the educational process teaching is student-centred *and* teacher-centred. We have just seen that teaching always 'starts from where the students are', acknowledging the value of their experience, their ideas, beliefs and aspirations, and promoting their active participation. And what is ultimately achieved in education is of course what the students achieve – with the assistance of teachers (the people who have made it their business to learn about, understand and 'speak' the public discourses in which the students wish to participate). As teachers we help students achieve most by teaching them in ways that are consistent with such an understanding of the nature and purposes of higher education, and by making courses of study as positively engaging, accessible and interesting as we can. Clearly, that takes sympathy and imagination as well as knowledge.

So, how can teachers think sympathetically and imaginatively about the ways they teach? The answer, we would say, is by putting students at the centre of their thinking. Instead of surveying a range of possible teaching-learning methods and selecting among them on the basis of abstract principles or beliefs about their effectiveness, or instead of cleaving to what is traditionally done, let's think about what the discussion so far has suggested our students (as students) really *need* a teacher's help with. Then we can think about the best ways to provide that assistance.

WORKING METHODS: METHODS THAT WORK

In summary, what we have seen that the students need is a teacher who:

- provides frameworks for their understanding each time a new subject/topic is encountered – presents ideas and devises activities that help focus the students' minds on the topic to be studied, sets them thinking constructively about it and along fruitful lines (providing less scaffolding over time);
- keeps those frameworks before the students as they progress and their understanding develops – invents core questions and a teaching narrative for each course of study: a storyline that encompasses the different kinds of subject matter and activity involved in it (both methods and media); sustains strands of meaning; summarises progress regularly and provides frequent reminders of key ideas and issues;
- does *not* make assumptions about their knowledge and skill (of subject matter or of how to go about their studies) – explains and illustrates new/difficult concepts, technical and other terms; devises a realistic study timetable, maintaining a steady pace that enables sufficient time for reading primary and secondary sources, thinking about and assimilating new ideas, completing activities and assignments . . ., and is prepared to adjust it;
- helps 'translate' students' verbal and written contributions into terms closer to those of the target, literary-analytical and critical

discourses – acts as a model of how debate is conducted in the discipline and how scholarly argument works;

● provides a structured, and staged, approach to reading different literary texts/genres – with processes of analysis-interpretation-evaluation at its heart – and to writing essays, using appropriate illustration and evidence from both primary and secondary sources, and being precise and 'objective';

● helps them discuss their thoughts with other students, communicate ideas effectively and work productively with others – leads seminar-style discussions and offers student-led sessions; devises small-group and team work;

● helps them think about study practices and reflect on their learning and achievements – offers opportunities for discussion of self-organisation and time management, making useful notes, approaching various study tasks . . . (both early on and when they have had some experience of trying to do these things).

It looks likely that these various needs will be better met via some teaching-learning methods and media than others. We will explore that idea in what follows. The discussion is again structured around the students' learning needs, as students of Literature. Accordingly, abstracting from the list above, we can see that our students learn to do all these things in four main ways: by reading, listening, speaking and writing. (And, of course, thinking; but we will assume that thinking is going on all the time.)

Reading

In Literature courses students do almost all their reading independently, in private study. To their teachers, then, reading is largely an invisible process – even though it is what the students spend most of their time doing. Furthermore, we tend to assume that our students, who have chosen to study Literature, can just do it: that they already know how to read literary works of all kinds. We are, of course, wrong in making that assumption. And even more wrong nowadays than once we were, bearing in mind the student-demographic changes discussed earlier (and see under 'The student's point of view' in Chapter 2 the broader cultural changes that have tended to marginalise reading, especially among younger people). Many students find it difficult to read critically (analytically and interpretatively). McGann et al. (2001: 144), for example, have found that while reading poetry ('a frankly intransigent medium') and non-fiction are acknowledged as relatively difficult, students approach classic novels 'with pleasure and a certain kind of understanding' – as long as the novels are not 'self-consciously reflexive or experimental'. However, the authors continue:

> That pleasure and understanding ... proved a serious obstacle to the students' ability to think critically about the works and their own thinking. It generated a kind of 'transparency effect' in the reading experience, preventing the students from getting very far towards reading in deliberate and self-conscious ways.

Here they refer to the 'problem' of fiction's tendency to draw the reader away from 'the world of its words' and towards character (which students interpret as if it were 'real'), plot (as if it were a sequence of events), scene and ideas or 'themes'. The challenge is 'to develop awareness of the fictionality of fiction with writers like Austen and Scott, Eliot and Hardy' (pp. 145–6). Clearly, students cannot just read even classic texts.

But difficulty is not necessarily a negative, 'a sign of failure and inadequacy, to be suppressed or hidden' (Parker, 2003: 144). Parker cites Salvatori (2000: 84) as saying:

> My own approach to reading and to interpretation of texts is very much shaped by the work I do with phenomenology and hermeneutics, reader response and reception theory. [So] the questions I ask as teacher are the distillation of my understanding of reading as a process involving difficult moments, which I see not as a sign of inadequacy on the reader's part, but rather as signs that the reader has sensed and/or identified a textual difficulty that she needs to capture and engage, interpret and respond to.

That said, there are broadly two different things that teachers can try to do in this situation: (1) help students to read different literary texts/genres appropriately and well; (2) help them make good use of all the time they spend reading.

Genre

As regards the former, teachers may take a direct role by devoting class time to discussing the different literary genres (prose, poetry, drama), with a focus on their purposes, forms and formal elements, and also offer guided reading exercises for some representative texts. Exploration of the genres and sub-genres could be tackled in lectures during the first year of study, often in period- or theme-based courses and preferably alongside the students' work on particular texts that represent the genres. Or seminar time could be devoted to it: teacher-led explanation followed by class discussion of the texts from the generic point of view.

Guided reading

With respect to guided-reading exercises, other possibilities present themselves. Here we have in mind ways of 'talking students through' the process of reading a short story or poem, for example – indicating where they might stop and think, and why; just what they might be thinking about at various points; where they might want to refer back to earlier lines or passages . . . – all the while employing the relevant analytical categories and terms. Since these kinds of exercise will be needed for each intake of new students, it might well be worth investing time in developing materials that can be used by them outside class – an audio-cassette (which students can stop and start whenever they wish) or an online interactive programme, for example. Also, it is now possible to access a vast library of digital resources and texts from around the world – e-books such as in Project Gutenberg (www.gutenberg.net)[3] – and digitised material that may be analysed using text analysis software packages which can count the number of occurrences of words or phrases even in long, complex texts such as novels. A concordance or KWIC (Key Word in Context) list, or a TextArc view of *Hamlet*, for instance, takes minutes when done via the Internet and can enable students to see the locations and uses of any specified name, word or phrase in the play. In this context, then, guided reading of a short text might take the form of the teacher supplying a few of his or her key words or phrases which students can explore for themselves using a concordance facility.

Reading strategies

In the second case, of helping students make good use of the time they must spend reading, by contrast the teacher might play the role of facilitator – providing the time and a forum for students to discuss among themselves how they approach their reading of different text genres, how much time they devote to reading, when and where they do it, and so forth. If seminar discussion time is at a premium, good use can be made of the kinds of course website that most university departments now host. Apart from their use as repositories of information about the department's policies and courses, spaces on a course website can be devoted to discussion among the students in a (synchronous or asynchronous) computer conference. In this case, a conference could be dedicated to discussion of reading (and other study methods too, perhaps especially essay writing). And if teacher time is also scarce, this might be a private conference which the teacher does not visit. However, a couple of students could be charged to report back the gist of the discussion periodically, in class time, thus enabling some contribution from the teacher.

Workload

These suggestions of course apply to reading primary, literary texts. But literature students must also read a range of theoretical and critical works reading that is very different in kind and must be tackled differently, as we discussed in Chapter 3. Here, we would just add that it is important not to overload the students with reading material of this secondary kind, especially with long book lists of unannotated items among which they are expected to select (on what possible basis?). Indeed, by applying the following rules of thumb, teachers can work out in advance how long it will take the 'average' student to read secondary texts:

- fairly familiar text/easy reading: *c.*100 words per minute;
- moderately difficult text/close reading: *c.*70 words per minute;
- dense, difficult text/unfamiliar reading: *c.*40 words per minute.

These are not reading speeds but 'study rates' – reading for under-standing – which allow time for thinking and a fair bit of rereading. On this basis, assuming a working week of *c.*40 hours, we may calculate the time we are *actually* asking our students to spend reading each week.[4] Making this calculation is a salutary experience, especially when many secondary texts can be read only at around 40 or in some cases 70 words per minute (Chambers, 1992).

1. *Reading online for any length of time can cause eye and back strain.* Whenever possible, teachers and students alike are advised to read lengthy texts in print, and especially literary works, since they are portable, they can be annotated and, in any case, it's more pleasurable.
2. *Reading online is different.* People tend to scan the screen rather than read every word sequentially, picking out key words, paying attention to the format of the presentation and looking for links to other websites and materials. Material usually needs to be redrafted for presentation on the web, in short 'chunks' with important points made at the start to aid scanning (see Nielsen (1997), accessed October 2004).
3. *Online materials and resources must be integrated into the course design* for them to be worth using (see Kirkwood (2003), accessed October 2004).
4. *It is important that we all respect intellectual property rights when using the Internet and the copyright on information made available through the electronic media.* Your university will be able to advise you about the laws and conventions governing this.

FIGURE 5.1   *Online reading: four caveats.*

Accessing texts

Accessing such secondary material can also present difficulties, especially for students who have responsibilities other than study or who work unsocial hours. Here, electronic access may be vital. Course websites can of course include links to other relevant sites and materials on the Internet – including online dictionaries and encyclopaedias, which, along with literary works and databanks of information, are also often available on CD-ROM (but see Fig. 5.1). Sometimes, texts may be downloaded to the site so that students can print material directly from it. And there will almost certainly be a link to the university's searchable library catalogue, via its intranet, and perhaps also to an electronic library from which articles can be downloaded. Such flexible and speedy access to materials can make the difference between students successfully completing their studies and dropping out.

Finally, we would re-emphasise something that applies to reading both primary and secondary texts. If a text of either kind is to be the focus for discussion, in a lecture or seminar/computer conference, it is very helpful to students if they are asked to *prepare themselves* for their listening or speaking by thinking about two or three questions while and after they read it. These questions, identified by the teacher in advance, should be few, short, clear and related to matters of significance: the kinds of question that might focus the students' attention appropriately, keep them actively engaged in their reading and help them think along fruitful lines. When a reading list is provided on paper/on a website before the course begins or at the start (as in the sample course outlines in Appendix 3 on the book's website) then such questions could be included under each item. Generally, this is a much more productive strategy – for the development of students' understanding and the quality of any ensuing discussion session – than taking the students unawares during the session or (worse) showing them up in front of their peers and so running the risk of alienating them (which of course would be unethical as well as counterproductive). And, as a result, students may begin to generate their own good questions.

Listening

Students mostly listen to lectures, but they may also need to listen to audio-cassettes, the radio, CDs and (while also watching) TV programmes, DVDs and multimedia packages on computer or CD-ROM – for performances of plays, poetry and story readings, discussions with authors, critics' forums and novel serialisations, screen adaptations, etc. As this list suggests, a major task for teachers these days is seeking out and reviewing all the potentially useful materials that are available across a range of media. But online 'portals' or gateways to digital resources that have been assessed for teaching-learning quality can take away much of the pain, considerably reducing the time and effort involved – see, for example, the Humbul Gateway (www.humbul.ac.uk/english), Voice of the Shuttle (http://vos.ucsb.edu) or the Australian E Humanities Gateway (www.ehum.edu.au). The Moving Image Gateway (www.bufvc.ac.uk/gateway) provides recordings of TV programmes for use in teaching, along with a database of stage and screen resources, and TRILT (Television and Radio Index for Learning and Teaching – www.trilt.ac.uk) offers a comprehensive record of British broadcasting. As we saw just now, resources such as these can often be linked electronically to a course website so that students can access them easily.

Listening in lectures
Generally speaking, listening is not a skill we have to learn. It is a capacity that most of us (whose hearing is not impaired[5]) just have, and we do it all the time. However, students listening in a lecture or

to a CD are a special case; here, listening usually means not just attending to someone or something but really concentrating and taking it in. Perhaps that's why in education people often refer to listening 'skills'. Students do have to practise this kind of 'listening hard' to get the most out of any of the teaching-learning methods that rely on it, just as teachers should be aware of the advantages and difficulties involved in those methods.

To take the example of listening to a good lecture, the great advantage is that the burden of establishing a framework for understanding the topic and sustaining a flow of meaning is largely borne by the speaker. (The corollary is of course that teachers must provide these things.) Student listeners certainly need to work at making sense of what they hear, but even when they are not familiar with some terms or don't understand parts of what is said, they can often follow the gist of it – unlike reading a critical essay, for example, when because the reader can rely only on his or her own resources the enterprise may not even get off the ground, or at any stage glimmerings of understanding may simply fade away. As speakers, teachers invest meaning in their utterances – through their emphases and tones of voice, facial expressions, gestures and such like – all of which can help support the students' understanding. And sometimes an accompanying visual display, using slides or PowerPoint is similarly helpful.

But we all know that lectures are not always successful. In fact, they get very bad press in the higher education literature. Since Donald Bligh's *What's the Use of Lectures?*, first published in 1971 and now in its fifth edition (Bligh, 1998), the lecture method has been denigrated, almost ritualistically. It is nowadays often seen as self-indulgently teacher-centred, preferred by those who like to strut their stuff, in the process rendering their students mute and passive. Students can't keep up with the speaker, we are told, they can't concentrate for longer than ten minutes together, they can't take notes, think and listen at the same time, and afterwards they can barely remember anything that was said. Some of these things certainly present difficulties. The pace at which the argument is developed may indeed be misjudged. And students do have to learn how to listen, think and jot down ideas more or less simultaneously. But mostly these charges simply miss the point, because they are based on the assumption that the primary function of a lecture is to *impart information* – even though information is much more easily and reliably gained from books, articles and websites.

Rather, the lecture is particularly helpful in engaging the students' interest and enthusiasm for a new topic, in providing the broad context for study of it (which they cannot gain from books), and, after study, in offering a summation and a weighing up of significance. Crucially, what lectures offer students is the opportunity to hear an argument developed, without interruption, by an 'expert speaker' of the discourse – a live model of how the ideas of the discipline are used: how arguments take shape, are illustrated and supported with evidence; how they connect to wider debate within the discipline; how conclusions are drawn. If at the same time the lecture is stimulating, even inspiring, because teachers communicate genuine enthusiasm for their subject, so much the better. The lecture, as one among very many teaching-learning methods, must play to its strengths. Far better that students should emerge from it reinvigorated, or feeling that they have 'seen' something significant, than that they should be able to reproduce dollops of information.

Planning lectures

As teachers, our first thoughts about a series of lectures are often, understandably, to do with what (of the syllabus) is going to be 'covered' in them rather than what in particular this method of teaching-learning can offer the students and what may get in the way of that. From the students' perspective, if the lecture is to be experienced as interesting and helpful then teachers need to bear in mind some issues surrounding the conditions of their listening – for example, density of ideas and pace of delivery. Such matters involve judgement about the rate at which students can absorb ideas: too thick and fast and they will flounder, too slow and they will become bored and distracted. Teachers must also make allowance for the fact that at the same time as listening to what is said the students are trying to think about it, and also jot down some notes to remind them of the main points of interest. In view of all this, students surely should not be expected to listen hard for more than about 30–40 minutes. If the timetable stipulates longer sessions in a lecture theatre, then listening can be punctuated by, for example, short readings (sometimes tape-recorded), interludes of discussion (if only with the person in the next seat), jotting down notes in answer to a question (preferably one that is about to be raised, again to channel the students' thoughts appropriately), doing a little quiz or some other mildly entertaining activity.

But what students are mainly trying to do in a lecture is *follow the argument*. All that was said earlier in discussion of the Words module, about the need to provide (contextualising) frameworks for students' understanding and to make clear the structure of the developing argument, reiterating key points and summarising progress frequently applies here – and applies to every lecture. When planning a lecture series, an all-encompassing teaching narrative needs to be plotted, otherwise each lecture is likely to be perceived by students as a discrete entity. The series will seem like bits of this and that rather than a coherent 'story' which, through its structuring, helps develop their understanding.

Speaking

The opportunity for students to learn through speaking usually means offering group work of some kind: seminars, tutorials, workshops, team projects. Of these, literature teaching in the UK undoubtedly relies most heavily on the seminar (usually of between 11 and 20 participants) which often involves student presentations, as evidence from the English Subject Centre survey shows (and as we see in the sample course outlines in Appendix 3). Sixty-four per cent of the literature departments offer 'half and half' lectures and group discussion classes, while 34 per cent of them offer 'mainly group discussion' – and, if you've done the sum, you will have deduced that only 2 per cent of departments offer 'mainly lectures' (Halcrow et al., 2003: 28–9). Also, 'almost all respondents provide one-to-one dissertation tutorials and consultations on demand' (p. 32). What all such sessions have in common is that they normally interact with the students' reading of primary and secondary texts, and they allow students to negotiate meaning and understanding with others. In the words of the English Benchmark Statement (QAA, 2000: 5):

> *Teaching arrangements in English programmes should provide a balance of direct instruction . . . and the opportunity for active assimilation, questioning and debate. The focussed discussion of reading lies at the heart of learning in the subject. It is important that students are able to engage in dialogue, and develop and negotiate conclusions with others . . .*

Dialogue

The 'Araby' vignette in Chapter 2 illustrated the value to us of the seminar as a teaching-learning method (as well as some of its pitfalls). Through discussion, students can experience new ideas 'in action', in others' and their own talk, fairly informally. Compared to reading and listening, discussion among peers is usually easier to follow, dynamic, spontaneous and potentially exciting. Students may positively enjoy the feeling of being part of a lively community of thinkers. Carried along in a flow of discussion, in which others share in the task of constructing and sustaining frameworks for understanding, they can find themselves saying things they did not even know they thought. Together, the students can push their understanding further ahead than they might on their own – as they hear others trying to sort out their ideas, they rework their own or glimpse new ways of understanding the topic. Questions are asked and answered, and understandings shared. The students know instantly whether they have communicated well and been understood, and they can try again. Crucially, such talk gives students rough and ready, first-hand knowledge of how to 'speak' the academic discourse and how to develop arguments appropriately, which helps them do so more formally in written assignments. Taking their cue from teachers, over time they may learn to adopt the detached, precise 'voice' of critical analysis.

Managing discussion

'May' is the operative word here, since of course everything depends on how teachers set up and conduct these sessions. We saw in Chapter 2 how uncomfortable and relatively fruitless the experience can be when a class is not prepared for the subject of discussion and the session itself is not sufficiently structured. The novice teacher of 'Araby' would have done well to ask the students to focus on a few questions when reading the text before the class, and to begin the seminar by exploring one of those questions (rather than with the mind-boggling, 'So . . . what do you think of this story?'). Following the vignette, we discussed a number of pedagogic strategies that promote intelligible, meaningful discussion which we will not repeat here. Rather, we will focus on the pressing question of how to engage the students and get them all working cooperatively together – rather than not participating at all, communicating only with the teacher or having a few verbose students crowd out the rest.

We saw in Chapter 2 that a helpful strategy is to break up the class into groups, each with a well-focused question to discuss or task to do, along with instructions regarding reporting back to the class as a whole – prior to plenary discussion in which the teacher, building on their contributions, plays a central role in restructuring, extending and summing up the discussion. In small groups of four or five it is almost impossible for any student to remain disengaged or silent. The teacher is absent from these discussions and so cannot be the focus of attention at that stage (which also has the effect of placing limits on the teacher's own enthusiasm to contribute). And very talkative or aggressively dominant students may be allotted the formal, and circumscribed, role of spokesperson for the group at the reporting-back stage, which should occupy them usefully during the discussion or work period – a role that could of course be rotated among group members over time. In any event, we should not underestimate how maddening these students can be, especially those who constantly either focus on themselves, their experiences and ideas or seem unable to focus on the topic at hand. It is of course the job of the *teacher* to find ways of stemming the flow or redirecting proceedings in the interests of everyone. The problem may be addressed during a seminar by tactfully changing tack or trying to draw other students into the discussion. But if this is too socially embarrassing, it is always possible to take such a student aside afterwards and talk things over. An equivalent move in a computer-conference discussion might be to communicate with the student 'outside' the conference via private e-mail (in this connection and others to do with the conduct of computer conferences, see Salmon, 2002).

But, in whatever manner, teachers *must* address this problem. If we fail to take that responsibility then, no matter how well prepared the seminar, many students will tune out; they will not benefit from it and, worse, they may (understandably) be reluctant to attend in future.

The 'communicative virtues'

Or the students may get so frustrated that they become abusive to some of their fellow students. An important educational purpose of seminar discussion and teamwork is development of the so-called communicative virtues – tolerance of other people's points of view, respect for differences among the group, willingness to listen to others (in the spirit that one might be wrong), and patience and self-restraint so that others may have a turn to speak or act. If these principles are breached then the teacher's role is not just a 'technical' one of policing the ground rules of cooperative work but the more fundamental one of ensuring that all the students learn this important aspect of the discipline (indeed, of any discipline). And of course this means that we, as teachers, must demonstrate these principles in our own behaviour towards students and colleagues. In particular, respecting differences among people should guide our behaviour towards those at the other end of the spectrum from the verbose student, those who are shy and do not readily participate.

Earlier we touched on the issue of whether we should be especially concerned about these students, pointing out that silence does not necessarily indicate lack of engagement. However, in view of the constructive gains to be made from well-focused, lively discussion, if students are not *actively encouraged* to participate then they will miss important opportunities to learn – a view supported in the QAA Subject Overview report (1995): 'In a number of observed seminars, students were given too few opportunities to contribute, and were consequently encouraged to become relatively passive'. The reviewers continue:

> *Lectures and seminars remain the most frequently employed means of . . . teaching . . . They are generally most successful when supplemented by student presentations that are often explicitly linked to the development of skills as well as to the evolution of discipline-specific knowledge.*

Another common ploy to involve all the students, then, is to require them to take turns, in twos or threes, to make presentations in seminars and/or to lead the discussion.

Seminar presentations

We saw this strategy adopted in the sample course outlines, where a formal 'oral presentation' is an *assessed component* of courses at every level. In part, this requirement is no doubt designed to ensure that all the students participate actively. At Level 1 (Appendix 3(a)), the purpose of the 15-minute presentation is explained to the students and also the presenters' responsibility to their audience:

> *Presentations help you clarify and structure your thoughts on some aspect of the module – you decide which topic to work on – and they*

*make you think about ways and means of expressing yourself orally.
Unlike essays, they are a part of the learning experience for the whole
group. An effective delivery benefits not only the presentees but also the
audience; please bear this in mind as you prepare for this part of your
assessment . . .*

In both these cases, small-group discussion and oral presentations, the
students are also learning how to work together on specific tasks to
deadlines. But of course group or team projects may take a variety of
other forms: for example, bibliographic or IT/web-based exercises,
performances, creating resources (such as audiotapes or videos),
written assignments (from book or film reviews to research-based
projects involving the students' own investigations). In all such cases,
students will need guidance from teachers on how to go about the task
and some ground rules for their collaborative efforts. Of perhaps
greater concern, however, is how to assess such group work appropriately and fairly, as we shall see in Chapter 6.

Student preparation

Meantime, teachers often complain that students *cannot* participate in
seminars and other discussion or group-work sessions, however well
they are conducted, because they are ill prepared for them: that
students simply fail to do the reading or carry out the tasks required
of them in advance. And this is seen as a growing problem which is
largely beyond the teacher's control, exacerbated by rising fees and the
need for many students to work part-time in order to support
themselves. However, there are a few things that teachers may do in
this situation. First, the onus is on us as teachers to make sure that
what we ask of students is, in fact, doable in the time allotted to their
studies. As we saw, we can ensure this only by carefully controlling
the amount of reading and other work that we set. That achieved, it is
then reasonable to adopt some of the measures identified earlier and
justified there solely on educational grounds: to make seminar/
workshop attendance compulsory and keep a register; to include
student-led sessions such that at some time during the course each
student must present a paper, individually or with one or two
partners; formally to assess the students' contributions to seminar and
group work. In this context of discussion, such measures perhaps take

a more draconian turn: in the first two cases, a penalty for failure to comply may be attached; in the last, a penalty is inbuilt.

Engaging students

But, ultimately, as teachers it must be our aim to interest and engage our students to the extent that they *want* to participate fully in their courses of study. Should this sound hopelessly unrealistic or even utopian to your ears, we recommend that you revisit the notion of a 'framing, existential pedagogy' explored in Chapter 1. There we discussed the importance of making connections between literature and the enduring terms and conditions of human existence – keeping in view serious and permanent issues of human physicality and sociability – such that studying literature is experienced by students as not only interesting but also *important*. After all, if it is not seen as important, why – given the many demands, desires and distractions that beset us – would any of us bother to study it seriously? In short, we believe that an approach to teaching in which literary experience is taken to be an important form of *human learning* is both most valid and most likely to inspire our students. One such approach is discussed in Chapter 1 (under 'A framing pedagogy: existential "sidebar" issues') and another is exemplified in this chapter in our discussion of the socio-cultural principles and practices governing teaching in the Words module.

We give the last word here to Ben Knights. In focusing on the 'study group', he acknowledges that this focus 'is in some degree to counter the culture of the subject, since the ideology of "English" is strongly individualistic even where it ostensibly proposes co-operation'. Nevertheless:

> The students' institutional experience is one of groups. This experience is intersubjective; the forms of dialogue practised there become the forms of thinking that characterise the subject. ... To build on the group nature of learning in our subject, consciously to construct experimental cultural communities, may be ... an alternative to what is frequently seen as the rigid opposition between solid knowledge and objective skills on the one hand and the personal response and creative engagement of the individual reader on the other. Students and teachers need to learn about the narratives within which self and learning are constructed. Those narratives are simultaneously cognitive and affective – learning

cannot be dissociated from the emotional matrix within which it takes place.

(Knights, 1992: 3)

Writing

Of all the activities discussed here, writing is usually experienced by students as the most difficult – and especially essay writing. As we saw in Chapter 3, academic writing is not mainly a matter of acquiring skills but, rather, is intimately bound up in the students' knowledge and understanding of the discipline and involves a focus on making meaning appropriately within its terms (Swales, 1990). Furthermore, in essay writing, the student is the sole author of that meaning making. And this form of writing is omnipresent. Indeed, in the UK:

In order to develop and demonstrate the skills [of communication of ideas], to engage in informed written debate and to present ideas in a sustained discursive form, English students must be required to write essays as a fundamental part of their learning experience'.

(QAA, 2000: 5, emphases added)

Writing essays as part of studying a literature course is, then, primarily a method of *learning*, and we would say the most profound method of learning.

Understanding the assignment

Each essay assignment offers students the opportunity to focus on a particular part or aspect of the syllabus (often of their choosing), study it in depth, draw together their knowledge and understanding from all sources, make appropriate selections from these sources and put them to use. That is, they practise arguing a case (often in answer to a specific question or for/against a given point of view), illustrating that argument adequately and offering appropriate evidence in support of it. Ultimately, students are offered constructive-critical feedback on their performance by a teacher, from which they may learn further – *if* that feedback is seen not just as a matter of correction but, primarily, as an answering response to the meanings the students have attempted to make. So it is not surprising that when students look back on their studies, the texts or topics on which they have written an essay are very often the ones they understood and remember best.

- *The straightforward 'true' question* – such as: 'How do the characters of *Howards End* increase our understanding of issues related to class and gender?'; 'What does Morris have to say about the process of change in *News from Nowhere*?'
- *The combined quote/question* – 'In what ways has Marlow, at the end of *The Heart of Darkness*, departed from a "straightforward world of facts"?'; 'Dick's work has been described as embodying "in miniature all the complexities, contradictions, hopes and anxieties of our post World War II world". How far would you agree with this statement with reference to *Do Androids Dream . . .?*'
- *The task* – 'Compare and contrast the exploration of difficult moral choices by *two or more* Victorian writers.'; 'Analyse the relationship between repression and biology as presented by Atwood'.
- *The discussion/for and against* – ' "*Great Expectations* is a moral tale told by an amoral narrator". Discuss this statement with detailed reference to the novel.'

FIGURE 5.2 *Sample essay-question types.*

Students experience writing an essay of, say, 1,500–2,000 words as a far more difficult task than, for example, arguing in speech, because the writer is *solely* responsible for providing and sustaining the framework of meaning for the reader, for the process of writing itself and for the eventual outcome. Furthermore, essay writing is a lengthy and complex process. First of all, the students must understand the task – what the essay question or title actually requires of them. A wide range of such questions is included in the Appendix 3 sample course outlines, and we can discern from these lists several types of 'question' that literature students are commonly asked to tackle (see Figure 5.2). The last of these examples is probably the most ambiguous, because 'Discuss' does not make it explicit that argument 'for and against' a statement or quotation is what is required. And often teachers set the complex task or cryptic question rather than the more straightforward, even at First level – perhaps out of a desire to challenge the students intellectually and a corresponding fear of spoonfeeding them. In short, precisely what is required of the students is by no means always readily apparent to them. And that is just the start.

Understanding the tasks

Once students think they understand what is being asked of them, they must then (although not necessarily in the order presented here):

1. Read the literary texts in question or choose them appropriately, and engage in the necessary analytical, interpretative and evaluative activities.
2. Find, read and apply relevant critical material.
3. Make notes from all sources towards their essay.
4. Think about and plot the line of argument they will develop in the essay – including appropriate illustration of major claims and evidence in support of them.
5. Structure the essay accordingly.
6. Write stylishly, persuasively and accurately.
7. Make good use of the scholarly apparatus.
8. Reflect and review: revise and polish their work.

Each of these elements may be experienced as difficult and time-consuming. And students may not even conceive of the essay writing process as a number of different (if overlapping) 'tasks', which must make it all the more daunting as they set out to muddle through somehow. For purposes of discussion we may identify the first task as 'reading', the second as 'researching' (2 and 3), the third as 'arguing/ structuring' (4 and 5), the fourth as 'writing' (6 and 7) and the last as 'reflecting and reviewing'. In Chapter 3 of the book a focus was the teaching of writing, and we presented there a process/staged approach to it that encompassed some of the tasks which are identified here from the students' point of view, while others have been explored in this chapter. The elements of the process that remain to be discussed are 'researching' and 'reflecting'.

Researching

In fact we did touch on this matter in 'Accessing texts' (above), which is obviously an important aspect of research. Even if, in the context of essay-writing, 'research' is a rather grandiose term for what is a relatively small-scale activity, nevertheless as an integral part of the students' study of Literature it is a set of skills that they must be taught. In fact, most UK literature departments do regard this teaching as essential, with 75 per cent of them claiming to offer training in 'research-related skills' (Halcrow Group et al., 2003: 52). In answer to more specific questions, it emerged that over half the departments include 'Library use' as a compulsory element at Level 1 and 'Academic use of the Internet, e.g. RDN, Humbul, Literature online' and 'General Internet searching skills' as optional elements at all Levels, in most cases with the assistance of library and technical staff (p. 44). So on closer inspection it seems that, in fact, in almost half the departments no such teaching is provided at all. And, further, when we consider that in *98 per cent* of departments students are required to 'engage in independent research-based (dissertation or project) work' (p. 51), this level of provision seems positively paltry. In addition, if literature academics are serious about engaging their students with the wealth of digital and web-based material available to us all, then making sure that the students are trained in the necessary procedures must be more than an optional extra. It is surely essential that students are taught to approach e-resources (just as any source) critically – to be able to discriminate between good resources and all the junk that is available on the Web (see the MLA Handbook, 2000) – rather than simply being let loose to Google their way around.

Reflecting/reviewing

By 'reflecting' we do not mean the kind of assignment in which students are asked to reflect on their study of aspects of a course and review their learning, their development, their strengths and weaknesses, etc. (see Thorpe, 2000, for example). Rather, in the context of essay writing, we are referring to the stage at which the student looks back over the draft essay and reviews what he or she has achieved with an eye to improving it prior to submission. This necessarily involves critical analysis of the essay draft – which, in turn, presupposes that the student has some knowledge of the criteria that might apply to it (i.e. what would make for a good response to the question or essay title). But this is precisely what most students, especially beginning students, do not have. Lacking such knowledge, how can they possibly improve the essay (beyond correcting spelling, grammar, etc.)? And if we as academics find it tough being critical of our own work, which most of us do, how much harder must it be for beginning students to be so self-critical? As teachers we do well to remember that good writing is a goal, not a starting point. So, critical review is also something that needs to be taught.

We suggest that it would be amenable to the kind of heuristic exercise discussed in Chapter 3 (under 'Writing pedagogy'). Specifically, students could be asked to critique essays by other (anonymous) students and, as an outcome, to discuss the criteria that might be

- Have you set out to answer the question/address the issues in the essay title, as it is worded?
- Have you presented an argument? Is it clear that you have done so? Is your argument developed throughout the essay, in a series of main points that are linked, and do you reach a conclusion/sum up at the end?
- Have you drawn on relevant parts of the course and other relevant material for the content of your essay to illustrate and provide evidence for the main points of your argument?
- Is the organisation of your essay (i.e. in sections or paragraphs) appropriate? Can each sentence be read and understood (i.e. have you said what you meant to say)?
- Have you paid attention to the conventions for quoting from sources, to correct grammar, spelling, etc.? Have you provided references in the approved way?

FIGURE 5.3 *Some basic criteria for critical review of the draft essay.*

applied to these essays. This would help them to understand essay requirements without first having to subject their own writing to scrutiny. They might perhaps start out with a 'generic' list of criteria, such as those in Figure 5.3, which would be applied to the *particular* essays being critiqued, enabling the meanings and implications of each question to be explored in context (what is meant by 'relevant' material, 'appropriate' organisation, etc., in the context of *this* essay question/title). Subsequently, students would undoubtedly also benefit from the kind of practice constructive exercises described in Chapter 3, at this as at the other stages of writing.

Balancing voices

A different way of looking at the list of essay writing tasks is to observe that, although the essay is a single-voiced expression, within it the writer must encompass and find a balance between a number of different 'voices': the texts concerned, the sources on which he or she draws, her or his own voice. This is a major difficulty for students, and most anxiety surrounds the last of these – the extent to which, or even whether, the writer's own voice should be heard. Furthermore, like any writer, students are attempting to address an audience, which is very often an unknown quantity as far as they are concerned. How often have you as teacher asked a student why he or she didn't explain some matter of central importance in an essay only to be told something like 'Well, I didn't think I had to say that because you already know it'? All these matters need to be discussed explicitly with students.

The most important thing to be said here, then, is that it is part of the teacher's job to *teach* students how to write essays in Literature – and, indeed, any other form of writing that is required of them (some of which we discuss in Chapter 6). As in the case of reading literary texts appropriately, we cannot just assume, as we once perhaps did, that they already know how to do it. This educational researcher sums up:

> ... *research suggests that literacy practices are complex, contested, specific, and, above all, contextualised* ... *These studies suggest that the development of students' thinking and writing is often hampered by a lack of explicitness* within the teaching of the subject *with regard to the literacy norms* ... *Such an idea challenges traditional fears that explicitness about the details of academic practice is a form of 'spoonfeeding', which will lead to the erosion of standards and a 'dumbing down' of higher education. [The studies] suggest the need for a shift from a view of success/failure based on 'ability' and 'preparation', to one that sees study at this level as an apprenticeship into new ways of thinking and expression for students* ... *such new forms of expression* ... *need to be explicitly modelled and explored.*
>
> (Haggis, 2003: 100)

Writing in the Disciplines

Finally, we will just draw attention to this movement, based originally at Cornell University's Knight Institute for Writing in the Disciplines (WiD), in case it should offer some inspiration. WiD is expressly concerned with writing as a form of learning, with 'writing to learn' (Monroe, 2002; Donohue, 2004). What makes the movement distinctive is its insistence on the discipline 'as that which is written, and therefore as that which is *practised* (rather than that which is ... researched)':

> ... *each Faculty's writing course is taught not by 'composition' teaching assistants but by the discipline's writers at all stages of their career* ... *The conviction underpinning the programme is that* ... *academics do not 'do' and then 'write up' their work; rather they practice and write the discipline. Thus the discipline is continuously being rewritten and*

. . . by leading academics, graduates and students together . . . [This] new inclusive definition brings together all into one community of practice.

(Parker, 2003: 146–7)

This is a radical and time-consuming programme since WiD courses are by definition writing intensive. Course content is greatly reduced to make way for weekly writing and revising assignments that, it is hoped, will ultimately transform the students' understanding of the discipline.

ELECTRONIC TEACHING METHODS

Scattered about the chapter are references to electronic and digital resources, to websites and the Internet. These mentions have been made in the context of the technologies' uses in the teaching and study of Literature, which is of course how we should as teachers think about them. Here we offer a brief overview.

Broadly speaking, it is helpful to distinguish between two different uses of information and communications technologies (ICTs) in this context:

1. *Broadcasting* – delivering content/resources, including digital library resources (via the Internet) and material on DVD or CD-ROM, largely for 'knowledge transfer' (teacher or writer to student) and for research purposes.
2. *Communicating* – in online (two-way) dialogue, including e-mail discussion lists, computer-mediated communication (CMC), List-serves, etc., for purposes of discussion and collaborative learning.

Further information about these ICTs and addresses for useful websites are included as Appendix 7 on the book's website (www.sagepub.co.uk/chambers.pdf).

Few Literature teachers are interested in these technologies as such. What we want to know is how using ICTs might enable us to teach our discipline more effectively, more efficiently or more imaginatively. In other words, we should begin by thinking about the ways in which ICTs might best serve our needs as Literature educators, that is, thinking *from* the discipline *to* the available technologies. It will do us no good simply to import e-teaching methods developed in other disciplines for other purposes; for example, from disciplines that emphasise the computer's extraordinary capacity to quantify or to store and reproduce 'information', when what we are most interested in is the analysis and evaluation of ideas, theories and processes – in challenging, questioning and creating knowledge. In view of our purposes and priorities we may wish to resist pressure to substitute multiple choice or question and answer assessment for the essay form, for instance, even if electronic assessment works well in other academic contexts and is comparatively cheap. As a paper on the uses of computers in history (in a special issue of the journal *Computers and the Humanities* (Chambers, 2000)) demonstrates: 'The crucial issues in the use of computers in teaching are pedagogical and not technical' (Spaeth and Cameron, 2000: 325). Or, as Charles Ess puts it, we must not allow 'the technological tail [to] wag the pedagogical dog' (Ess, 2000: 298).

Common themes and recommendations that emerge from the papers in this special issue are as follows.

1. Electronic methods and resources should be integrated with existing teaching practice, ensuring that they serve well-defined 'higher order' purposes. Digital resources can complement classroom activities, library use and existing teaching methods (i.e. 'blended' learning) – and even offer new possibilities.
2. Communications technologies offer increased opportunity for discussion among students and between them and their teachers, formally (seminar-style) and informally (chat), whether synchronously or asynchronously. These technologies also enable collaborative work among groups of students, especially in distance education and among international groups.
3. Digital texts of all kinds allow access 'wherever and whenever' and eliminate the need for libraries to hold multiple copies (see AHDS, Literature Online and the Oxford Text Archive, among others, in the Bibliography at the end of the book, under 'Websites'). Text 'searching' software offers new opportunities for textual analysis, from the small to grand scale.
4. Databases of cultural artefacts can include rare or otherwise inaccessible primary sources of all kinds (e.g. pictures, maps, audio and video recordings). A range of different text-types may be brought together on a website or on multimedia CD-ROM. These are especially valuable towards independent work/research and study of multidisciplinary fields.

5. The Internet and hypertext offer opportunities for creative work by students, which may be assessed, e.g. constructing a web page; guided exploration for good websites and source materials; exercising discrimination and skills of critical evaluation. The students' choice of their own path through hypertext material may foster self-reliance and a spirit of inquiry.

Finally, the caveats. As we saw, students need training in approaching electronic resources critically, and teachers need training and time to explore both the new possibilities and their integration in teaching programmes. Teachers also need to learn to work more closely and collaboratively with other staff, librarians and technical staff in particular. Therefore some institutional change is entailed if ICTs are to become a normal part of the curriculum and of teachers' priorities. These changes are well underway in universities in many countries and will only accelerate.

POSTSCRIPT

Here and in earlier chapters of the book we have made reference to the following teaching-learning methods: audio-visual, bibliographic, collaborative group/team work, creative writing, performance, essay writing, ICTs (DVD, CD-ROM, databases, search engines) and web-based methods (computer conferencing, the Internet, websites), lectures, oral presentations, project work/dissertations, reading (both primary and secondary texts), seminars, small-group discussion, tutorials, workshops. And others are discussed in Chapter 6. Plenty to choose from?

While it is not the point of this list that surveying it we may congratulate ourselves on the range of methods we use, it is no doubt more interesting for our students if we offer them a *variety* of ways of studying and learning in any given course. Indeed, some would say that a variety of methods should be offered because students have characteristic, and various, 'learning styles' – predominantly verbal or visual – which educators must take account of. But can it be so, we wonder, when a distance teaching institution such as the UKOU enrols 4–8,000 students every year in each of its introductory courses (Arts, Social Sciences, Health and Social Care, the Sciences, Technology, Maths and Computing . . .), all of whom study by means of the *same* methods and most of whom study successfully? Even if it were true that students have different learning styles, the variety of teaching-learning methods we have discussed here, as a result of considering the students' needs in relation to the study of Literature as a discipline, would surely suffice? And such consideration of the students' needs ensures that the chosen teaching methods have the added advantage of some rational justification.

So, we reiterate here what we have attempted to demonstrate in the course of the chapter: we need to know *why* we use the various teaching-learning methods we do, *when* and *to achieve what*. The point is to make appropriate connections between what our students are likely to need from us and the means available to us to help them fulfil their potential as students of Literature. That there may be great tension between these developmental and supportive aspects of our role as teachers and the requirement that we also act as judge and assessor of our students' work is one of the issues discussed in the next chapter.

Notes

1. See Lyotard (1984), in particular 'Education and its legitimation through performativity'. Performativity is expressed in the 'competency' and 'vocational skills' movements in the UK and the Outcomes Based Education movement in South Africa, for example. These and movements like them (right back to the behaviouralism applied to education in the mid-twentieth century) have long been seen as the mistaken attempt to apply ' "scientific" … principles and procedures in dealing with questions which fall outside the scope of science as commonly understood' (Standish, 1991: 171). For more recent critique see Barnett (2003).

2. 'Kinema' refers to cinemas and 'torches' to the lights used by attendants to show cinema-goers to their seats. 'Cornish ripple' is a type of ice cream.

3. For this and other useful websites see Appendix 7, the annotated website list on the book's website (www.sagepub.co.uk/chambers.pdf). The authors would like to thank Simon Rae (UKOU) for compiling this Appendix, and for his contributions to discussion of electronic methods in the text of the book.

4. Such a calculation may be made on the basis of any requirement regarding total hours of study, and over any period (a term, a semester, a month, etc.). A more sophisticated, and realistic, calculation would also involve estimating the time needed for reading primary texts, and include the time students are expected to spend in class, writing essays, etc. Research into student workload at the UKOU suggests that our courses tend to be overloaded, perhaps especially literature courses (given the length of many primary texts), so that often students cannot possibly do the work expected of them in the time available, let alone in the time advertised in course descriptions. There is no reason to suppose that the situation is any different in conventional universities.

5. Special arrangements must of course be made for students whose hearing is impaired, and indeed for all those who have any kind of disability. In the UK, the SENDA (Special Educational Needs and Disability Act) 2001 spells out the requirements (www.hmso.gov.uk/acts/acts2001/20010010.htm – accessed 25 October 2004). The TechDis website (www.techdis.ac.uk) provides resources and tools, and discussion of the impact of SENDA on the UK further, higher and specialist education sectors. See the Bibliography at the end of the book under 'Websites'.

Key references

Monroe, J. (2002) *Writing and Revising the Disciplines*. Ithaca, NY: Cornell University Press.

Northedge, A. (2003) 'Enabling participation in academic discourse', *Teaching in Higher Education*, 8(2): 169–80.

Websites

Australian e-Humanities gateway, at www.ehum.edu.au
Humbul Gateway, at www.humbul.ac.uk/english
Voice of the Shuttle, at http://vos.ucsb.edu

6

Student assessment

We have seen that thinking about what will be assessed and the ways teachers will assess students' (mainly written and oral) work is *a part of* the planning cycle for teaching – not something tacked on, to be considered when everything else is settled. And such decisions are of course closely bound up with our teaching-learning aims and objectives for the programme; as these become formulated we need to be thinking about how each one might best be assessed. That is, we must aim to assess in ways appropriate to the discipline all those things that are centrally important for students to be able to do, to know and to understand in the course of their education in Literature. Thus as teachers we ensure that our assessment practices are *valid*: well founded, sound and to the point.

The UK English Benchmark Statement puts assessment matters in a nutshell, as shown in Figure 6.1.

4.2.1. The assessment of students should be explicitly linked to the learning processes and outcomes of their degree programmes, which should recognise that assessment significantly influences how and what students learn. Assessment inheres in and informs the learning process: it is formative and diagnostic as well as summative and evaluative, and the process should provide students with constructive feedback. Students should be given the opportunity to pursue original thought and ideas, and encouraged to question received opinion.

4.2.2. The diversity of material and approaches, as well as programme objectives which value choice and independence of mind, suggest that it is desirable for students of English to experience a variety of assessment forms. Programmes should specify and make explicit the overall rationale for their approach to assessment, make clear the relationship between diagnostic and final assessment, and ensure, within the variety of approaches taken, that assessment is consistent in the demands it makes on students and the standards of judgements it applies.

(QAA, 2000: 5)

FIGURE 6.1 *4.2. Assessment.*

If it is pretty obvious that assessment should be aligned to the teaching-learning objectives of programmes and courses, it is equally obvious that there is indeed a strong relationship between what will be assessed and what students pay greatest attention to and give most time to as they study. This is not meant as a cynical observation, implying that all or even many students take a purely instrumental approach to their studies (although, of course, we know that some do). A function of any assessment regime is that it *should* act as a guide in this way, reinforcing teachers' priorities and helping the students to identify what activities, knowledge and understanding are centrally important to their progress.

But many other ideas are packed into this Statement – criteria and standards of assessment; the transparency of assessment regimes; formative and summative modes of assessment; feedback to students; consistency and fairness; variety in forms of assessment – all of which are discussed in this chapter. We begin with the crucially important question, how do we decide what to assess, when and to what standards?

TRANSPARENT ASSESSMENT CRITERIA AND STANDARDS

It turns out that the Benchmark Statement's first injunction, that assessment of students 'should be explicitly linked to the learning processes and outcomes of their degree programmes', is not so much an invitation to teachers to work these things out for themselves as it may seem at first sight. For its authors go on to identify what the assessment criteria for English programmes should be. This marks a sea change, in two respects: the idea that student assessment should be planned at the overarching level of the Literature programme; and that any external body (such as the QAA) might recommend just what higher education teachers should be assessing.

Until fairly recently it was customary for UK English departments to have an assessment policy but individual teachers were largely responsible for the form and conduct of it in 'their' courses. The sum of the students' achievements across all or certain of these courses then determined their final grade/degree classification. However, attention is now being focused on assessment of the programme as a whole: on identifying programme-based learning objectives from which the assessment criteria for the various courses that make it up can be derived. This vantage point is said to ensure a less piecemeal approach to assessment and to enable more systematic planning of it throughout the programme. It is regarded as far preferable from the point of view of students. For when programme-based criteria are not identified there is a danger that the criteria and standards of assessment applied to individual courses are applied inconsistently by their teachers, even to courses at the same level – with the students (especially in modular study) having to try to anticipate what each teacher they encounter expects and may favour. Criteria and standards may also be applied inconsistently within the same course if more than one person is involved in assessing the students' work (for example, a lecturer and graduate assistants). On the other hand, when the criteria and standards of assessment of individual courses are derived from the aims and objectives of the entire programme and are published, then the students can be more confident that a team of teachers is assessing their work on an agreed, consistent basis over the whole programme.

As regards academic departments and teachers, a requirement to agree on assessment criteria and standards for the three- (or four-) year programme should encourage debate about the modes and various forms of assessment that might be appropriate, at what levels and in which courses or modules in the programme. Further, apart from the expected gains in consistent application of the criteria and in reliability of marking, the idea is that once the learning objectives of the programme are identified a *selection* of them can then be allocated to its component courses – so reducing the number of different objectives prioritised in any one course or module. As a result, it is said, our assessment practice will become more focused and specific.

So, how might all this work out in Literature?

Programme assessment

According to the English Benchmark Statement, the core assessment criteria for an English programme should be as shown in Figure 6.2.

Standards of achievement of these criteria are then identified at two levels: threshold (the minimum requirement for honours graduates) and modal (the level reached by 'the typical student whose results fall into the main cluster', pp. 6–7). For example, as regards the first criterion (breadth and depth of subject knowledge ...), at the threshold level students will demonstrate 'an appropriate knowledge' while at the modal level they will demonstrate 'an extensive knowledge'.

- breadth and depth of subject knowledge, including relevant contextual knowledge and the demonstration of powers of textual analysis as appropriate;
- the management of discursive analysis and argument, including the awareness of alternative or contextualising lines of argument;
- rhetorical strategies which demonstrate the convincing deployment and evaluation of evidence;
- independence of mind and originality of approach in interpretative and written practice;
- fluent and effective communication of ideas and sophistication of writing skills;
- critical acumen;
- informed engagement with scholarly debates.

(QAA, 2000: 6)

FIGURE 6.2 *Core assessment criteria.*

While there is surely nothing objectionable about this list, on reflection it is not easy to see how it could in fact enable teachers to identify *different* assessment criteria to be applied, even at the various levels of the programme let alone in all the component courses or modules that might make it up. Rather, wouldn't these very broad criteria need to be met at every level, and in every course, to some extent? The criteria might be weighted differently at different levels: we might not attach as much value to 'independence of mind and originality . . .' at Level 1 as at Level 3, for example, and in the final year this criterion might be assessed especially in a dedicated project or dissertation course. And the standards applied would certainly differ from level to level – for example, the breadth and depth of knowledge, the degree of sophistication of writing and of engagement with scholarly debate expected at Level 3 would not be the same as that expected at Level 1. Nonetheless, these are indeed all characteristics of the study of Literature *tout court*.

So, it looks unlikely that core criteria of assessment in Literature can be carved up and served at discrete levels, and in particular courses, in the way recommended. Students begin to develop all the attributes in the list from the start of their undergraduate studies (and often well before), and through all the courses they study. True, some courses may to a greater extent aim to deepen the students' knowledge and others to broaden it, and this emphasis will be reflected in the syllabus and the activities the students are asked to undertake. But such items and activities will not be different in *kind* – as we shall see shortly in the discussion of assessment in our anonymous English department (Appendices 3 and 4 on the book's website). Curiously, the Benchmark Statement's more detailed lists of 'Subject knowledge' and 'Subject-specific skills' discussed in Chapter 4 may actually be more helpful as a basis for drawing up such core assessment criteria just because they are more detailed. What is also interesting is that the skills in the third list discussed there, the 'Generic and graduate skills' (of IT, time-management and organisation, and 'employability') are nowhere to be found in the QAA's list of assessment criteria!

However, including these skills would raise another issue – that of 'core' and 'optional' programme elements. If the programme aims and assessment criteria included the acquisition of certain IT skills, for example, where might they be taught and assessed? Unless such an element were present in every course in the programme, which might be thought an overemphasis or simply be impracticable, these skills would have to be taught in a dedicated course or in a few particular courses – and this course, or all/some of these courses, would presumably have to be made compulsory. If we were also to include as criteria the other 'generic' skills the QAA urges us to include, how many core, compulsory courses would be needed in the programme? And if these were many, how could we continue to offer the students choice by designating some courses optional?

Returning to the core assessment criteria, if 'independence of mind and originality . . .', for example, is deemed a core criterion of assessment, could it continue to be assessed mainly in an optional dissertation course? As regards the last two QAA assessment criteria ('critical acumen' and 'informed engagement with scholarly debates'), would literary theory/criticism courses need to be made compulsory in all institutions? And the problem would only be compounded if very many more subject-specific aims were identified. A solution might be differential weighting of programme aims and assessment criteria, with some regarded as more important than others . . .? In any event, it seems likely that such a system would create as many problems as it seeks to solve.

So, if the core criteria of assessment we are offered are not after all precise, do not enable us to assess different criteria among our courses, have the effect of complicating our existing procedures and present us with difficulties regarding the exercise of student choice, then what, we may reasonably ask, is the *point* of these criteria?

Criterion- versus norm-referenced assessment

We have seen that assessing students on the basis of agreed criteria (that is, criterion-referenced assessment) is said to have certain advantages – clarity, consistent application of assessment criteria and standards, reliable marking and transparency. In this kind of assessment system the aim is to *measure* the students' learning through a process that is precise, objective and reliable. Norm-referenced assessment, by contrast, is an art rather than a science – a kind of connoisseurship in which experienced teachers in a particular discipline acquire a shared understanding of both what they should be assessing and the standards that should be applied. Through their induction into the discipline, and their experience as a teacher of it, they absorb the norms; they learn to *make judgements* appropriately between levels and within particular courses of study. Clearly, then, the Benchmark Statement's lists of assessment criteria and threshold and modal standards is an attempt at criterion-referenced assessment which, as such, aims to make assessment in English a more objective, 'scientific' business.

Against this, we argued just now that the criteria identified there seem unlikely to help us much, because they are broad rather than precise and because they will apply to some extent to any and all the courses that might make up the Literature programme. However, perhaps that won't matter too much if we can identify the precise standards that apply to the programme. We saw, for instance, that an 'appropriate' breadth and depth of subject knowledge should be demonstrated at the threshold level and an 'extensive' knowledge at the modal level. But what is meant by 'appropriate' knowledge and 'extensive' knowledge'? What exactly is the difference between them? We are not told. And we are not told because these are the kinds of descriptor that only those on the inside of the discipline can interpret; they belong in a norm-referenced assessment system. What this suggests is that 'rational' practices are cloaking continued reliance on what are after all socio-academic judgements. It implies that this attempt to introduce a criterion-referenced assessment system is more symbolic than real (Woolf, 2001). What are we to make of that?

Our answer would be that to the extent that the criterion-referenced approach to assessment can make it a more consistent, reliable and transparent process for teachers and students, it is a good thing to attempt. In principle, teachers *should* know as clearly as possible against what criteria they are assessing students and what standards they are applying. And these things *should* be agreed among all those involved in teaching the programme so that they may apply the criteria as consistently as possible and mark or grade as reliably as possible. The fact that ultimately our judgements are indeed norm-based makes it even more necessary that we undertake to reach agreement about what those norms are. Group grading exercises, in which team members mark the same assignment and exam answers, and subsequently discuss their thinking and judgements, can be powerfully effective towards reaching greater understanding and consensus among the team – and also in training newcomers to teaching, including graduate assistants.

Also, because norms are not of themselves transparent, teachers *should* make their criteria and standards as transparent to students as they can, describing what is required to gain particular marks, grades and degree classifications, so that students understand both what they are aiming for and why their present work attracts a particular grade. Appendix 6(a) on the book's website provides an example of assessment criteria and standards for seminar presentations in a form that is presented to the students (preceded by a description of the role of the seminars in the course as whole). Note that grading criteria are presented in positive terms of what is required of students at each grade, and not in terms of 'deficit' from the top grade down – of what students fail to do or demonstrate at the lower grades. In addition, we should offer the students discussion sessions in which all these things are explained and explored. They too will benefit greatly from exercises in which the peer group grades anonymous scripts and together discusses the outcomes.

Nonetheless, we would say that the extent to which the criterion-referenced system can make assessment in English more 'scientific' is soon reached – beyond that, as we saw, matters are likely to become so complex and subtle as to undermine that system's very aims of validity, consistency and reliability. And that is because of the *nature* of Literature as a discipline. In a discipline that is hermeneutic, intertextual, participatory, value-laden, context-dependent and relatively indeterminate (Chapter 1) – involving critical engagement, insisting on problematising and also on creativity – it is simply not possible (even if it were desirable) to predetermine all the outcomes of the students' learning, at the programme or any other level. This is 'complex learning' (Knight, 2001) which cannot be assessed by means of 'tame' tasks that are structured and simplified such that little challenge is involved. Nor is it possible to replace the teacher-assessor's judgements with 'objective' standards. And it appears that the academics who compiled the English benchmark assessment criteria understand all this very well.

In summary, what we would say is that as Literature teachers we should aim to devise assessment regimes in which our criteria and standards are as clear and precise as we can make them, while retaining the proper scope for exercise of our professional judgement. We turn now to some of the main considerations involved in the design of such a regime.

DESIGNING AN ASSESSMENT REGIME

Learning versus measurement

Perhaps the most helpful distinction made in the Benchmark Statement is between *formative* assessment (designed primarily to contribute to the students' learning throughout the programme of study) and *summative* assessment (designed primarily to judge the results of their learning). In practice the two modes are not mutually exclusive – assessment regimes almost always include assignments that have both functions simultaneously – nevertheless it is crucial that we understand these essentially different purposes and are fully aware of the implications of employing one, the other or both modes together.

These days, many literature programmes aim to achieve a balance between formative and summative assessment (broadly, between coursework and end-of-course exam), or may even place greater emphasis on coursework. However, according to Gibbs and Simpson (2004–5: 3–4, emphasis added),[1] this practice seems to run counter to certain structural forces at work on and in higher education.

> When teaching in higher education hits the headlines it is nearly always about assessment: about examples of supposedly falling standards, about plagiarism, about unreliable marking or rogue external examiners, about errors in exam papers, and so on. The recent approach of the Quality Assurance Agency (QAA) to improve quality in higher education has been to focus on learning outcomes and their assessment, on the specification of standards and on the role of external examiners to assure these standards. Where institutional learning and teaching strategies

focus on assessment they are nearly always about aligning learning outcomes with assessment and about specifying assessment criteria. All of this focus, of the media, of quality assurance and of institutions, is on assessment as measurement.

But, the authors add:

The most reliable, rigorous and cheat-proof assessment systems are often accompanied by dull and lifeless learning that has short-lasting outcomes – indeed they often directly lead to such learning.

They conclude that, while they are not arguing for unreliable assessment, 'we should design assessment, first, to support worthwhile learning, and worry about reliability later. *Standards will be raised by improving student learning rather than by better measurement of limited learning.*' (Discuss.)

Coursework versus *exams*

Non-assessed coursework is clearly of the formative kind referred to in the Benchmark Statement – perhaps the paradigm case of it – having the sole purpose of focusing students' attention and, through judicious feedback from teachers, helping them to understand the central ideas and engage in the processes involved in their studies. Although all these matters *will* undoubtedly be assessed formally at some points, the problem is that in the meantime the very absence of assessment may 'signal' relative lack of importance, ironically, students may pass up such opportunities for stress-free practice and guidance. Put baldly, 'students will rarely write unassessed essays' (Gibbs and Simpson, 2004–5: 8). However, the authors continue, 'if coursework is taken away from a module due to resource constraints, students simply do not do the associated studying . . . It is argued that [teachers] have to assess everything in order to capture students' time and energy.' This is an argument they do not support. Describing some research conducted in the 1990s, in which teacher marking of coursework was replaced by peer review, they note that:

. . . the students' exam marks increased dramatically to a level well above that achieved previously when teachers did the marking. What achieved the learning was the quality of student engagement in learning tasks,

not teachers doing a lot of marking. The trick when designing assessment regimes is to generate engagement with learning tasks without generating piles of marking.

This is all the more important as student numbers increase because, unlike the costs of teaching – which can be kept fairly steady, mainly by increasing class sizes – the costs of assessment tend to rise in direct proportion to student numbers, as does the burden of marking on teachers. So, how can literature teachers engage their students in this way without unduly burdening themselves?

First, if we want to try to make sure that students pay attention to what we regard as important developmental activities it may be that we have to abandon the widespread practice of assessing their progress only at seminal points – on completion of major pieces of work, such as full-blown essays – and find ways of encouraging serious engagement in activities leading up to those points. For example, in 'The Patchwork Text' project (www.apu.ac.uk), an essay is built up over a number of weeks from a variety of sources and, during this period, aspects of it are discussed with fellow students and teachers in scheduled meetings. Some time may be devoted to such activity in writing workshop sessions too, before the final product is submitted. And we might even decide to award a percentage of the total coursework marks to developmental activities. For instance, Appendix 6(b) on the book's website ties a class presentation, marked at the time of delivery, to preparation of a coursework essay that is marked at a later point. Or, *two-stage assignments* may be set with some marks reserved for the first, draft stage – also on the assumption that prevention of poor performance is better (for the students' learning and morale) than later, more time-consuming correction of it. Further, this clearly signals writing as a *means* of understanding, not just a result of it. And this kind of assignment (like the Patchwork Text) also has the effect of distributing students' efforts more evenly across the weeks of study.

But the two-stage strategy would generate a rather heavier marking load – unless it were designed as a *group assignment*, which could be more efficient in terms of the time spent both teaching and marking. Appendix 6(a) 'Procedure' on the book's website outlines a three-stage strategy in which small groups of students: (a) collaborate to produce pieces of writing; (b) deliver them orally; and (c) subsequently together prepare an analytical commentary and a self-assessment.

Or we may try to ensure students' engagement by other means, such as the approach taken to attendance at seminars in the English department whose course outlines are included in Appendix 3. There, seminar attendance is clearly regarded as a major part of the students' education in literature; although attendance itself does not attract marks, nevertheless it is not optional.

Seminar attendance

Attendance at seminars is compulsory. There are several reasons for this. Student absences may: compromise the assessment of, and adversely affect the learning of, other students; disrupt the planned delivery of the seminar (which is essentially participatory and collaborative in nature); disadvantage the absentee by missing essential parts of the module; jeopardise the successful assessment of the absentee. **Therefore, students who do not attend at least 75% of seminars on a module will be deemed to have failed that module (even if a mark of 40% or higher is attained overall through formal assessment), unless there are clear mitigating circumstances supported by documentary evidence. Students who fail a module because of poor attendance will normally be required to be entirely reassessed in that module.**

Please note that the attendance of individual students will be very carefully monitored. Ensure that you sign an attendance register for each seminar attended. If, for whatever reason, you are unable to attend a seminar, it is important that you contact me (before the seminar, if possible) to inform me of your situation, and to discuss the details of any work which may need to be done as a result.

Out of courtesy to other members of the class, **please be punctual.**

Note that the assessment policy is made explicit ('transparent') in the way the Benchmark Statement advocates; students are not only told what the policy is but are also given reasons for it. A sanction for non-attendance is then spelt out clearly.

Second, if a main aim of assessing students' work is developmental then we may also need to think in terms of less monolithic assessment regimes. In many UK literature programmes the regime involves a combination of assessed coursework (mainly essays) and unseen examinations each usually of two or three hours' duration in which students are asked to write several essays – though in modular systems both the duration and requirements of the exam and the number of coursework essays are scaled down.

Unit title: *Introduction to Prose Fiction*, Level 1

Assessment design: diagnostic essay (0 per cent); 2,000-word essay (50 per cent); two-hour (unseen) examination (50 per cent).

This course focuses on texts from the late eighteenth and early nineteenth centuries. The exam is designed to assess breadth of subject knowledge. Students may not repeat material used in the assessed essay, and they may not focus on a single text in answer to a question.

Unit title: *Critical Theory and Practice*, Level 3

Assessment design: 3,000-word written assignment (50 per cent); two-hour examination (50 per cent).

In the written assignment students must demonstrate understanding of the significant aspects of a particular critical theory and also critically evaluate that theory.

In the exam, students are asked to put theory into practice. The paper is divided into two sections, each carrying equal weighting. In section 1 the candidate must answer a general question (from a choice of five), demonstrating the ability to think critically about an issue in relation to literary examples. In section 2 s/he must produce a critical analysis of a literary extract provided in the examination paper (from a choice of three).

(www.english.heacademy.ac.uk, accessed August 2004)

FIGURE 6.3 *Examples of assessment design.*

Practice varies with respect to the proportion of the overall marks awarded to coursework and exams, but it is still fairly unusual for coursework to be weighted more heavily (and see the example assessments in Figure 6.3). In this respect, practice in our anonymous English department is what some would term 'progressive' – here, the emphasis is on coursework, which also includes an oral component. In each module a 1,500-word essay attracts 40 per cent of the total marks and an oral presentation a further 30 per cent; the remaining 30 per cent of marks is awarded to one essay produced in a summative, end-of-module unseen examination. (However, in all three assessment components the pass mark is 40 per cent, which is the standard commonly applied in the UK.)

As regards coursework essays, note that submission is about three-quarters of the way through each module – as explained in Appendix 3(c), 'so that you can profit from the marking of your essay before revising for your exam'. So, although perhaps a little late in the day for a formative assignment, this work clearly has that function – as does the oral presentation, which may be assessed at any point in the semester. We may suspect that students who happen to make their presentation earlier rather than later on perhaps derive greater benefit. But that also depends upon what feedback they receive from the teacher and how it is viewed, matters to which we will return.

Progression in assessment

Meantime, we can also see from these course outlines that, although the assessment model is the same across the programme (70 per cent coursework; 30 per cent exam), progression from one level to the next is built in. At Level 1, for example, the coursework essay questions/titles are tightly focused, on specific texts that have been studied in the module and (although students are clearly expected to have contextual knowledge) they are quite narrow in scope, for example: 'Choosing two poems of the First World War that we have studied, assess, in detail, their *particular* contribution to the writing of the period.' Contrast that with the Level 2 question, 'How effectively does Browning present different kinds of obsession in his poetry?' Here there is no indication of such restriction, but whether the students select poems appropriately is no doubt itself an aspect of the test. At Level 3 the questions are at once broad and more abstract: 'Analyse the relationship between repression and biology as presented in Atwood'; 'What part do gender and sex play in the struggle for utopia as constructed by Lessing?' Note, too, that at Level 3 the students are offered greater choice in that they may if they wish negotiate with the teacher an essay question/title other than those listed.

Similarly, progression is evident in the examination papers set at Levels 2 and 3 (see Appendix 4(a) and (b) on the book's website). The Level 2 exam offers students a wide choice – in fact, the first eight questions cover the syllabus – and these questions are quite circumscribed, for example: 'Tess has been described as a striking embodiment "of the woman realised both as object and as consciousness". Consider the validity of this statement, with close reference to the text.' The last few questions are broader in scope, offering the possibility for comparisons and contrasts to be drawn, but within specified limits: 'Explore the representation of childhood in *at least two* Victorian novels.' At Level 3, by contrast, the questions are thematic and open-ended, with the rubric including the instruction always to refer to two or more texts (which the students know must extend beyond the relatively few 'set' texts): 'In what variety of ways, and for what reasons, do the writers of utopias challenge or extend notions of reality?'; 'How far do the dystopian texts you have read represent an attack on idealism?'

Notice, too, that it is clear from the rubric under 'Assessment' in Appendix 3(b) that it is possible for the students to achieve less than 40 per cent for their performance in any *one* of the assessed components (coursework essay, oral presentation, exam) and still pass the module as a whole if they attain 40 per cent overall; an overall mark of 40 per cent will not do – the students must also achieve at least 40 per cent in two of the three components. What this means is that the examination is not privileged in any way, which is quite unusual (especially in a regime in which an exam attracts only 30 per cent of the total marks). It suggests that, in this regime, the exam is not seen as particularly significant in educational terms. Rather, a main purpose is likely to be verification – to ensure that the work is undertaken by the named student and (especially in the distance teaching context) that the student is who she says she is. So, various forms of cheating are made more difficult and, subsequently, any very marked discrepancy between performance in coursework and exam can be investigated.

Furthermore, exams are regarded as an important guarantee of academic standards. In UK universities, for example, they are normally blind double-marked, and the exam papers, the distribution of grades awarded and cases at the boundaries between grades are subject to scrutiny by an external examiner – a colleague of standing in the discipline from a different institution. These strategies are designed to assure high standards within Literature departments and also comparable standards in departments across the country. By contrast, coursework is not normally double-marked (except for dissertations), and only if there is a discrepancy between it and the exam mark will it be scrutinised by an exam board including the external examiner. Exam boards are expensive to convene; in general, having one programme board and a system with fewer assessment boundary points (a pass/fail or a class awards system, e.g. first, second, third) rather than the scale 0–100 per cent make for easier decisions, less scope for disagreement between markers and fewer cases at the boundaries that need to be reviewed.

Although verification and assurance of standards are functions of exams generally, in many assessment regimes exams are indeed also justified on educational grounds. They are thought to have the particular and distinct merits of prompting students to revise the course, reviewing their work and pulling together their knowledge of it from all sources, a process that has the effect of considerably increasing their understanding. Some would also justify the unseen nature of exams as giving students practice at working under pressure, memorising and having to 'think on their feet', supposedly real-world abilities that will be valued in the workplace. In Literature pro- grammes, however, the burden of pure memorising is sometimes relieved by means of 'open-book' exams, in which students can bring along (un-annotated) set texts. It is claimed that, given the time-limit of the exam, this is no substitute for the kind of knowledge and understanding gained through the revision process, that, in fact, students will do less well in the exam if they waste time consulting the texts for more than the precise wordings of quotations. However this may be, exams are not on the whole popular with students (see Figure 6.4).

Yet, according to Gibbs and Simpson (pp. 8–9), in general coursework assessment is in decline in the UK: owing to resource

---

Students prefer coursework – they consider it to be fairer, to measure a greater range of abilities and allow them more scope to organise their own work patterns.

Students do better at coursework assignments – all combinations of kinds of coursework produce up to 12 per cent higher average marks than exams alone: in English, one-third of a degree classification higher; three times as many students fail exam-only modules.

Coursework is valid – coursework marks are a better predictor than exam scores of long-term learning of course content and of any subsequent performance (e.g. success at work).

The quality of students' learning is higher in assignment-based courses – including greater emphasis on thinking, more sophisticated conceptions of learning, greater ability to make comparisons and to evaluate.

Whether or not higher education teachers give helpful feedback on coursework assignments makes more difference than anything else they do – 'helpful' feedback focuses students' attention on important aspects of the subject, helps them monitor their own progress, encourages active learning, provides understanding of results, helps the students feel a sense of accomplishment and aids student retention.

Adapted from Gibbs and Simpson (2004–5).

FIGURE 6.4 *What do we know about coursework assessment versus exams?*

constraints, assignments are set less frequently and the amount, quality and timeliness of feedback offered to students is reduced – especially in shorter, modular courses. Indeed, as we saw in the anonymous English department, only one assignment per module is set and that towards the end of each semester, not long before the exam. Modularisation and semesterisation have generally also led to an increase in the number of examinations. And a great increase in the use of graduate assistants (mainly a consequence of the now intense focus on research and research funding through the Research Assessment Exercise) may, they argue, have an adverse effect on the quality of the feedback students are offered. The authors conclude (p. 9, emphasis added):

> *At the same time the diversity of students has increased enormously, so that previous assumptions of the level of sophistication of knowledge background, study skills, conception of learning (Säljö, 1982) or conception of knowledge (Perry, 1970) of students are now likely to be very wide of the mark.* Far more guidance is likely to be required by these students, who need more practice at tackling assignments and more feedback on their learning, not less.

FEEDBACK AND LEARNING

If we do not care much whether the students learn or whether they abandon their studies, then the best thing we can do is give their coursework assignments low marks and provide no comment at all, especially in the early stages of higher education. But if we want coursework assessment to help our students *learn*, then offering them feedback on their work is of the essence.[2] Matters are as clear cut as that.

However, it is also clear that we must try to think about these matters in the present circumstances of institutions. For example, in an effort to retain coursework the argument that it increases student retention is likely to be a strong one – retaining students is, after all, a lot cheaper than losing them and having to recruit afresh. And any ideas we may have about the frequency and quantity of feedback that should ideally be offered must be tempered by the knowledge that in most institutions teachers have even less time to give to this aspect of their job than before. That said, we know that there are several principles involved in providing feedback that should be adhered to – which are also conditions of the students' making good use of the feedback offered.

● Set a formative assignment and offer feedback on it as early in a course as possible. This is good for the students' development, since they will have time in the course to learn from it, and it is good for their morale, and for retention, if they receive guidance and support early on – particularly at Level 1. The feedback should of course be encouraging rather than very critical at that early stage; from the students' perspective, it is a long-term project they're embarking on.

● Provide feedback as quickly as possible. Certainly students should receive feedback on an assignment before they get started on the next, or well before they sit an exam, otherwise it's of little use to their development.

● In feedback, focus on the students' performance of the task rather than on them or their abilities as individuals, and comment constructively. It is hard for students (indeed, for anyone) to receive critical comment calmly, fully take it in and use it well. But that is exactly what we want them to do. Lea and Street (1998: 169) remark on teachers' frequent use of ' "categorical modality", using imperatives and assertions, with little mitigation or qualification . . . as a categorical assertion that the point is not "correct" ' ('Explain', 'A bit confused', '?', '!'). Here, the teacher 'clearly and firmly takes authority, assumes the right to criticise directly . . . on the basis of an assumed "correct" view of what should have been written and how'. They argue that use of a more provisional modality, such as 'you might like to consider . . .', 'have you thought about . . .?' or 'could this be interpreted differently?' would 'evoke a different interpersonal relationship between student as writer and teacher as marker . . .'

● Provide feedback in such a way that the students can understand it given their current level of sophistication, as we have just seen. Also, offer advice that is specific and doable. 'Avoid ambiguity by eliminating pronouns that have no clear referent and by moving or eliminating misplaced modifiers or dangling phrases' will leave students gaping. 'Read the literature on X' is not very helpful; 'read A's article on X' is much more so. 'Use evidence appropriately' is no doubt something the students would do if only they knew how.

- Offer feedback selectively, not copiously. There is only so much that a student can take in at a given time and hope to practise and improve at. A focus on three or four issues is probably sufficient with respect to any one assignment.
- Offer feedback that looks forward to the next and subsequent tasks (not simply corrects the present performance) so that it will help towards the students' future work. Indeed, Knight (forthcoming) argues that such 'feed forward' is *more* valuable than feedback because it has greater power 'to stimulate transfer' from one type of task to another and to improve future performance.

There are ways of putting some of these principles into practice that will undoubtedly save the teacher's time and effort. For example, to take the last point: there will often be occasion to remark on the students' writing or aspects of their study skills that are of ongoing importance. So, commenting on these things is worth investing time in. Furthermore, they may be things that many students get wrong or could do with some advice about. In this case it will be worth preparing comments fairly carefully and fully which may then be circulated to *all* the students, on paper or posted on the course website. Such a practice could extend to substantive matters too; often students will misunderstand the same aspect of an essay question, or choose similarly to focus on a rather peripheral matter at the expense of something more important. It may well be a more efficient use of the teacher's time also to prepare this kind of feedback for all, adding just a few further points on each individual student's script. Over time, a bank of comments could be compiled and used in successive presentations of the course.

Also, it is less time-consuming to direct students to some explanatory source material when possible rather than explain something fully oneself, which has the added advantage that the students can then work out for themselves where they may have gone wrong. In the case of a very poor essay, it may be best to mark only the first page or so in any detail and then return it for correction and resubmission; this strategy both saves the teacher time and forces the student to think about how to do better. And, finally, students are themselves a constructive-critical resource – we shall see shortly the kind of contribution that peer review of students' work can make to their development.

We have focused here on students' written work. But where there is an oral component of the course then the students will also need feedback on their performance of it. Here, we would recommend even greater sensitivity to the students' feelings, especially when critical comment is made person to person. Such comment may feel like an attack on the very person – to a much greater extent than critique of written work – because a presentation is more directly self-expressive: nobody enjoys hearing that they bored everyone silly or simply failed to communicate with their classmates. Feedback on an oral presentation can be attended and reacted to in privacy if it is presented in written form after the fact.

Plagiarism

We raise plagiarism as an issue in its own right because it undermines the educational purposes of coursework; to the extent that if students plagiarise they fail to address for themselves literary ideas and study processes. In this time of Internet plagiarism, with lurid stories of coursework downloaded, essays bought and sold, it may seem naïve to point out that many students are confused by the meaning of 'plagiarism'. But in their study of student writing, Lea and Street (1998: 167–8) found that students 'expressed anxieties about plagiarism in terms of their own authority as writers ... Their overriding concern was that the texts they read were authoritative and that they as students had little useful to say.' They cite a student: 'I don't know anything about the subject other than what I've read in books so how on earth could I write anything which was not someone else's idea?' They continue, 'For this student, as with others, the relationship between plagiarism and correct referencing was not transparent and he was worried that he would plagiarise unknowingly.' However, the institution treated plagiarism 'as clearly definitive and unquestionable'. Its discourse 'is that of the law and authority rather than of tutor and student engaged in the learning practices of educational discourse', which 'affirms the disciplinary and surveillance aspects of the writing process ... backed by the heavy weight of an institution with boards, regulations and, ultimately, legal resources'. Although universities and departments must both define the meaning of plagiarism and make their policy regarding it widely known, Lea and Street's research suggests that a more sensitive approach to these matters is required of teachers in the interests of their students' learning.

That said, institutions and teachers cannot take a relaxed attitude to the trade in student work on the Internet. But this and less wholesale cheating can be very difficult to detect since material from electronic sources can so easily be cut and pasted into assignments, and there are very many sources available. Furthermore, the plagiarised essays are student essays – good ones perhaps, but not the polished products of critics, extracts from which teachers may recognise and are anyway much more likely to spot. However, that same Internet hosts a number of plagiarism detection services, some of them programmes developed by universities (see www.jisc.ac.uk/mle/plagiarism). Other than our own noses, this is indeed the main line of defence.

The role of teacher and assessor

Policing our students in this way is not an appealing prospect, and it raises a broad issue touched on in earlier chapters – that we may experience considerable tension between the role of nurturing teacher and that of judge and assessor of the students' work. In the former role we are fully involved with our students, guiding their learning and attending to their development as students of Literature; in the latter role, it seems we must stand back from them, as it were 'forget' all that and judge the work they produce according to the agreed criteria and standards.

Indeed, post-Foucault we cannot be unthinking about the forces that act upon our institutions and the power relations that permeate them. Jones et al. (2005) suggest that the role of teacher itself contains such tension. Teaching, they argue, has a double function – of conveying ideas and managing communication – and these 'ideational' and 'interpersonal' functions may conflict. Exploring in some detail the workings of first- and second-year text-based seminar classes, they observe that in ideational terms 'the skirmishes tend to take place between certain kinds of language – academic versus non-academic', with teachers acting as exemplars of literary discourse, carrying out both 'modelling' work and 'reframing' work. This they acknowledge involves a kind of 'coercion' or 'authority-backed persuasion'. In the first-year class the teacher was seen to downplay ideational conflict (e.g. did not insist on historicising the text) in order to establish fruitful interpersonal relationships with and among the students; in the second-year class, where 'the language is held more in common', there was much more ideational cut and thrust. These authors conclude that the coercive element

> seems to us an important part of the teacher's role. Even though it is complicated and perhaps compromised by other roles . . . it is not one

*which can in any facile way be counterpoised to a teaching style based
on the recognition of difference, or the encouragement of subaltern voices
... The teachers are doing necessary work – raising the students'
capacities to read, reason, argue, write, and so on ... But [although this
is so], students' willingness to enter into the process is provisional.*
Lecturers have to earn the right to teach, so to speak, on the basis
of the intellectual productivity of their relationship with students.

(Emphasis added)

Given the power that teachers inevitably have – an authority on the
discipline and (backed by institutional might) an authority over the
student – it seems that they have to earn the students' trust if they
want to foster serious engagement with the subject. Perhaps this is a
solution to the conflict between the roles of teacher and assessor too.
Perhaps it is less a matter of the teacher somehow overcoming such
conflict and more a matter of students 'granting' the role of assessor,
'agreeing' to overlook its threatening aspect. The authors suggest that
this will happen only if the students feel their teacher is trustworthy
in the teaching role – genuinely has their interests at heart. Further, in
the role of assessor, we can surely earn that trust only by sincerely
trying to make our assessment practices as valid, reliable and
transparent as possible.

Specialisation versus multidisciplinarity revisited

In Chapter 4 we noted that students in a combined/joint honours or
modular programme, of which only a part is devoted to Literature, are
'rarely taught or assessed separately from their peers in single honours
at the level of course or module', and questioned whether these
students could indeed possibly be expected to acquire the same
breadth and depth of knowledge given that they spend half the time
or less studying Literature than their specialist peers. We also
questioned whether these students' knowledge and understanding
would be similar in kind to the specialist literature student's. We
asked, 'should we apply the same *criteria of judgement* to these
students' achievements?' – and answered, 'No'. We speculated there
that different assessment criteria might be identified or different
standards of achievement applied. However, since we concluded
earlier that assessment criteria in Literature are likely to be broad and
relatively indeterminate, applicable in any and all courses, it seems

more likely that we could achieve this discrimination by applying standards differentially. Once the various assessment criteria have been agreed upon, the standards expected of specialist Literature students might first be stipulated. Then it would be a matter of qualifying those standards where appropriate for application to multidisciplinary students. For example, different degrees of 'breadth' and 'depth' of knowledge may well be identified; these students might perhaps be expected to have greater contextual knowledge than Literature specialists, but less experience of in-depth textual analysis. We invite you to think further about this in an Activity at the end of the chapter.

VARIOUS FORMS OF ASSESSMENT

As we saw, the English Benchmark Statement assumes that a variety of approaches will be taken to assessment. We would just reiterate here what we concluded about diversity in teaching methods in Chapter 5: the point is not to hold fast only to the traditional methods we are familiar and comfortable with (the essay, the exam, the project/dissertation . . .) nor to offer variety for variety's sake, but to know *why* we use the methods of assessment that we do, *when* and *to achieve what*. For example, in many subjects multiple choice testing is used, and increasingly so now that the tests can be marked by computer (see the national Computer Assisted Assessment Centre, University of Luton: www.caacentre.ac.uk). Computer-marked testing (CMT) could perhaps replace essay-based exams in Literature and so considerably save teachers' time and effort. So, should English teachers use CMT?

First we must ask: why use it? What aspects of our students' knowledge, understanding and/or skill would it enable them to demonstrate? How would using it impact on their understanding of Literature as a discipline and their study practices? The UK Subject Centre for English is currently experimenting with this form of assessment[3] – testing students' knowledge of texts (displaying literary extracts or entire poems followed by multiple choice or yes/no options), their awareness of literary techniques, knowledge of literary history and basic critical terms – for diagnostic purposes, or in formative or summative mode. Either way, and even though such tests are tricky and time-consuming to construct, the scores make up 'only a fraction of a student's overall degree' and thus 'threaten in no way the hegemony of the essay as the focus of assessment in English studies'. The authors continue:

> *The terrible literalness of computers means that, in general, questions have to deal in matters of right and wrong in a way that is perhaps alien to thinking about and discussing literature. The reduction of critical subtleties to 'yes' or 'no' may indeed be offensive in itself. On the other hand, if we want students to read texts and remember something about them, why not test their knowledge?*

You will of course have to answer our questions, and theirs, for yourself.

Leaving aside the staple forms of assessment and also oral assessment, then, about which enough has probably been said, what other methods might we consider using because they promote our students' learning and/or enable us to judge their knowledge and skill appropriately?

Group work

We have seen that collaborative group work is highly valued in a discursive subject such as Literature as a means of encouraging cooperative research, the pooling of ideas and knowledge among peers, and also offering them opportunities to discuss texts and debate aspects of the subject together in a focused, task-oriented way. More generally, confident, articulate expression of ideas is at the centre not only of our research and teaching but also of our students' ability to progress in the discipline.[1] However, as we noted earlier, difficulties can arise in assessing group work fairly especially as regards variable inputs to the work by individual students – notably, those who see it as a licence to take things easy. A number of strategies have been devised for coping with this, most of which depend on some combination of a whole-group mark for the finished product – whether written work or oral/visual presentation or both – plus assessment of individually prepared work (see Appendix 6(a) under 'Procedure'). For example, the group members may be required to keep a log or build up a portfolio of their research notes and various contributions to the project from start to finish, which is marked separately from the group product (for which each member gains the same, threshold, score); the group score and individual score are then summed to yield a probably different final score for each group member. Or the mark awarded to each group member may be negotiated openly and agreed by the whole group in discussion with the tutor. Individually prepared work may also take the form of an account of the development of the work, a critique of the outcome or a self-assessment (see below).

A difficulty that arises with regard to group presentations towards summative assessment concerns verifiability. Short of audio or video recording the presentations and subjecting them to double marking at a later date, the only guarantee is when written work is submitted in support of the presentation – another reason why it is so often required. Finally, a tendency has been noted among students to spend longer at work on group projects (especially preparing for presentations) than the marks available warrant. No doubt the desire not to let fellow students down or a fear of being humiliated in front of them can create a lot of anxiety. All these issues need to be aired in Literature departments and also discussed with students.

Peer assessment

Peer assessment is almost exclusively used formatively and rarely reduces the marking burden on teachers in any direct way. It is often used, for example, precisely to help students understand the assessment criteria and standards that apply to their work, especially in their first year as undergraduates. These exercises usually take the form referred to earlier, of each student independently marking the same anonymous essays (of varying standards, produced by students in previous intakes) against the stated criteria, and subsequently discussing their thoughts and judgements together and with a tutor. In rounding up the discussion, the tutor can be sure to raise any significant issues not covered in the discussion.

Generally, peer assessment is based on the belief that students have much to learn from each other's experience, knowledge and understandings. So it is also often used to help develop the students' skills as critics and writers, notably in writing workshops (as we saw in Chapter 3). Here, the students may bring along an outline of an essay or talk for critique by a partner or small group of fellow students. If the work in preparation is posted on the course website beforehand, the session itself can be used very productively. In the case of remote students, 'discussion' and critique can be accomplished via a dedicated computer conference (see below).

But peer assessment can also be used to help improve the students' subject-specific learning, as the case in Appendix 6(c) demonstrates. Notice that in this design the student's performance as a peer assessor is itself assessed by the tutor, on the basis of its potential to help the fellow student whose work is under scrutiny. The exercise thus includes an element of training in how to make judgements appropriately and equitably, and how to criticise in a constructive, un-threatening manner – experiences that no doubt pay off in other settings, such as the seminar. It underlines the obvious point that students *learn* over time how to conduct themselves in the role of assessor. If this form of assessment is to be used then opportunities to learn must be included in the Literature programme. This should counteract the possibility of prejudiced treatment of some students (those from ethnic minorities, for example), especially at a time when there is increasing pressure to make assessment fairer by making it anonymous.

Self-assessment

We have just seen how self-assessment may be used, summatively, in the context of collaborative group work. Here, as elsewhere, its use emphasises the importance for the students' progress in reflection on their own performance, their developing understanding and skills. Self-assessment invites students to put some critical distance between the experience of carrying out their work and the finished product – applying to that product the standards of judgement they would apply to any other written material or oral performance. When they do so sincerely, they may acquire deeper understanding of what is expected of them as students and a surer grasp of their present strengths and weaknesses.

Self-assessment aimed at improving students' essay writing was a focus of the 'Assessment and The Expanded Text' project (see note 3). In this scheme, students are required to complete a self-assessment sheet to accompany each essay they submit. The sheet

> ... *provides students with a structured way of reflecting on, and critically evaluating, their own written work. It breaks the essay down into its constituent parts and invites students to assess their performance in each ... part. Accompanying [this] are explanations of what constitutes stronger or weaker performance in that category ... [using]*

*the common terminology of assessment (e.g. 'persuasiveness', 'argu-
ment', 'originality') ... in well-defined language that is intelligible to
students. The sheet also provides space for them to make a general
comment on their work in their own words, and invites them to estimate
a percentage grade ... tutors tick the boxes and make their own
comments on the essay. Thus they use the sheet as the main form of
written feedback ... The sheet is accompanied by a short guide for
students on how to self-assess their work.*

These materials are available for adaptation and use (www.unn.ac.uk/
assessingenglish).

Self-assessment may also take the more subject-centred form of a
'personal statement' in which the students critically review their own
position on a topic or text. The requirements for statements such as
this may be as rigorous as for any other piece of written work: as
carefully focused, clearly structured, referenced, etc. As we shall see,
such statements are often required as an accompaniment to and
overview of a portfolio of work.

Portfolios

Appendix 6(d) on the book's website provides an example of portfolio
assessment. Here, the students bring together their coursework (three
essays), written and marked at intervals during the course, which they
resubmit at the end of the year along with a review of the seminars
they have attended and the contributions to them they have personally
made. This design, then, combines essay-assessment and self-assessment. It also neatly avoids the main pitfall of portfolio assessment –
the extra burden of marking it usually entails for the teacher – by not
requiring any remarking of the essays in the portfolio; at the end of
the course the only marking needed is of the seminar review.
Nevertheless, at that stage teachers can review the sum total of the
students' work in the course which, in this case, they may modify by
10 per cent up or down. Often, however, portfolios contain coursework
that was read by the tutor and, on the basis of the feedback provided,
is rewritten and resubmitted for grading at the end of the course.
Clearly, this is designed to enhance the students' learning and no
doubt does, but (like the two-stage assignment discussed earlier) it
doubles the work for the tutor – unless, as we saw, the first stage is
peer- or group-assessed.

There are looser and more creative uses of portfolio assessment too, at the extreme to a kind of reflective 'learning diary' the students keep throughout their courses. Some of these approaches are also documented on the English Subject Centre website (www.english. heacademy.ac.uk).

1. Level 2 course, 'Texts and Textuality'

The portfolio [of 4,000 words] is intended to be a space where students record, reflect on and select their coursework . . . They can rewrite seminar work so it's all one thing, or they can include lots of snippets and cut ups of their own work . . . The portfolio provides them with the opportunity to apply principles to things which interest them, rather than having a prescribed question to answer . . . [It] includes copy of the exercises done for class. Students are encouraged to edit these pieces in ways which show a development of learning . . . [Workshops are used] to discuss and redraft work . . . Implicit in the workshop method is the belief that by presenting their work in progress students are likely to increase both their understanding of critique as a genre and develop skills of persuasion, negotiation and argument which improve their essay writing.

2. Level 1 course, 'The City, Real and Imagined'

The portfolio can assume many forms. It might be a scrapbook of materials collected from media sources. It can include or be comprised substantially of interviews on audio or video tape. It can include photographs taken by students or photomontages. All of these forms have been presented to students in the teaching sessions . . . Whatever form [it takes]   students must include a written commentary that outlines the theme chosen and reflects on how the themes relate to materials presented on the unit, as well as . . . in the course reader . . . The extent to which [it does so] forms a crucial measure of the portfolio's success or failure in terms of marks out of 100. [It must also] show evidence of wider research – in media archives or libraries.
    . . . The portfolio is flexible enough to let students take further any one of the approaches introduced to them on the unit. The flexibility of the assessment makes it well suited to diverse classes including people from very different backgrounds, abilities and with very different study profiles. The portfolio is also researched and compiled across the semester, giving plenty of opportunity for feedback, advice, tutorial sessions. Time is built into the programme for seminar and workshop feedback and final presentation of results.

Online discussion and group work

For remote students an asynchronous computer conference may be the only means of 'discussing' ideas about the texts they read with other students and their tutor: 'discussing' because, as we noted in Chapter 5, many of the features of face-to-face discussion are not possible in this medium, particularly its spontaneous flow and cut-and-thrust. However, from the point of view of student assessment the conference has the distinct advantage of yielding a transcript. By its nature, live seminar discussion cannot be captured in its entirety and subjected to scrutiny after the event. The conference transcript, by contrast, not only provides an accurate record of the event but also identifies each of the 'speakers'. Indeed, when a conference discussion is included in the assessment design students are often required to make a certain number of contributions, and of particular kinds: initiating a topic/ offering a point of view; 'listening' and responding to others' points of view; synthesising or summarising aspects of the discussion, and so on. It is then a relatively easy matter to assess their various contributions. And these (and any other) requirements may be communicated to remote students in just the ways we saw earlier of making the assessment regime transparent.

Via the Internet remote students can also engage in collaborative group work. In dedicated spaces (which the tutor may observe) they can work together on a project over a specified period, making use of a range of online source material (in such an integrated medium, including visual and aural sources) as well as primary texts in print. In the virtual setting, just as in the real world, they must discuss the issues, organise themselves, distribute tasks, negotiate the outcomes and, together, structure and present the final piece of work. The main difference is that time-scales for this kind of work (as for discussions) are inevitably longer, allowing for remote access and students' occupying different time zones. As before, not just the finished product but also the workings of the group are evident and open to scrutiny. Thus issues surrounding fair allocation of marks for the different group members are somewhat less problematic.

Formative assessment and two-stage assignments may also be accomplished online. For example, draft essays can be posted elec-tronically and peer-reviewed prior to reworking and final submission. Submission of assignments of all kinds is of course also electronic, which can considerably speed up the process of marking and providing feedback to the students – something that is becoming common in campus universities too, even where little reliance is made on the web for other purposes. And use of html, for example, enables students to include a wide variety of assignment formats and a range of media.

Online scenario

Students studying a playwright are provided with set texts, readers and DVDs of performances of the play(s). They also have access to a range of online resources and engage in a number of online activities based around discussing certain themes, in computer conference with the tutor and each other. At intervals different 'experts' are brought in to the online forum to discuss particular issues, with whom the students may also engage.

Assessment is based on a collaborative activity in which the students work together, in groups of 4–5 over a ten-week period, to produce a proposal for staging a play of their choice. An outline structure for the proposal is provided, indicating what issues *must* be addressed; the word limit for the assignment is 3,000 and students are encouraged to include other media as appropriate. At the mid-point, each small group must post a draft extract from their proposal on the course website (text only, max. 700 words) for review and comment by the tutor and other students. The tutor has access to the small-group discussions throughout the period and may, on occasion, intervene to offer guidance. On the due date, each group must post its finished proposal.

The virtual learning environment supports a range of media including audio, video, text, images and stage simulations, a threaded discussion board and a webcasting facility so that the experts can make their contribution from their own locations. The students also have access to a range of collaborative tools, such as shared whiteboards, instant messaging and annotation tools, that allow them to share comments on text and visuals.

Or, students may work together on whole-group developmental tasks, such as analysing a literary extract or summarising a critical text, posting their critiques or summaries on the website and discussing each other's versions in a conference. Such formative activities also help students build up the specifically online skills of discussion and group working they need, along with the (usually not too demanding) technical ability.

An example of the assessment design for an online course is included in Appendix 6(e). Unlike the other designs there, this is not a course in Literature. It is in fact a course in the UKOU's Masters in Open and Distance Education, first presented to 60 students worldwide in 1998 and subject to ongoing updating and revision. The students either plan to be or are already involved in the design and delivery of online courses. Notice that the types of coursework assessment included are various: seminar-type discussion subsequently incorporated in an essay; collaborative group work involving research (web search); creative work (designing a multimedia programme); and an extended essay encompassing all aspects of the course. The course ends with an examinable component.

POSTSCRIPT

We have argued in the chapter that, in assessing students, teachers of Literature should be aiming to devise regimes in which our criteria and standards of assessment are as clear and precise as possible and are applied consistently, without compromise to the exercise of our professional judgement. In a complex, problematising and creative discipline such as Literature, it is neither possible nor desirable to try to determine all the outcomes of students' learning in advance. We may feel strongly that the essay continues to be the best way to offer students the opportunity to argue a case at some length, and so both learn and demonstrate their growing understanding and skill. But this does not mean to say that teachers are unable to introduce other methods of assessment, especially in the context of (formative) coursework. We have seen that there are a number of possibilities here. However, whatever the task, timely and constructive feedback to students on their performance is vitally important for their learning. It would be a shame if such trends as modularisation and semesterisation were allowed to reduce these opportunities. In conclusion, we reiterate Gibbs and Simpson's belief (2004–5: 4) that 'standards will be raised by improving student learning rather than by better measurement of limited learning'.

Activity?

If you are setting out to design or reappraise an assessment regime, preferably with a group of colleagues, we suggest that you take as your starting point the Benchmark Statement's short list of assessment criteria (this chapter) *and* the longer lists of 'Subject Knowledge' and 'Subject-specific skills' (see Figures 4.2 and 4.4 in Chapter 4) and 'Generic and graduate skills' (Appendix 5 on the book's website).

Try devising assessment criteria for your literature programme as a whole. And then the standards required at two or three grades/degree classifications – first for specialist Literature students and, separately, for students in multidisciplinary programmes.

Try deriving from this the assessment criteria and standards for at least one course at each level of study. (If you carried out the activity at the end of Chapter 4 and re/designed a course or module, you might like to build on that work.) Will any of the courses be compulsory or optional? Will any include online elements?

Finally, work out how you could make all this transparent to students. What information will you need to give them, in what form(s)? And how will you try to make sure that the students fully understand the information and its implications for them?

Notes

1. Extensive reference is made to the Gibbs and Simpson article throughout the discussion. Written as part of a report of a large-scale project funded by the Higher Education Funding Council for England (HEFCE), it provides a review of the literature – including significant contributions made in the 1970s on both sides of the Atlantic, by such as Snyder (1971) on the 'hidden curriculum' and Miller and Parlett (1974) on 'cue-consciousness' – as well as recent research into assessment. We are grateful to the authors for permission to use their work.

2. Gibbs and Simpson (2004–5: 10) again: 'In the Course Experience Questionnaire (Ramsden, 1991), used extensively in Australia and elsewhere to evaluate the quality of courses, the questionnaire item that most clearly distinguishes the best and worst courses is "Teaching staff here normally give helpful feedback on how you are going" (Ramsden, 1992: 107).'

3. See: www.english.heacademy.ac.uk/resouces/topic/assessment/cmt/index. htm (accessed March–September 2004). In what follows frequent use is made of the English Subject Centre's website, which has a searchable index (www.english.heacademy.ac.uk). It offers an excellent review of newer methods of assessment, along with examples and case studies – as of many other aspects of the teaching of Literature. Many of the assessment case studies are derived from the work of the 'Assessment and The Expanded Text' consortium, based at Northumbria University (see the Bibliography at the end of the book under 'Websites').

4. See: www.anglia.ac.uk/speakwrite. The Speak-Write Project (HEFCE, Fund for the Development of Teaching and Learning), based at Anglia Polytechnic University 1998–2001, focused on oralcy and rhetorical skills in English studies and developed related material for use by teachers.

Key references

Gibbs, G. and Simpson, C. (2004–5) 'Conditions under which assessment supports students' learning', *Learning and Teaching in Higher Education*, 1(1): 3–31.

Knight, P. T. and Yorke, M. (2003) *Assessment, Learning and Employability*. Maidenhead: Open University Press.

Websites

Computer Assisted Assessment Centre, University of Luton at www.caacentre.ac.uk

UK Higher Education Academy English Subject Centre at www.english.hea.ac.uk

7

Evaluating teaching; future trends

Once the process of curriculum planning and course preparation is complete, what remains is of course to put all the plans into action and actually teach the programme. However, as we saw in Chapter 4, that is not quite the end of the story. As teaching proceeds and afterwards, faculty will be trying to find out how all the decisions they made work out in practice. Specifically, the Literature department (and no doubt university authorities) will be interested in such matters as whether the courses make up a coherent whole, expressing curriculum aims appropriately, whether the teaching-learning objectives are apt and achievable and what kind of progress the students make. And the staff responsible for teaching each of the programme's courses will want to know whether all the elements of the course are well designed in relation to its objectives, whether the syllabus is fruitful, the course stimulating and interesting to the students, whether the teaching methods and study activities are effective and whether the methods of student assessment are appropriate and fair. In other words, the design and conduct of our courses need to be evaluated in some way and, in light of the results of such evaluation, adjusted or revised. And so the course design process comes full cycle.

Evaluative inquiry is our subject in this short final chapter of the book. The chapter ends with some thoughts about the directions literature teaching might take in coming years, in the context of trends in the wider academy and internationally.

EVALUATING COURSES AND TEACHING

Here we focus on some of the issues surrounding the evaluation of courses and teaching as it affects academics as teachers. We saw earlier in the book that in many countries regimes for assuring quality of provision at the levels of the department and institution are centrally inspired and controlled: audit or inspection systems, with requirements for data of certain kinds to be gathered by university authorities from staff and students. For instance, universities in Australia and the UK routinely collect and analyse huge data sets of, variously, patterns of student enrolment and attendance, dropout rates, continuous assessment and exam pass rates, grade distribution patterns, employment destinations of graduates, and so on. And routinely students are surveyed to gauge their satisfaction with their courses and their teaching as well as with university facilities such as library, study accommodation, etc. We are not concerned here with this kind of mega-inquiry, which in any case will be carried out by educationalists, statisticians and other suitably qualified people according to whatever governmental and institutional policies prevail. Rather, we are interested in what teachers can do to satisfy themselves about the courses they offer and their own performance. In other words, we are interested in 'action research'.

Action research

This type of inquiry involves teachers' both investigating a course *in* action throughout, and reflecting *on* their own actions (see Schön, 1983 – and Bleakley's critique of Schön: ' "Reflective practice" is in danger of becoming a catch-all title for an ill-defined process' (Bleakley, 1999: 317)). It is formative inquiry, aimed at improving aspects of the course as it proceeds or next time round, in which teachers compare their aspirations and intentions to what actually happens on the ground. But of course what 'actually happens' can't simply be read off the surface of events. Things may not be quite as they seem, especially when the inquirer and the course designer/teacher are one and the same person. So, various strategies and techniques have been proposed for carrying out good research of this kind more objectively.[1] But it may be that in this context 'research' is too grand as a term for the approach teachers want to take to monitoring and improving what they do. A number of options are open to us, from the informal all the way to full-blown investigation.

Self-monitoring

Being observant about how students are engaging with the course texts and teaching methods, what goes on in the classroom or online and the students' progress in assignment work and so on, and mulling over what we might do better, is at the informal end of the range of possibilities. And these are things that surely all of us do while going about our business, as intelligent people who care about the quality and effectiveness of our teaching and our students' learning. But as an aid to such critical reflection, or in order to conduct it on a more objective and secure footing, some teachers find it helpful to go one step further: for example, to keep a journal in which they record the main events of the session (or week, month) along with their thoughts about these things and any ideas they have for future action. We are not talking here only about recording teaching-learning problems or 'failures'. It is equally important to record strategies and events that worked well, and to reflect on the reasons for their success, so that they can be replicated with confidence.

Beginning teachers may find this idea particularly helpful, and even more so if they can team up with a Literature colleague, or better still a group of them, to talk over some of the issues that emerge. Often, teaching is not discussed much in the staff room, unlike one's research, so being open about these matters no doubt takes a bit of courage to begin with. Indeed, it may be foolhardy or downright impossible in departments where the fiction is maintained that teaching is not only 'no problem' but is relatively unimportant, and where any attempt to discuss it is taken to reveal the academic's failings and unworthiness for tenure or promotion. Sadly, this happens. However, to us, the advantages to be gained from a group of people discussing the issues at the heart of their work – especially people with a similar, and cooperative, job to do – are blindingly obvious. A perhaps less obvious but even more valuable outcome in the long run is that the community of Literature teachers may develop a shared 'language' for talk about their pedagogic practice that is both apt and enabling.

Peer review

In departments in which teaching is rightly valued colleagues may be able to enlist each others' assistance somewhat more formally, as reviewers of proposed course designs (syllabus, teaching-learning methods and assessment practices) who can offer critique and helpful advice before a course starts. Once it is underway, a sympathetic colleague may then act as an occasional observer in the classroom, recording his or her observations of particular incidents and discussing them subsequently with the teacher. This is a convincing way of having one's own teaching strategies and habits uncovered, and a more productive way of learning about teaching in general than being offered injunctions or prescriptions about it by disinterested parties. Examining video recordings made of teaching sessions can achieve similar results, especially when they are viewed and discussed by the teacher in the company of others.

In saying here that these are rather more formal roles for colleagues, no suggestion of surveillance is in any way intended. Subjecting a course and teaching to scrutiny by colleagues is a way of making reflection on one's own activities a more objective and fruitful process, and it depends upon trust. Any hint of 'evidence' being gathered or of management's interest in this process would of course scupper the very possibility of openness – and of acquiring the insights into teaching that can benefit all concerned.

Student review

Quite apart from information that the department and institution will gather from students, teachers themselves may well want to check whether their perceptions of the course design, of their teaching and the students' learning, are similar to those of the students involved (and of a colleague-observer's, if this has been solicited). Such comparisons between the views of different parties is known as 'triangulation', a process that yields a more rounded and hence reliable view of whatever is being investigated.

To gather the students' views, teachers may ask them to complete a short *questionnaire* (anonymously) about their experience of the course at or near its end, whether in class, online or in their own time. The teacher may ask which parts of the syllabus the students most enjoyed studying and think they learned from well (and vice versa), which teaching methods/sessions they found most interesting and helpful, what they thought of the essay and other course assignments and so on. Depending on the size of the group, the questions may be 'open' (students write in their answers) or 'closed' (e.g. 'yes/no' answers or ticking one response among several given options). Open questions have the advantage of allowing students to raise the issues that matter most to them, to illustrate and give reasons for their views. But, as this suggests, far too much information may be generated, or information that is too diffuse for the teacher to analyse comfortably when the class is large. And because the students have to write their responses, this is a time-consuming task which they may complete only perfunctorily or not at all. Coded questionnaires of course take less time both to complete and analyse, but although they allow the teacher to sum the students' 'votes' they do not yield much information beyond that. And the teacher receives answers only to the questions he or she has thought to ask. So a questionnaire that combines closed *and* open questions may be the most satisfactory option.

Another way of canvassing students' views is to hold a *discussion* about the course among a representative group, a 'focus group', either face to face or in computer conference. In such discussion it is obviously easier to follow up an observation or criticism and really to get to the bottom of any perceived difficulties. And groups will, in the nature of things, tend to reach a consensus – or, at least, any major differences of opinion will be clear enough. But the main drawback is that the students are identifiable so they may be reluctant to be honest about their experiences and judgements. A way round this is to have someone other than the teacher conduct the discussion, but this person will not be as familiar with the course as the teacher and may not pursue the issues that would be of most interest to the teacher. In any event, if the discussion is in person it must either be tape recorded or notes must be scribbled down as fast and as comprehensively as possible while it proceeds; a computer conference has the advantage of providing a transcript. And analysing the outcomes will be time-consuming.

Conflicting messages

But what if on some issues no consensus emerges from the students' responses in questionnaires or discussion, or they even conflict? What if, on reflection, teacher A does not agree with teacher B's judgement about some aspect of her teaching they are reviewing together on video tape? How does the teacher decide which views to accept, which to act upon? The notion that a teacher may not agree with another's perceptions of an event gives us a clue here, for that disagreement implies certain criteria of judgement. That is, teacher A has *reasons* for her disagreement with teacher B, and these reasons are most likely to be based on her broad (even if unarticulated) philosophy of education and the teaching aims that flow from it. To take an obvious example, if teacher A believes that teaching should be learner-centred she is unlikely to be persuaded by teacher B that it is a waste of everyone's time asking the students to discuss together a matter about which they know very little. Quite rightly, what teachers do in this situation is accept feedback and advice that accords with the educational beliefs that guide their actions, or at least does not conflict with them.

The corollary of this is that it behoves practising teachers to be aware of and to be able to articulate their underlying beliefs. What evaluation then reveals is any differences between teachers' 'espoused theories' (what they think they believe) and their 'theories-in-action' – what they actually seem to be doing in practice (Argyris and Schön, 1974). In this connection, a (suitably adapted) 'cycle' of monitoring and reflection such as that proposed by Kolb (1984) may recommend itself: do some teaching; reflect on the experience/gather others' views about it; *conceptualise it*, including reading the relevant educational literature; plan future strategies . . . and so back again to the beginning of the cycle. But perhaps this sounds like a lot of effort – yet more planned, purposeful activity on the teacher's part that begins before a course starts, continues throughout it and, seemingly, never ends – when already the academic's job (teaching, research, administration *and* service to the wider university and society) is overwhelming. So, teachers might be inclined to ask, why go to all that trouble?

Professionalism

Technical professionalism

There are several possible answers to this question, some of them closely related to the contemporary situation of the academy. As we have seen, widely and increasingly academics are being held accountable for the quality of their teaching by funding bodies, by governments and their agencies. In this situation, as George and Cowan (1999: 2) put it, 'It is to the advantage of academics to retain . . . involvement in the evaluation of their activity, and to ensure continuing respect for their evaluations. They are more likely to do so if they engage in the process rigorously and from a basis of sound and objective self-criticism.' Furthermore, from 2006/7 the UK government intends to introduce a system of accreditation for new university teachers, in accordance with certain 'national professional standards' which are presently being devised and will eventually be applied to all academic staff (DfES, 2003: §4.14). At this stage it looks as if initial accreditation will be based largely on portfolio evidence of the teachers' work over a period, which will include formative evaluation of aspects of their teaching along with evidence of reflective self-criticism. In short, as professional teachers we are 'required' to evaluate and try to improve our performance in some way or another.

But surely there are better reasons for attending seriously to our role as teachers? And a truncated, technical or 'performative' professionalism, in which our purposes and values as teachers may appear to play little part, cannot be the most satisfactory conception of what it means to be professional.

Commitment to students

By contrast, it might be said that we should bother to be self-critical and to educate ourselves about teaching because, as teachers, we are necessarily committed to students (the direct objects of our teaching) and their learning: to their learning well and to their well-being. Further, since the contexts in which students study (higher education systems) have changed quite radically in recent years, and continue to change – especially as regards the curriculum and the range of new e-teaching methods available to us – we are of necessity experimenting to a large extent, and we need to know how well we are doing it. For these reasons alone we may want to keep investigating and trying to improve our courses and teaching.

Vocation

But, of course, there is more than this to be said about the question of professionalism. Mills and Huber (2005: 20–2), for example, point out that the 'shifting relationship' between expertise and teaching seen as a vocation is a complex one which 'has implications for the status of academics and for the teaching of the disciplines'. Lately, the shift has been away from 'social trustee professionalism' to 'expert professionalism' (Brint, 1994: 11) and, in this move, the technical aspects of professionalism have been split off from the moral aspects 'with [the] moral and non-market aspects ... becoming steadily less important'. The authors continue:

> ... most [academics] would imagine themselves as experts in their own field, with all the command of disciplinary knowledge, practices and dispositions that this involves. Yet they would also wish to invoke a sense of professionalism as a moral vocation to challenge any move towards standardization.

> (Mills and Huber, 2005: 21)

So, educators must insist that disciplinary purposes and values are at the heart of their professionalism properly understood. One size does not fit all, in this matter as in many others. And, in general, being professional in the role of teacher means being 'reflective, imaginative and scholarly' about teaching one's discipline (p. 20). What the authors promote, then, is a scholarship of teaching and learning in the different disciplines. This, they argue, may be one way of 'side-stepping the tensions that surround the politicization of learning and teaching policies in the UK, and between education and the disciplines in the US'[2] (p. 22).

The Scholarship of Teaching and Learning (SoTL) movement

Described by Mills and Huber as a nascent movement, the SoTL is nonetheless burgeoning – the founding Council includes members from Australia, Canada, New Zealand, South Africa and the UK as well as the USA, and a first, well attended, international conference was held in October 2004 in Bloomington, Indiana. Perhaps the SoTL appeals so widely for the reasons these authors suggest: after all, who better than discipline-based academics to explore and evaluate their own discipline's pedagogy? As they characterise it:

> The [SoTL] invites disciplinary faculty to approach their teaching and their students' learning with a sense of 'problem' in mind ... This may involve a sense that one's pedagogy is not working, or that one would like to try something new, but it may also involve 'problems' of a more descriptive or visionary sort: what, in fact, are my students learning, or what kinds of learning might be desirable, possible?
>
> (Mills and Huber, 2005: 23)

Bass sets out some of the movement's central concerns:

> Changing the status of the problem in teaching from terminal remediation to ongoing investigation is precisely what the scholarship of teaching is all about. How might we make the problematization of teaching a matter of communal discourse? How might we think of teaching practice, and the evidence of student learning, as problems to be investigated, analysed, represented and debated?
>
> (Bass, 1999: Introduction, para. 1)

No particular methods of such investigation are preferred. They may include desk work (literature analysis), questionnaire and interview studies, participant-observation or other ethnographic methods (for example, see Gunn, 2003), scrutiny of students' written work or of video/audio records of classroom interaction (as in Jones et al., 2005), and so on.

The movement emerged out of the Carnegie Foundation for the Advancement of Teaching's long interest in higher education pedagogy, and is promoted by the Carnegie Academy for the Scholarship of Teaching and Learning (CASTL). Its intellectual foundations are in Boyer's distinction (based on work by Eugene Rice – see Rice (2002) for a retrospective account) between four forms of scholarship integral to academic practice: the scholarship of discovery (research), of teaching ('transmitting, transforming and extending knowledge'), of integration and of application (Boyer, 1990: 24), and in the work of Shulman (1997), who identifies and characterises 'pedagogical content knowledge'. Subsequently, Huber and others developed the notion of distinct disciplinary 'styles' and ideas, which, though distinct, may nevertheless be 'traded' across discipline boundaries to everyone's advantage (Huber and Morreale, 2002). The Huber and Morreale volume comprises chapters by authors in different disciplines 'doing' the SoTL in their field (see, in particular, Salvatori and Donohue on English studies: and see Hutchings (2000), also a collection of papers).

A number of researchers and educators who share these concerns and were already exploring similar ground have recently been attracted to the SoTL movement: in the UK for instance, see Healey (2000) on scholarship, Jenkins (1996) and Jenkins et al. (2003), the latter on relationships between teaching and research. In the past year the *AHHE* journal has published three such papers: Jones et al. (2005), which well exemplifies the kind of investigation that can contribute to our understanding of teaching and learning Literature; Knights (2005) which illuminates a 'crossover area' between discipline-based research and a scholarship of teaching in Literature; and Booth (2004) on the scholarship of teaching in History.

Teaching and research
As reference to Jenkins's and Knights's work suggests, the teaching-research nexus is of particular interest to these scholars. On one hand, the SoTL movement clearly strives to promote the importance of

teaching in the academy, as a corrective to the great emphasis placed on the highly (some would say over-) valued and rewarded activity of specialist disciplinary research. On the other hand, it appears to want to claim the SoTL as *a form of* research, and as valid and productive a form as any other. In any event, it certainly tries to be clearer about relationships between teaching and research. Where this relationship is marked, it is commonly conceived in one of three main ways. That is, teaching may be:

- *research led* – the content of the curriculum is based on the research interests of the teaching staff,[3] with an emphasis on students understanding research findings rather than processes of research;
- *research oriented* – the curriculum places as much emphasis on understanding the processes by which knowledge is produced as on learning the knowledge made; skills of inquiry are taught and practised;
- *research based* – in large part the curriculum is designed around inquiry-based activities, with research processes integrated in the student learning activities (for example, problem-based learning: see Hutchings and O'Rourke (2002) for this approach to teaching Literature).

To these a fourth conception may be added (i.e. the SoTL):

- *research informed* – teaching draws consciously on systematic inquiry into the very processes of teaching and learning.

(Adapted from Healey, 2003.)

However, it seems to us that this last conception is different in kind from the other three, in that those others all make reference to curriculum and content (the 'what' of teaching) – that is to say, to the academic's disciplinary knowledge and expertise – whereas the fourth refers to processes of teaching-learning, the 'how' of it. Traditionally, academics are much more comfortable grappling with the former than the last – which is pretty much SoTL's point. So, we may ask, what might persuade academics-as-teachers to take processes of teaching and learning more seriously? The answer, according to Diamond and Adam (2004), is nothing short of reconceptualising scholarship 'for the 21st century' and associated institutional change.

Scholarship redefined

Since around 1990 Robert Diamond has undertaken a number of large-scale inquiries into relationships between scholarship, professional service and academic reward systems in US universities, among faculty (of all disciplines), disciplinary associations and academic administrators, on behalf of the American Association for Higher Education among other bodies (Diamond and Adam, 2004: 35–6). The main problem he unearthed concerns the very narrow definitions of scholarship that operate in the academy, which 'influence faculty priorities and engagement' (p. 34), and a corresponding lack of recognition of other, important, aspects of the academic's work which *also* have the characteristics of traditional scholarship. Consequently, the authors conclude:

> *If we can focus on the qualities of scholarly work and use an approach that is accepted by the academic disciplines, we may have a definition of scholarship for the 21st century . . . what we propose as a model . . . has the advantage of addressing both the product and the process of scholarly work.*
>
> (p. 37)

The 'Criteria for Scholarly Activity' that emerged from all these studies and negotiations are as follows.

- Requires a high level of discipline-related expertise.
- Conducted in a scholarly manner with clear goals, adequate preparation and appropriate methodology.
- The work and its results are appropriately documented and disseminated. This reporting includes reflective critique addressing the significance of the work, the process of inquiry and what was learned.
- Has significance beyond the individual context.
- Breaks new ground or is innovative.
- Can be replicated or elaborated.
- The work – both product and process – is reviewed and judged to be meritorious and significant by a panel of peers.
- It will be the responsibility of the academic unit or department to determine if the activity or work falls within the priorities of the department, school/college, discipline and institution.

(Diamond and Adam, 2003: 37–8)

'Interestingly', the authors add, 'some of the studies or articles published in recognized journals today may not meet the criteria just listed.'

However, when these conditions are met, they argue, *whatever the focus of the work* it is scholarly and should count as such in the institution's reward/promotion system. Thus 'valuing work based on dollars generated or numbers of publications accumulated will be replaced with institutional guidelines stressing significance of work' and 'it will be possible, perhaps for the first time, for faculty priorities to come together with institutional missions and vision'. Such an inclusive definition of scholarly work would encompass both research as traditionally understood *and*, for example, the scholarship of teaching and learning.

Conclusion

Discussion of a *scholarship* of teaching and learning has of course taken us well beyond the much more modest aims with which we began this chapter: to suggest effective and efficient ways in which all teachers can monitor, evaluate and try to improve their course designs and teaching practices. As we remarked, this process completes the curriculum development 'loop' – for the first time that is, since teachers will want to satisfy themselves that any changes they make to their courses as a result really are improvements. By contrast, the formal and systematic kind of inquiry that the SoTL movement proposes will not be an attractive proposition to all teachers, although all of us should surely be aware of the scholarly work that has been carried out in our discipline or field. But we would say that the movement's emphasis on recognising and rewarding the full range of scholarly activity that goes on in our universities is a meaningful and overdue corrective. The kind of institutional change that Huber and Diamond call for would open up much wider possibilities for our work as academics, offering opportunities for individuals to be rewarded for putting their knowledge and talents to best use and pursuing the interests that best express their and their discipline/ department's concerns. A view of professionalism related to the academic vocation – grounded in the discipline or field, in its purposes, values and scholarly activities – is, we would say, far preferable to the notion of 'expert' professionalism, in which teachers are required to perform their work according to generic prescriptions and predefined standards shorn of academic significance.

TRENDS

We end this chapter, and indeed the book, with a brief discussion of the direction higher education seems to be taking and how this might impact on the discipline. As the term 'trends' suggests, we are here extrapolating from observations made throughout the book. But rather than simply repeat these observations in summary form, we will present instead some issues and unifying questions posed by a major international conference on the Humanities sponsored by the Social Sciences and Humanities Research Council of Canada.

Central concerns

At the conference 'Alternative Wor(l)ds: The Humanities in 2010' (Demers, 2002), over 100 delegates from all constituencies in more than 30 Canadian universities, along with representatives of the US National Endowment for the Humanities, the MLA and the (then) UK Arts and Humanities Research Board, spent their time considering questions put to them by a panel who had read and consulted widely beforehand in order to identify a set of central themes for discussion. These questions, then, represent the concerns of a large and varied body of humanists. Adapting Demers's account, they may be re-presented under three main headings: the nature and purposes of humanities disciplines; new paradigms and fields; new methods of teaching and learning.

Disciplinary purposes

Discussion about the nature and purposes of the Humanities focused on this question (Demers, 2002: 18):

Who should set the academic agenda for the universities?

The issues that arose and were explored included many of the 'external pressures' discussed throughout this book. Almost every-where the academic agenda is tending to be set by others than academics themselves, whether they like it or not. In many countries the 'needs' of the economy are the pre-eminently shaping force, which has led to wider participation in higher education/massification and an accompanying decline in resource for it, and to an emphasis on the teaching and learning of marketable skills. While increasing governmental control over the higher education sector as a whole is a far less marked outcome in North America than in Australia, South Africa and the UK, greater 'accountability' is a noticeable trend everywhere. And public funding for research into teaching and learning follows this external agenda, tending to focus on student recruitment and retention (e.g. students' transition from schooling and, via 'study skills' teaching, their preparedness for university), on students' acquisition of marketable skills and their employability upon graduation. In this situation, humanities academics are of course asking themselves whether recent department mergers and closures are driven solely by this agenda or whether there may indeed be growing scepticism among the public about the value of their disciplines. In any event, the prognosis hardly seems encouraging. Unless, that is, the Humanities can and will accommodate to the external agenda?

New fields and paradigms

> What are the elements that make a humanities/liberal arts degree important today – and attractive to the student population? . . . What new models for . . . the humanities should we examine?

On an accommodating view of things, the skills honed in study of the Humanities – skills of analysis, interpretation, evaluation, synthesis and communication in speech and writing – are both widely needed in and transferable to the workplace. It would suggest examination of issues-, problem- or practice-based curriculum models and, in general, a broader educational offering (e.g. multidisciplinary, modular) rather than discipline-specific study. In this connection, a 'cultural studies' umbrella, or study of Literature combined with creative writing and modern cultural forms such as film, television or media, might be preferred. As we saw, curricula such as these are in fact popular among students in the UK and, as we shall see in a moment, the possibilities for study of postcolonial and world literatures may receive a fillip from a perhaps unexpected quarter.

New teaching-learning and assessment methods

> What new methods of teaching and learning in the humanities should we examine?

Continuing to pursue this line of thought, our students' use and mastery of ICTs would of course be seen as essential. Even in conventional universities, 'blended' teaching-learning methods would become the norm – that is, traditional methods combined with e-tuition and e-learning (the kinds of media and method discussed in Chapter 5 – DVD and multimedia CD-ROM, databases, the Internet, digital resources such as e-books, text-search software, and e-mail discussion, computer conferencing, online collaborative work, resource-based learning . . .). We might also expect greater emphasis on group work and presentation skills in preparation for what is required in many jobs. Methods of assessing students' work would need to become correspondingly broader, to include portfolio and even practice-based modes, self- and peer-review, and assessment of group work.

'No change'

But, if humanities educators reject the idea of accommodating the external agenda, then:

> How can [they] build and promote a shared vision of the contribution of a humanities education to students, employers, governments and the general public?

In other words, assuming that as humanities educators we can agree among ourselves, how could we convince all these parties of the value to them of *our* conception of what we offer? We will not repeat here ideas about unity of purpose and direction discussed in Chapter 1 of the book but, perforce, leave this important question open for the moment. In any case, there is one development – currently not much remarked upon within the academy – that just might cast the concerns discussed here in a different mould.

The trend towards globalisation

The all-encompassing trend we wish to draw attention to is the 'globalisation' of higher education, in the context of the advent of GATS – the 1995 General Agreement on Trade in Services. While we may all be familiar with the notion of liberalisation and globalisation in trade, these ideas are fairly new as applied to services. The Agreement is operated by the World Trade Organisation (under the auspices of the UN), the 145 member countries of which account for 97 per cent of world trade:

GATS is the first multinational agreement [between member countries] to provide legally enforceable rights to trade in all services. It has a built-in commitment to continuous liberalization through periodic negotiations. And it is the world's first multinational agreement on investment, since it covers not just cross-border trade but every possible means of supplying a service, including the right to set up a commercial presence in the export market.

(World Trade Organisation Secretariat, 2002)

Education is among the services concerned. And, according to Hawkridge (2005: 7), 'In the medium- to long-term, GATS has serious organisational, cultural, legal, political and economic implications for . . . education.'

Under the Agreement, countries are expected to file requests for liberalisation of services in other countries and also to offer to liberalise their own services. So far, the USA has requested access to higher education, adult education, training and educational testing services in all countries and, along with Australia and New Zealand, is pressing for full liberalisation of the education market. The UK and Canada, however, have declared that they are not offering access to their publicly-funded education services. As yet many countries have not made their position on GATS known, though they will have to before long. And the stakes are extremely high for countries that export education (that is, the richer western countries): in 2000, for example, exports of educational services were worth over $10 billion to the USA, $3.7 billion to the UK, $2.1 billion to Australia and $0.8 billion to Canada (Larsen et al., 2002). These countries are no doubt planning to reap far greater rewards once the Agreement is fully underway.

Some internationalisation of education, then, seems inevitable and is indeed underway – although whether the effects in exporting countries will be felt right across the higher education system, will be more or less confined to distance education institutions and some existing 'flagship' universities or will mainly give rise to new, commercial forms of higher education is a matter of conjecture. In any case, such globalisation is predicated on extensive use of ICTs. When an institution has these technologies at its disposal it is of course possible to attract and educate students from locations anywhere in the world, provided the necessary technology is available or can be made available there, without the trouble and expense of setting up satellite campuses in those locations. This might be an attractive proposition for many universities in a situation of inadequate public funding for higher education: they may want to seek new global markets to maintain their income or, in the case of distance teaching universities, to achieve greater economies of scale. As Hawkridge (2005: 2) remarks:

> *Proponents [of globalisation] see knowledge as a commodity and education as a service, to be traded globally, and students everywhere as customers whose needs can and must be met through globalisation, which is a creative gale.*

And they would claim positive advantages for it: enrichment of the curriculum, wide provision of high-quality courses and scarce staff expertise made available to students in many countries. Indeed, perhaps some of these considerations underlie MIT's decision to make its 'courseware' freely available (OpenCourseWare at MIT (US): http://ocw.mit.edu/index.html). But globalisation of higher education has many detractors too, who see it as more of a destructive than a creative force.

Some regard cognition in e-learning as different from that in embodied forms of education and inferior to it (see Dreyfus, 2001, and also critique of his argument in Blake, 2002). Others fear that global education will tend to impose common curricula, teaching-learning methods and indeed the English language, ultimately reducing cultural diversity (see Chambers, 2002b; Ess, 2001). Furthermore, it is seen as incompatible with social objectives in many countries (Stromquist and Monkman, 2000): 'nowhere are the poor able to benefit from services they cannot pay for' (Hawkridge, 2005: 2). Finally, the 'nightmare scenario' of a takeover of higher education by private companies is said to threaten us all: corporations such as Microsoft, publishers like McGraw-Hill and Pearson, and private for-profit universities.

Interestingly, this threat is sometimes taken as a reason for publicly-funded universities to enter the global marketplace as soon as possible in order to do the job properly, despite any misgivings they may have. In that process, it is thought that mergers or collaborations between institutions might be needed, producing some reconfiguration of higher education in the provider countries. And, paradoxically, the greater emphasis on cultural and intercultural issues that would ensue might be expected to offer extra business for the Humanities.

In short, if a public higher education institution decided to enter the global market then some quite radical changes might be implied.

- *Change to curricula and the contents of courses in order to accommodate students from other countries and cultures.* In Literature, this might accelerate moves towards redefining the discipline, from a national/culture-based conception (English, Canadian, Australian literature, etc.) to something like Literatures in English or post-colonial literatures – accompanied by the teaching of correspondingly wider literary traditions and texts. (And, in this connection, see Cornwell, 2006.)
- *Changes in staff recruitment.* With ever greater emphasis on ICTs and e-tuition, one might expect not only compulsory training in this kind of teaching to be introduced for all faculty, but also recruitment of educational technologists, library and technical staff in greater numbers and much closer working relationships between them and faculty. Indeed, 'learning design' might tend to be taken out of discipline-based academics' hands to a greater degree than many expect or wish.
- *More stringent quality assurance measures.* These would be of the essence in a competitive global market in order to attract large numbers of overseas students, so one might expect government to exercise even tighter controls over institutions and they, in turn, over academic departments and individual employees.
- *Commercialisation/standardisation.* The tendency for universities to be treated as businesses would become a reality – they would indeed *be* global businesses, presumably run primarily on economic principles. So if the Literature department (and any other discipline or field) failed to recruit students in sufficient numbers then presumably it would be merged with other departments or axed. That is, unless these businesses preferred to sacrifice public funding altogether and become private institutions – a move that some 'premier' UK universities are already threatening to make, with the intention of removing themselves from government regulation precisely in order to reinstate the educational principles they see as being compromised at present. But whether, as businesses, they would be successful in this is debatable.

Seen in this context, for Literature (and the Humanities more widely) to adopt a position of 'no change' is a non-starter. As we have seen throughout the book, many such changes are either already underway or the groundwork for them is laid. But, whether we find these ideas exciting or depressing, we should remember that they are only possibilities for the future of the academy. What we may be able to do – as so often before – is to bend them to *our* purposes. And for that we need to be clear about, and in agreement about, what our purposes as educators are.

This takes us right back to the beginning of the book. Ideas discussed in Chapter 1, regarding unity of purpose and a 'speaking with one voice', only gain added urgency. The question that should concern us now is: are we prepared to take this challenge to the Humanities seriously?

Notes

1. We will not go into these strategies in great detail here. George and Cowan (1999) discuss a range of examples in different academic settings, many of which may be adapted to literature teaching. Parlett and Hamilton (1972) offer a basis in theory; Angelo and Cross (1993) and Calder (1994) suggest a variety of techniques. Also see Hatfield (1995) and Hillier (2002).
2. Prior to this account of professionalism the authors discuss the rise of 'faculty development' in the USA (its UK equivalent being 'staff/educational development'), and reasons for the relatively low status that 'education' has among discipline-based academics – a fascinating discussion but tangential to this theme.
3. Whether or not the curriculum is *based* on staff's research interests, in Chapter 4 (under 'Normal provision') we saw that, in the UK at least, staff's research interests are certainly a major influence on the curriculum (Halcrow Group et al., 2003: 55).

Key references

George, J. and Cowan, J. (1999) *A Handbook of Techniques for Formative Evaluation: Mapping the Student's Learning Experience*. London: Kogan Page.

Huber, M. T. and Morreale, P. (eds) (2002) *Disciplinary Styles in the Scholarship of Teaching and Learning: Exploring Common Ground*. Washington, DC: American Association for Higher Education and the Carnegie Foundation for the Advancement of Teaching.

Schön, D. A. (1983) *The Reflective Practitioner*. New York: Basic Books.

Websites

World Trade Organisation Secretariat (2002) *Trading into the Future*, at: http://www.wto.org

Bibliography

Agathocleus, T. and Dean, A. (eds) (2002) *Teaching Literature: A Companion.* Basingstoke: Palgrave Macmillan.

Angelil-Carter, S. (ed.) (1998) *Access to Success. Literacy in Academic Contexts.* Cape Town: University of Cape Town Press.

Angelo, T. A. and Cross, K. P. (1993) *Classroom Assessment Techniques,* 2nd edn. San Francisco: Jossey-Bass.

Argyris, C. and Schön, D. A. (1974) *Theory in Practice: Increasing Professional Effectiveness.* San Francisco: Jossey-Bass.

Bakhtin, M. (1981) *The Dialogic Imagination.* Austin, TX: University of Texas Press.

Ballard, B. and Clanchy, J. (1988) 'Literacy in the university: an "anthropological" approach', in G. Taylor, B. Ballard, V. Beasley, H. K. Bock, J. Clanchy and P. Nightingale (eds), *Literacy by Degrees.* Milton Keynes: SRHE/Open University Press, pp. 7–23.

Barnett, R. (2003) *Beyond all Reason: Living with Ideology in the University.* Buckingham: SRHE/Open University Press.

Barnett, R. and Coate, K. (2005) *Engaging the Curriculum in Higher Education.* Maidenhead: SRHE/Open University Press.

Barrow, R. (2004) 'Language and character', *Arts and Humanities in Higher Education,* 3(3): 267–79.

Barry, P. (1995) *Beginning Theory: An Introduction to Literary and Cultural Theory.* Manchester: Manchester University Press.

Barry, P. (2003) *English in Practice: In Pursuit of English Studies.* London: Arnold.

Bass, R. (1999) 'The scholarship of teaching: what's the problem?', *Inventio: Creative Thinking about Learning and Teaching,* 1(1). Available at: www.doit.gmu.edu/Archives/feb98/randybass.htm.

Becher, T. and Trowler, P. (2001) *Academic Tribes and Territories: Intellectual Enquiry and the Cultures of Disciplines,* 2nd edn. Buckingham: SRHE/Open University Press.

Bernstein, B. (1975) *Class, Codes and Control: Towards a Theory of Educational Transmission,* Vol. 3. London: Routledge & Kegan Paul.

Berry, W. (1983) *Standing by Words.* San Francisco: North Point Press.

Bérubé, M. (2003) 'The utility of the arts and humanities', *Arts and Humanities in Higher Education,* 2(1): 23–40.

Bérubé, M. and Nelson, C. (eds) (1995) *Higher Education Under Fire: Politics, Economics and the Crisis of the Humanities*. New York and London: Routledge.

Birkerts, S. (1994) *Gutenberg Elegies*. New York: Random House.

Birkerts, S. (1996) *Tolstoy's Dictaphone: Technology and the Muse*. St Paul, MN: Graywolf Press.

Bizell, P. (1982) 'Cognition, convention, and certainty: what we need to know about writing', *RE TEXT*, 3(3): 213–44.

Blake, N. (2000) 'Paralogy, validity claims and the politics of knowledge: Habermas, Lyotard and higher education', in P. A. Dhillon and P. Standish (eds), *Lyotard: Just Education*. London: Routledge, pp. 54–72.

Blake, N. (2002) 'Hubert Dreyfus on distance education: relays of educational embodiment', *Educational Philosophy and Theory*, 34(4): 379–85. (Symposium on Hubert Dreyfus's 'On the Internet'.)

Blake, N. and Standish, P. (eds) (2000) *Enquiries at the Interface: Philosophical Problems of Online Education*. Oxford: Blackwell.

Blake, N., Smeyers, P., Smith, R. and Standish, P. (1998) *Thinking Again: Education after Postmodernism*. Westport, CT: Bergin & Garvey.

Bleakley, A. (1999) 'From reflective practice to holistic reflexivity', *Studies in Higher Education*, 24(3): 315–30.

Bleich, D. (2001) 'The materiality of language and the pedagogy of exchange', *Pedagogy: Critical Approaches to Teaching Literature, Language, Composition, and Culture*, 1(1): 117–41.

Bligh, D. (1998 [1971]) *What's the Use of Lectures?*, 5th edn. Exeter: Intellect.

Booth, A. (2004) 'Rethinking the scholarly: developing the scholarship of teaching in history', *Arts and Humanities in Higher Education*, 3(3): 247–66.

Boughey, C. (2003) 'From equity to efficiency: access to higher education in South Africa', *Arts and Humanities in Higher Education*, 2(1): 65–71.

Bourdieu, P. (1988) *Homo Academicus*. Cambridge: Polity Press.

Boyer, E. (1990) *Scholarship Reconsidered: Priorities of the Professoriate*. Princeton, NJ: Carnegie Foundation for the Advancement of Teaching.

Brint, S. (1994) *In an Age of Experts: The Changing Role of Professionals in Politics and Public Life*. Princeton, NJ: Princeton University Press.

Brookfield, S. D. (1986) *Understanding and Facilitating Adult Learning*. Buckingham: Open University Press.

Bruner, J. (1983) *Child's Talk: Learning to Use Language*. Oxford: Oxford University Press.

Bruner, J. (1986) *Actual Minds, Possible Worlds*. Cambridge, MA and London: Harvard University Press.

Bruner, J. (1996a) *The Culture of Education*. Cambridge, MA: Harvard University Press.

Bruner, J. (1996b) 'Frames for thinking: ways of making meaning', in D. R. Olson and N. Torrance (eds), *Modes of Thought: Explorations in Culture and Cognition*. Cambridge, New York and Melbourne: Cambridge University Press, pp. 93–105.

Calder, J. (1994) *Programme Evaluation and Quality*. London: Kogan Page.

Chambers, E. A. (1992) 'Work-load and the quality of student learning', *Studies in Higher Education*, 17(2): 141–53.

Chambers, E. A. (ed.) (2000) 'Computers in humanities teaching and research: dispatches from the disciplines', *Computers and the Humanities*, 34(3): Special Issue.

Chambers, E. A. (2001) 'Critical humanism', in E. A. Chambers (ed.), *Contemporary Themes in Humanities Higher Education*. Dordrecht: Kluwer Academic Publishers, pp. 1–20.

Chambers, E. A. (2002a) 'Understanding students' learning "from the inside"', in T. Evans (ed.), *Research in Distance Education 5*. Geelong: Deakin University Press. Available at: http://www.deakin.edu.au/education/RIPVET/RIDE_Papers/.

Chambers, E. A. (2002b) 'Cultural imperialism or pluralism? Cross-cultural electronic teaching in the humanities', *Arts and Humanities in Higher Education*, 2(3): 249–64.

Chambers, E. A. and Northedge, A. (1997) *The Arts Good Study Guide*. Milton Keynes: Open University.

Channon, G. (2000) 'Tailor-made or off-the-peg? Virtual courses in the humanities', *Computers and the Humanities*, 34(3): 255–64. (Special Issue: 'Computers in Humanities Teaching and Research: Dispatches from the Disciplines'.)

Coffin, C., Curry, M. J., Goodman, S., Hewings, A., Lillis, T. M. and Swann, J. (2003) *Teaching Academic Writing: A Toolkit for Higher Education*. London and New York: Routledge.

Cornwell, G. (2006, forthcoming) 'On the "Africanisation" of English Studies in South Africa', *Arts and Humanities in Higher Education*, 5(2).

Crème, P. and Lea, M. (2003 [1997]) *Writing at University: A Guide for Students*, 2nd edn. Buckingham: Open University Press.

Crowley, S. (1999) *Composition in the University: Historical and Polemical Essays*. Pittsburgh: Pennsylvania University Press.

Crowther, J., Hamilton, M. and Tett, L. (eds) (2001) *Powerful Literacies*. Leicester: NIACE.

Dahlgren, L. O. and Marton, F. (1978) 'Students' conceptions of subject matter', *Studies in Higher Education*, 3(1): 25–35.

Delbanco, A. (1999) 'The decline and fall of literature', *New York Review of Books*, 4, November: 32–8.

Demers, P. (2002) 'Horizon of possibilities: a Canadian perspective on the humanities', *Arts and Humanities in Higher Education*, 1(1): 11–26.

DfES (Department for Education and Skills) (2003) *The Future of Higher Education* (White Paper). London: DfES. Available at: http://www.dfes.gov.uk/hegateway/hereform/index.cfm.

Diamond, R. M. and Adam, B. E. (2004) 'Balancing institutional, disciplinary and faculty priorities with public and social needs: defining scholarship for the 21st century', *Arts and Humanities in Higher Education*, 3(1): 29–40.

Donohue, C. (2004) 'Writing and teaching the disciplines in France: current conversations and connections', *Arts and Humanities in Higher Education*, 3(1): 59–79.

Dreyfus, H. (2001) *On the Internet*. New York: Routledge.

Duguid, S. (1984) 'The humanities and higher education', *Canadian Journal of Higher Education*, XIV(1): 41–58.

Eaglestone, R. (2002) *Doing English: A Guide for Literature Students*. London: Routledge.

Eagleton, T. (1996 [1983]) *Literary Theory: An Introduction*, 2nd edn. Oxford: Blackwell.

Easthope, A. (1991) *Literary into Cultural Studies*. London: Routledge.

Edwards, R. and Usher, R. (2001) 'Lifelong learning: a postmodern condition of education?', *Adult Education Quarterly*, 51(4): 273–87.

Eisner, E. W. (1976) 'Educational connoisseurship and criticism: their form and functions in educational evaluation', *Journal of Aesthetic Education*, 10(3–4): 135–50.

Eisner, E. W. (1985) *The Educational Imagination: On the Design and Evaluation of School Programs*, 2nd edn. New York: Macmillan.

Elbow, P. (1998) *Writing with Power: Techniques for Mastering the Writing Process*, 2nd edn. New York: Oxford University Press.

Ellis, J. (1997) *Literature Lost: Social Agendas and the Corruption of the Humanities*. New Haven, CT: Yale University Press.

Entwistle, N. and Ramsden, P. (1983) *Understanding Student Learning*. London: Croom Helm.

Ess, C. (2000) 'Wag the dog? Online conferencing and teaching', *Computers and the Humanities*, 34(3): 297–309.

Ess, C. (2001) 'What's culture got to do with it? Cultural collisions in the electronic global village, creative interferences, and the rise of culturally-mediated computing', in C. Ess (ed.) with F. Sudweeks, *Culture, Technology, Communication: Towards an Intercultural Global Village*. Albany, NY: State University of New York Press, pp. 1–50.

Evans, C. (1993) *English People: The Experience of Teaching and Learning English in British Universities*. Buckingham: Open University Press.

Evans, C. (ed.) (1995) *Developing University English Teaching*. Lampeter: Edwin Mellen Press.

Feldman, C. F. and Kalmar, D. (1996) 'Autobiography and fiction as modes of thought', in D. Olson and N. Torrance (eds), *Modes of Thought: Explorations in Culture and Cognition*. Cambridge, New York and Melbourne: Cambridge University Press, pp. 106–22.

Gadamer, H.-G. (1989) *Truth and Method*, 2nd revised edn, trans. J. Weinsheimer and D. G. Marshall. London: Sheed & Ward.

Garrison, D. R. (1991) 'Developing critical thinking in adult learners', *International Journal of Lifelong Education*, 10(4): 287–303.

Geertz, C. (1975) *The Interpretation of Cultures*. London: Hutchinson.

George, J. and Cowan, J. (1999) *A Handbook of Techniques for Formative Evaluation: Mapping the Student's Learning Experience*. London: Kogan Page.

Gibbs, G. and Simpson, C. (2004–5) 'Conditions under which assessment supports students' learning', *Learning and Teaching in Higher Education*, 1(1): 3–31.

Graff, G. (1995) *Literature Against Itself*. Chicago: Ivan R. Dee.

Graff, G. (2003) 'Conflict clarifies: a response', *Pedagogy: Critical Approaches to Teaching Literature, Language, Composition, and Culture*, 3(2): 266–73. ('Symposium: Teaching the Conflicts at Twenty Years': 245–75.)

Gregory, M. (1995) 'The sound of story: narrative, memory and selfhood', *Narrative*, 3(1): 33–56.

Gregory, M. (1997) 'The many-headed hydra of theory vs. the unifying mission of teaching', *College English*, 59(1): 41–58.

Gregory, M. (2001) 'Curriculum, pedagogy, and teacherly ethos', *Pedagogy: Critical Approaches to Teaching Literature, Language, Composition, and Culture*, 1(1): 69–90.

Gregory, M. (2002) 'The politics of difference vs the ethics of essentializing: looking back and looking forward in humanities discourse about human nature', *Arts and Humanities in Higher Education*, 1(2): 125–44.

Guillory, J. (1993) *Cultural Capital: The Problem of Literary Canon Formation*. Chicago: University of Chicago Press.

Gunn, V. (2003) 'Transforming subject boundaries: the interface between higher education teaching and learning theories and subject-specific knowledge', *Arts and Humanities in Higher Education*, 2(3): 265–80.

Guy, J. M. and Small, I. (1993) *Politics and Value in English Studies: A Discipline in Crisis?* Cambridge: Cambridge University Press.

Haggis, T. (2003) 'Constructing images of ourselves? a critical investigation into "approaches to learning" research in higher education', *British Educational Research Journal*, 29(1): 89–104.

Halcrow Group with Gawthrope, J. and Martin, P. (2003) *A Report to the LTSN English Subject Centre: Survey of the English Curriculum and Teaching in UK Higher Education*. Royal Holloway, University of London: LTSN English Subject Centre (Report Series Number 8).

Halliday, M. A. K. (1985) *Spoken and Written Language*. Oxford: Oxford University Press.

Hardwick, L. (2001) 'Critical humanism in action: towards reading Aeschylus' *The Persians*', in E. A. Chambers (ed.), *Contemporary Themes in Humanities Higher Education*. Dordrecht: Kluwer Academic Publishers, pp. 45–64.

Hatfield, S. R. (ed.) (1995) *The Seven Principles in Action: Improving Undergraduate Education*. Bolton, MA: Anker Publishing.

Hawkridge, D. (2005) *Globalisation and Business Education*. Paper presented at the Open University, UK, February 2005.

Healey, M. (2000) 'Developing the scholarship of teaching: a discipline-based approach', *Higher Education Research and Development*, 19(2): 169–89.

Healey, M. (2003) *Linking Research and Teaching: A Disciplinary Perspective*. Paper presented to the Society for Research into Higher Education Annual Conference 'Research, Scholarship and Teaching: Changing Relationships?', Royal Holloway University of London, 16–18 December 2003.

Hillier, Y. (2002) *Reflective Teaching in Further and Adult Education*. London and New York: Continuum.

Hirst, P. H. (1974) *Knowledge and the Curriculum: A Collection of Philosophical Papers*. London: Routledge & Kegan Paul.

Hirst, P. H. and Peters, R. S. (1970) *The Logic of Education*. London: Routledge & Kegan Paul.

Hopkins, C. (2001) *Thinking About Texts: An Introduction to English Studies*. Basingstoke and New York: Palgrave.

Huber, M. T. and Morreale, P. (eds) (2002) *Disciplinary Styles in the Scholarship of Teaching and Learning: Exploring Common Ground*. Washington, DC: American Association for Higher Education and the Carnegie Foundation for the Advancement of Teaching.

Hutchings, P. (ed.) (2000) *Opening Lines: Approaches to the Scholarship of Teaching and Learning*. Menlo Park, CA: Carnegie Foundation for the Advancement of Teaching.

Hutchings, W. and O'Rourke, K. (2002) 'Problem-based learning in literary studies', *Arts and Humanities in Higher Education*, 1(1): 73–83.

Insko, J. (2003) 'Generational canons', *Pedagogy: Critical Approaches to Teaching Literature, Language, Composition, and Culture*, 3(3): 341–58.

Ivanič, R. (1998) *Writing and Identity: The Discoursal Construction of Identity in Academic Writing*. Amsterdam: John Benjamins.

Jay, G. S. (1997) *American Literature and the Culture Wars*. Ithaca, NY: Cornell University Press.

Jenkins, A. (1996) 'Discipline-based educational development', *International Journal of Academic Development*, 1(1): 50–62.

Jenkins, A., Breen, R. and Lindsay, R. (2003) *Reshaping Teaching in Higher Education: Linking Teaching with Research*. London: SEDA/Kogan Page.

Jonathan, R. (2000) 'Cultural diversity and public education: reasonable negotiation and hard cases', *Journal of Philosophy of Education*, 34(2): 337–94.

Jones, K., McLean, M., Amigoni, D. and Kinsman, M. (2005) 'Investigating the production of university English in mass higher education: towards an alternative methodology', *Arts and Humanities in Higher Education*, 4(3): 247–64.

Kelly, M. (2001) '"Serrez ma haire avec ma discipline": reconfiguring the structures and concepts', in R. di Napoli, L. Polezzi and A. King (eds), *Fuzzy Boundaries? Reflections on Modern Languages and the Humanities*. London: CILT, pp. 43–56.

Kirkwood, A. (2003) 'Going outside the box: skills development, cultural change and the use of on-line resources'. Internal report, Open University. Available at: http://kn.open.ac.uk/public/document.cfm?docid=3946.

Knight, P. T. (2001) 'Complexity and curriculum: a process approach to curriculum-making', *Teaching in Higher Education*, 6(3): 369–81.

Knight, P. T. (forthcoming) 'The local practices of assessment', *Assessment and Evaluation in Higher Education*, 31.

Knight, P. T. and Yorke, M. (2003) *Assessment, Learning and Employability*. Maidenhead: Open University Press.

Knights, B. (1992) *From Reader to Reader: Theory, Text and Practice in the Study Group*. London: Harvester Wheatsheaf.

Knights, B. (2005) 'Intelligence and interrogation: the identity of the English student', *Arts and Humanities in Higher Education*, 4(1): 33–52.

Kolb, D. (1984) *Experiential Learning*. New York: Prentice Hall.

Kress, G. (1998) 'Visual and verbal modes of representation in electronically mediated communication: the potentials of new forms of text', in I. Snyder (ed.), *Page to Screen: Taking Literacy into the Electronic Era*. London: Routledge, pp. 53–79.

Kress, G. (2003) *Literacy in the New Media Age*. London: Routledge.

Lakoff, G. and Johnson, M. (1999) *Philosophy in the Flesh: The Embodied Mind and its Challenge to Western Thought*. New York: Basic Books.

Larsen, K., Martin, J. P. and Morris, R. (2002) *Trade in Educational Services: Trends and Emerging Issues*, Working Paper. Paris: OECD.

Lave, J. and Wenger, E. (1991) *Situated Learning: Legitimate Peripheral Participation*. Cambridge: Cambridge University Press.

Lave, J. and Wenger, E. (1999) 'Learning and pedagogy in communities of practice', in J. Leach and B. Moon (eds), *Learners and Pedagogy*. Buckingham: Open University Press, pp. 21–77.

Lea, M. R. and Street, B. V. (1998) 'Student writing in higher education: an academic literacies approach', *Studies in Higher Education*, 23(2): 157–72.

Lentricchia, F. and DuBois, A. (2003) *Close Reading: The Reader*. Durham, NC: Duke University Press.

Levine, G. (2001) 'The two nations', *Pedagogy: Critical Approaches to Teaching Literature, Language, Composition, and Culture*, 1(1): 7–19.

Lillis, T. (2001) *Student Writing: Access, Regulation, Desire*. London: Routledge.

Lyotard, J.-F. (1984) *The Postmodern Condition: A Report on Knowledge*. Manchester: Manchester University Press.

McCurrie, M. K. (2004) 'From the edges to the center: pedagogy's role in redefining English departments', *Pedagogy: Critical Approaches to Teaching Literature, Language, Composition, and Culture*, 4(1): 43–64.

Macdonald, J., Weller, M. and Mason, R. (2000) *Innovative Assessment Practices in Networked Courses at the Open University*. Milton Keynes: Open University, Institute of Educational Technology Centre for Information Technology in Education (CITE) Report 260, July.

McGann, J. with Griffith, J., Kremer, J., Kroeger, R. L., Moriarty, B., Pikler, J., Simpson, B. and Stephenson, K. (2001) ' "Reading fiction/teaching fiction": a pedagogical experiment', *Pedagogy: Critical Approaches to Teaching Literature, Language, Composition, and Culture*, 1(1): 143–65.

McKibben, W. (1992) *The Age of Missing Information*. New York: Random House.

McLean, M. (2001) 'Can we relate conceptions of learning to student academic achievement?', *Teaching in Higher Education*, 6: 399–413.

Marton, F. and Säljö, R. (1976a) 'On qualitative differences in learning I – outcome and process', *British Journal of Educational Psychology*, 46: 4–11.

Marton, F. and Säljö, R. (1976b) 'On qualitative differences in learning II – outcome as a function of the learner's conception of the task', *British Journal of Educational Psychology*, 46: 115–27.

Marton, F., Hounsell, D. and Entwistle, N. (eds) (1984) *The Experience of Learning*. Edinburgh: Scottish Academic Press.

Miller, C. M. I. and Parlett, M. (1974) *Up to the Mark: A Study of the Examination Game*. Guildford: Society for Research into Higher Education.

Miller, M. C. (1988) *Boxed In*. Evanston, IL: Northwestern University Press.

Mills, D. and Huber, M. T. (2005) 'Anthropology and the educational "trading zone": disciplinarity, pedagogy and professionalism', *Arts and Humanities in Higher Education*, 4(1): 9–32.

Mitchell, S. and Andrews, R. (2000) *Learning to Argue in Higher Education*. Portsmouth: Boynton/Cook Publishers.

MLA (Modern Language Association) (2000) *Handbook for Writers of Research Papers*, 5th edn. New York: MLA.

Monroe, J. (2002) *Writing and Revising the Disciplines*. Ithaca, NY: Cornell University Press.

Moore, T. (2004) 'The critical thinking debate: how general are general thinking skills?', *Higher Education Research and Development*, 23(1): 3–18.

Murray, D. (1987) *Write to Learn*. New York: Holt, Rinehart & Winston.

National Committee of Inquiry into Higher Education (The Dearing Report) (1997) *Higher Education in the Learning Society*. Norwich: HMSO.

National Endowment for the Arts (2004) *Reading at Risk: A Survey of Literary Reading in America*. Washington, DC: National Endowment for the Arts (Research Division Report No. 46). Available at: http://www.nea.gov/pub/ReadingAtRisk.pdf.

Neilson, J. (1997) *How Users Read on the Web*. Available at: www.useit.com/alertbox/9710a.html.

Northedge, A. (2003) 'Enabling participation in academic discourse', *Teaching in Higher Education*, 8(2): 169–80.

Olson, D. R. (1996) 'Literate mentalities: literacy, consciousness of language, and modes of thought', in D. R. Olson and N. Torrance (eds), *Modes of Thought: Explorations in Culture and Cognition*. Cambridge, New York and Melbourne: Cambridge University Press, pp. 141–51.

Parker, J. (2001) 'Humanities higher education: new models, new challenges', in E. A. Chambers (ed.), *Contemporary Themes in Humanities Higher Education*. Dordrecht: Kluwer Academic Publishers, pp. 21–43.

Parker, J. (2003) 'Writing, revising and practising the disciplines: Carnegie, Cornell and the scholarship of teaching', *Arts and Humanities in Higher Education*, 2(2): 139–53.

Parlett, M. and Hamilton, D. (1972) *Evaluation as Illumination: A New Approach to the Study of Innovatory Programmes*, Occasional Paper 9. Edinburgh: University of Edinburgh Centre for Research in Educational Sciences.

Pascoe, R. (2003) 'An Australian perspective on the humanities', *Arts and Humanities in Higher Education*, 2(1): 7–22.

Paterson, R. W. K. (1979) *Values, Education and the Adult*. London: Routledge & Kegan Paul.

Perry, W. G. (1970) *Forms of Intellectual and Ethical Development in the College Years*. New York: Holt, Rinehart & Winston.

Peters, M. (1995) 'Education and the postmodern condition: revisiting Jean-François Lyotard', *Journal of Philosophy of Education*, 29(3): 387–400.

Postman, N. (1982) *The Disappearance of Childhood*. New York: Random House.

Postman, N. (1985) *Amusing Ourselves to Death*. New York: Penguin Books.

QAA (1995) *QO 12/95 Subject Overview Report – English*. Higher Education Funding Council for England, Quality Assessment of English 1994–95. Available at: www.qaa.ac.uk.

QAA (2000) *Subject Benchmark Statement – English*. Gloucester: Quality Assurance Agency for Higher Education.

Ramsden, P. (1991) 'A performance indicator of teaching quality in higher education: the Course Experience Questionnaire', *Studies in Higher Education*, 16(2): 129–50.

Ramsden, P. (1992) *Learning to Teach in Higher Education*. London: Routledge.

Readings, W. (1996) *The University in Ruins*. Cambridge, MA: Harvard University Press.

Rice, R. E. (2002) 'Beyond *Scholarship Reconsidered*: Toward an enlarged vision of the scholarly work of faculty members', in K. Zahorski (ed.), *Scholarship in the Postmodern Era: New Venues, New Values, New Visions*, New Directions for Teaching and Learning No. 90. San Francisco: Jossey-Bass.

Richardson, J. T. E. (2000) *Researching Student Learning*. Buckingham: SRHE and Open University Press.

Robb, M. (1994) *Living Arts: Words*. Milton Keynes: Open University.

Säljö, R. (1982) *Learning and Understanding*. Göteborg: Acta Universitatis Gothoburgensis.

Salmon, G. (2002) *E-Tivities: The Key to Active Online Learning*. London: Kogan Page.

Salvatori, M. (2000) 'The great educational divide', in P. Hutchings (ed.), *Opening Lines: Approaches to the Scholarship of Teaching and Learning*. Menlo Park, CA: Carnegie Foundation for the Advancement of Teaching and Learning, pp. 81–93.

Salvatori, M. and Donahue, P. (2002) 'English studies in the scholarship of teaching', in M. Huber and S. Morreale (eds), *Disciplinary Styles in the Scholarship of Teaching and Learning: Exploring Common Ground*. Washington, DC: American Association for Higher Education and Carnegie Foundation for the Advancement of Teaching, pp. 69–86.

SAQA (2000) *The National Qualification Framework and Curriculum Development*. Waterkloof: South African Qualifications Authority.

Scholes, R. (1985) *Textual Power: Literary Theory and the Teaching of English*. New Haven, CT and London: Yale University Press.

Scholes, R. (1998) *The Rise and Fall of English: Reconstructing English as a Discipline*. New Haven, CT: Yale University Press.

Scholes, R. (2001) *The Crafty Reader*. New Haven, CT: Yale University Press.

Schön, D. A. (1983) *The Reflective Practitioner*. New York: Basic Books.

Scott, J. W. (1995) 'The rhetoric of crisis in higher education', in M. Bérubé and C. Nelson (eds), *Higher Education Under Fire: Politics, Economics and the Crisis of the Humanities*. New York and London: Routledge, pp. 293–304.

Showalter, E. (2002) *Teaching Literature*. Oxford: Blackwell.

Shulman, L. (1997) 'Disciplines of inquiry in education: a new overview', in R. Jaeger (ed.), *Complementary Methods for Research in Education*. Washington, DC: American Educational Research Association, pp. 3–29.

Smallwood, P. (1997) 'Criticism and the meaning of "theory"', *British Journal of Aesthetics*, 37(4): 377–85.

Smallwood, P. (2002) '"*More Creative than Creation*": On the idea of criticism and the student critic', *Arts and Humanities in Higher Education*, 1(1): 59–71.

Smith, K. (2004) 'School to university: an investigation into the experiences of first-year students of English at British universities', *Arts and Humanities in Higher Education*, 3(1): 81–93.

Snyder, B. R. (1971) *The Hidden Curriculum*. Cambridge, MA: MIT Press.

Snyder, I. (ed.) (2002) *Silicon Literacies: Communication, Innovation and Education in the Electronic Age*. London: Routledge.

Spaeth, D. A. and Cameron, S. (2000) 'Computers and resource-based history teaching: a UK perspective', *Computing and the Humanities*, 34(3): 325–43.

Standish, P. (1991) 'Educational discourse: meaning and mythology', *Journal of Philosophy of Education*, 25(2): 171–82.

Strathern, M. (ed.) (2000) *Audit Cultures: Anthropological Studies in Accountability, Ethics and the Academy*. London: Routledge.

Stromquist, N. and Monkman, K. (2000) *Globalisation and Education: Integration and Contestation across Cultures*. Lanham, MD: Rowman & Littlefield.

Swales, J. (1990) *Genre Knowledge: English in Academic and Research Settings*. Cambridge: Cambridge University Press.

Taylor, G., Ballard, B., Beasley, V., Bock, H. K., Clanchy, J. and Nightingale, P. (1988) 'Introduction' to *Literacy by Degrees*. Milton Keynes: SRHE/Open University Press, pp. 1–6.

Thesen, L. (2001) 'Modes, literacies and power: a university case study', *Language and Education*, 15(2/3): 132–45.

Thorpe, M. (2000) 'Encouraging students to reflect as part of the assignment process', *Active Learning in Higher Education*, 1(1): 79–92.

Tyler, R. W. (1949) *Basic Principles of Curriculum and Instruction*. Chicago: University of Chicago Press.

VanZanten Gallagher, S. (2001) 'Contingencies and intersections: the formation of pedagogical canons', *Pedagogy: Critical Approaches to Teaching Literature, Language, Composition, and Culture*, 1(1): 53–67

Vygotsky, L. S. (1978) *Mind in Society: The Development of Higher Psychological Processes*, eds M. S. Cole, V. John-Steiner, S. Scribner and E. Souberman. Cambridge, MA: Harvard University Press.

Widdowson, P. (1982) *Re-reading English*. London: Routledge.

Widdowson, P. (1999) *Literature*. London: Routledge.

Woolf, H. (2001) *Assessment Criteria: Fuzzy by Design?* Paper presented to the Student Assessment and Classification Working Group Annual Conference, Wolverhampton, 15 November.

World Trade Organisation Secretariat (2002) *Trading into the Future*. Available at: http://www.wto.org.

Yorke, M. and Knight, P. T. (2004) *Embedding Employability into the Curriculum*. York: Learning and Teaching Support Network.

WEBSITES

Arts and Humanities Data Service (AHDS): at http://ahds.ac.uk

Arts and Humanities in Higher Education: An International Journal of Theory, Research and Practice, Sage Publications: at www.sagepub.co.uk

Assessment and the Expanded Text Project, Northumbria University, UK: at www.unn.ac.uk/assessingenglish

Australian Academy of the Humanities: at www.humanities.au

Australian e-Humanities Gateway: at www.ehum.edu.au

Carnegie Foundation for the Advancement of Teaching, USA: at www.carnegiefoundation.org

Carrick Institute for Learning and Teaching in Higher Education, Australia: at www.autc.gov.au/institute.htm

Council for the Humanities, Arts and Social Sciences, Australia: at, www.chass.org.au

Department for Education and Skills, UK: at http://www.dfes.gov.uk/hegateway/hereform/index.cfm

Department of Education, Science and Training, Australia: at www.dest.gov.au

Distributed National Electronic Resource (DNER), UK: at www.jisc.ac.uk/dner

English Association, The University of Leicester, UK: at www.le.ac.uk/engassoc/

English Department Home Pages Worldwide, USA: at www.nyu.edu/gsas/dept/english/links/engdpts.html

HEA English Subject Centre, UK: at www.english.heacademy.ac.uk

Higher Education Academy, UK: at www.hefce.ac.uk

Humbul (Humanities) Gateway, UK: at www.humbul.ac.uk/english

Literature Online: at http://lion.chadwyck.co.uk/

Moving Image Gateway, UK: at www.bufvc.ac.uk/gateway

National Computer Assisted Assessment Centre, UK: at www.caacentre.ac.uk

National Endowment for the Arts, USA: at www. nea.gov.

OpenCourseWare at MIT, USA: at http://ocw.mit.edu/index.html

Oxford Text Archive (OTA), UK: at http://ota.ahds.ac.uk/

Patchwork Text Project, UK: at www.apu.ac.uk

Plagiarism detection service, UK: at www.jisc.ac.uk/mle/plagiarism

Project Gutenberg: at www.gutenberg.net

QAA Subject Overview report – English, UK: at www.qaa.ac.uk

Sheffield Hallam University, UK: at www.shu.ac.uk

Speak-Write Project, Anglia Polytechnic University, UK: at www.anglia.ac.uk/speakwrite

Special Educational Needs and Disability Act (SENDA), UK: at www.hmso.gov.uk/acts/acts2001/20010010.htm

TechDis, UK: at www.techdis.ac.uk

Television and Index for Learning and Teaching UK: at www.trilt.ac.uk

University of Southern Queensland, Australia: at www.usq.edu.au

Voice of the Shuttle: at http://vos.ucsb.edu

World Trade Organisation Secretariat: at http://www.wto.org

Index

Added to a page number 'f' denotes a figure and 'n' denotes notes.